TAROT IN TEN MINUTES

TAROT IN TEN MINUTES

R.T. KASER

AVON BOOKS ◈ NEW YORK

TAROT IN TEN MINUTES is an original publication of Avon Books. This work has never before appeared in book form.

Illustrations from the Rider-Waite Tarot deck reproduced by permission of U.S. Games Systems, Inc., Stamford, Connecticut 06902. Copyright © 1971 by U.S. Games Systems, Inc. Further reproduction prohibited.

AVON BOOKS
A division of
The Hearst Corporation
1350 Avenue of the Americas
New York, New York 10019

Copyright © 1992 by Richard T. Kaser
Interior design by Robin Arzt
Published by arrangement with the author
Library of Congress Catalog Card Number: 92-18746
ISBN: 0-380-76689-2

Library of Congress Cataloging in Publication Data:
Kaser, R. T.
  Tarot in ten minutes : a new way of reading the cards & yourself / by R.T. Kaser.
    p. cm.
  Discography: p.
  Includes index.
  1. Tarot—Handbooks, manuals, etc.   I. Title.
BF1879. T2K34   1992   92-18746
133.3′2424—dc20   CIP

First Avon Books Trade Printing: November 1992

AVON TRADEMARK REG. U.S. PAT. OFF. AND IN OTHER COUNTRIES, MARCA REGISTRADA, HECHO EN U.S.A.

Printed in the U.S.A.

OPM   10 9 8 7 6 5

To the glory of God
and in memory
of
Mom Miller

PREFACE

Tarot in Ten Minutes is not your typical Tarot book. You aren't going to have to wade through this book from front to back and digest a lot of extraneous information before you begin to play with your cards. In fact, you'll be conducting your first Reading—asking your first question and getting your first answer—in less than **ten minutes,** aided by the book's prefabricated Answer sections.

These Answer sections are not your typical Tarot book answers, either. In other books, you have to struggle to relate general, all-purpose descriptions or heavy-duty mythological references to the question you asked. But with *Tarot in Ten Minutes,* if you ask about your love life, the book will answer in a way that talks about your love life. If you ask about your finances, the book will talk to you about money. There are 29 questions and 29 Answer sections in all. And they cover everything from your career prospects to your mission in life.

Within **nine minutes** you will be learning which Tarot card is your mascot in life—that is if you choose to start with Reading #1. Or you'll be exploring your employment situation, delving into your dreams, contemplating your life's purpose, because there is a Reading for just about everything here, and there are no rules about how you should proceed through the book. Starting at the beginning and working your way through to the end will result in a complete experience with the cards and a complete look at your life. But if you don't want to start with Reading #1, don't—just consult the Contents or the Index to find the Reading that deals with the question you want to ask.

The method you'll use as you follow this book is straightforward: Ask your questions; shuffle the cards; deal up the cards; and look up your answers.

To ask your question. The easiest thing to do is to ask one of the 29 questions listed in the Contents, or one of the 78 questions included in the Index. These lists will direct you to the Reading where your question is treated. If you don't find your exact question, pick the one closest to it. Most Readings allow you to tailor the question to your specific situation. Once you know what Reading you're going to do, consult its Tarot Tools section, which will tell you which cards to use. Many of the Readings use only the 10 or 20 cards that are best at answering the type of question you have asked. This is one way in which *Tarot in Ten Minutes* helps you get answers that are so relevant to your question.

To shuffle the cards. Some of the Readings in this book are so easy to do that they don't even require you to shuffle. And when it comes time to shuffle, the book will tell you how. But in general, there is absolutely no way you can shuffle the cards wrong. Ruffle them together. Shuffle them from front to back or back to front. Swirl them around on the table in front of you. With this book you *do not* have to cut the deck. You *do not* have to light candles or burn incense. You *do not* have to work on a black velvet cloth or keep your cards wrapped up in silk. You *do not* have to pick out a card to signify you or the person you are reading for. You can do these things if they make you feel more comfortable with the cards, but no complex rituals or extra procedures are required to get an answer. Just follow the instructions in the How To section in each Reading.

To deal up the cards. The cards are done shuffling when they don't want to go into one another, or when one leaps out of the deck. At this point stop shuffling, cut the deck if you are so inclined, and deal up the top card or cards. The How To section in each Reading will tell you how many cards to deal up and how to arrange them.

To look up your answers. The answers to each question are right with the Reading. When you are done dealing up your cards, just find the answers for the card or card combinations that have come up. The answers will relate directly to your question. Depending on the question you have asked and the type of layout you are using, some of the answers you receive will be detailed, and some will be short and snappy. Some Answer sections will trace your question back to its roots and look at the various aspects of a situation; other answers will read more like a single continuous thought. The How To sections will tell you what kind of answer to expect for each question. If you would like more detail on your question, shuffle and deal again. To find more information on the meaning of any card at any time, turn to the back of the book and consult the Quick Reference Guide.

In fact, if you prefer to follow a method you already know for shuffling, dealing, and reading the cards, use the Quick Reference Guide the same way you would consult any traditional Tarot book. The difference is, the answers you find here will be more down-to-earth, practical, and specific than what you are used to finding. And they will certainly add to your own understanding of the cards.

Either way, within **six minutes,** you will be reading your cards. To save six minutes, skip the rest of this preface. But if you'd like to know how and why this book originated, read on....

My first experience with the Tarot was a fiasco. I lit my incense. I had my bowl of water sitting by to keep the evil spirits away. I shuffled the

Preface

deck, asked my question, dealt up my cards into a Celtic Cross formation, and then went to look up the answers. The book gave me 10 or 15 different answers for every card. Each card, it seemed, could stand for many different things. What was I to make of this? Which was *my* answer? What did *my* cards mean?

I tried other books. Some told me how the cards were about an allegorical journey or vision quest. Some told me how the cards represented figures from Greek and Roman mythology. Some told me how they related to the stars and astrological signs or to numbers and numerological theories. Some taught me colors. Some taught me symbols. Some told me how the cards embodied ancient Egyptian ideas or the religious traditions of Mother India, the pagan customs of Europe, or Hebrew mysticism. Some spoke only of the cards' Christian symbols, some only of New Age spiritualism, and some of Jungian psychology. All of this was quite interesting—but when I dealt up my cards in a Celtic Cross, I still didn't know how to read them.

What I really wanted—needed, desired—was a book that helped me out with the answers, that helped me figure out what the cards meant in the context of real-life questions. *Tarot in Ten Minutes* is my humble attempt to give you the book I could not find anywhere else—the book with the answers.

How I finally learned to read the cards was by playing around with them and trying all different kinds of things. Through trial and error—and by borrowing techniques from other types of fortune-telling devices—I discovered that reading Tarot cards can be a lot easier than most Tarot experts admit. You simply do not need to spend a lifetime learning complex methods in order to enjoy the experience and learn something about yourself in the process. In fact, in less than **four minutes** you'll be well on your way to using your cards to get *real* answers to *real* questions, by using simple techniques not found in other Tarot books.

To make things easy, many of the Readings in this book borrow their technique from the way in which Celtic runes are read. With runes, three engraved stones are selected from a bag of stones in order to get a reading of the current situation, an action that is required, and a result that can be expected. The same technique works well with the cards.

From the Chinese I Ching—a rather philosophical method of reading fortunes by tossing coins—I have borrowed the idea of interpreting the cards as a continuous thought. Quite a few Readings in the book use this method in their Answer sections, where the first card that turns up is treated as the main idea, with each additional card supplying more detail. Readings conducted this way tend to answer your question more directly than traditional Tarot methods.

From the age-old tradition of numerology, I also discovered that cards can be selected for character readings by adding up the numbers in your name or birth date.

All of these techniques, as well as the traditional Celtic Cross method, are used in this book. If you'd like more information on the methods, consult the opening section of the Quick Reference Guide for details on each type of layout.

You don't really need to know or remember any of this to use the book and enjoy your cards. But if you're interested in knowing why *Tarot in Ten Minutes* is able to provide specific answers when so many other sources do not, read on.

One secret to the book is this: I stack the deck in your favor. Rather than working with all 78 cards at once, we use the cards that are best at answering specific kinds of questions—Coin cards for money questions, Cups for love, Wands for work, Swords for strategy, and so forth. This not only makes perfect sense, but it helps you focus in on your question. And it helps your cards focus on the answer.

Another secret is this: I stack the deal in your favor. Contrary to popular opinion, it seldom takes more than a few cards to answer a direct question decisively. So, with the more straightforward questions, you'll use vastly simplified card layouts. And you'll find these layouts prove to be just as reliable as the lavish, intricate multicard spreads recommended in so many other sources.

The final secret is this: I spare you the theory. The answers in this book are based on decades of study and research, but why bore you with pages and pages of theory? The Answer sections in this book tell you what the cards might mean in the context of a real question. Isn't that, after all, what matters? And why do these things always have to be so complicated anyway?

I want you to use your cards. I want you to have fun with your cards— for the Tarot is both serious and frivolous. It is both helpful and ludicrous. It is like everything else in the universe. It is like life itself. In **one minute,** I'll set you loose, but allow me one last thought.

Should you believe the answers in *Tarot in Ten Minutes?* Let me put it this way: You will know when the answers are right because they'll *feel* right. They'll be your own conclusions. At the least, *Tarot in Ten Minutes* will give you a fun way to spend the evening. At the most, it will help you decide things about and for yourself. This is what Tarot is best at. This is what Tarot does.

CONTENTS

Contents

Quick Reference Guide

INTRODUCTION TO THE CARDS

Tarot in Ten Minutes works with *all* Tarot decks. Your Readings will be accurate even if the images sometimes described in the book do not exactly match the pictures on your cards.

Since the Tarot is a work of art, you will have the best luck with the cards if you use a deck that is fully illustrated with pictures on every card, especially . . .

> The Rider-Waite Tarot Deck
> (pictured on pages 2–19)
>
> Hanson-Roberts Tarot Deck
> Barbara Walker Tarot
> Aquarian Tarot
> Morgan-Greer Tarot
> Sacred Rose Tarot Deck
> The Mythic Tarot
> Royal Fez Moroccan Tarot
> Deck
> The Norse Tarot
> Starter Tarot Deck

VERY IMPORTANT

You may have to alter the order of two cards in your deck. Some decks show Justice as Card XI, but we will be using it as Card VIII. Likewise, Strength, which is sometimes shown as Card VIII, will be used as Card XI. The names printed on your cards may vary slightly from the Rider-Waite deck titles used in this book.

The Cards

The first 10 Trumps . . .

THE MAGICIAN.

THE HIGH PRIESTESS

THE EMPRESS.

THE EMPEROR.

THE HIEROPHANT

THE LOVERS.

THE CHARIOT.

JUSTICE.

THE HERMIT.

WHEEL of FORTUNE.

...for Questions about Wants and Needs

3

The next 10 Trumps . . .

JUDGEMENT.

THE SUN

THE MOON.

THE STAR.

THE TOWER.

THE DEVIL.

TEMPERANCE.

DEATH.

THE HANGED MAN.

STRENGTH.

. . . for Questions about Emotions and Feelings

The first 10 Wands . . .

. . . for Questions about Work and Career

The first 10 Cups . . .

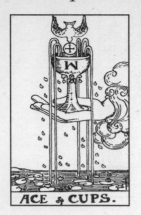

. . . for Questions about Love and Friendship

The first 10 Coins . . .

. . . for Questions about Money and Finance

The first 10 Swords . . .

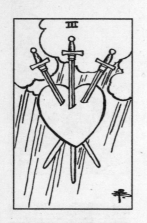

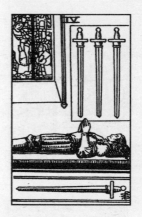

. . . for Questions about Tactics and Strategy

The Kings and Queens . . .

KING of WANDS

QUEEN of WANDS.

KING of CUPS.

QUEEN of CUPS.

KING of PENTACLES.

QUEEN of PENTACLES

KING of SWORDS.

QUEEN of SWORDS.

. . . for Questions about People and Places

PAGE of WANDS.

KNIGHT of WANDS.

PAGE of CUPS.

KNIGHT of CUPS.

... *for Questions about News and Messages*

THE WORLD.

. . . for Yes/No Questions

The Readings

Reading #1

WHO AM I?

In your life as a whole and at any given moment, you can be said to be living out one of the situations depicted by the Tarot cards. In this Reading, you will learn to identify which card *signifies* your life in general. This card is your mascot in life. It describes you. It can also be said to *cover you*. It is sometimes called your *Key Card*.

TAROT TOOLS

Take out your deck—any Tarot deck will do—and separate out the following cards:

I	*The Magician*
II	*The High Priestess*
III	*The Empress*
IV	*The Emperor*
V	*The Hierophant*
VI	*The Lovers*
VII	*The Chariot*
VIII *or* XI	*Justice*
IX	*The Hermit*
X	*Wheel of Fortune*

HOW TO

In this Reading, we will use the numbers associated with your birth date to determine the card that represents your general situation in this life, your Key Card or mascot. Here's how . . .

Simply add up the month, day, and year of your birth, like this:

August 29, 1952 = 8 + 29 + 1952 = 1989

Then add up the result:

1989 = 1 + 9 + 8 + 9 = 27

Now reduce this number by adding it up once more. You should get a number of 10 or less:

$$27 = 2 + 7 = 9$$

If this step adds up exactly to 10, reduce it again to 1, only if the day of the month in which you were born is an odd number; leave it as 10 if the day on which you were born is an even number.

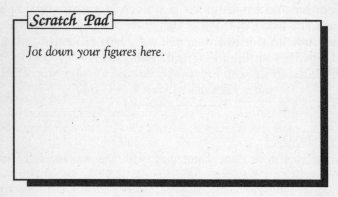

Scratch Pad

Jot down your figures here.

Now take out the card from your deck that signifies you. Look at it for a minute, then look up its meaning in the following Answer section. Just repeat the steps to learn about others.

For additional information on any card, consult the Quick Reference Guide.

THE ANSWERS

I The Magician. Look at your Key Card. This is the card of people who control their own destinies. *Magicians have the ability to make things happen.* If this is your Key Card, you are particularly good at influencing— even controlling—your own environment. You are capable of leading a highly directed, determined life by focusing your energy on achieving all the things that matter in this world: career and status, love and happiness, money and possessions, power and glory. If you are like most people, how-ever, you will need to choose one of these areas to master. The choice is yours.

II The High Priestess. Look at your Key Card. This is the card of people who know without knowing. *High Priestesses have the ability to know or feel things.* If this is your Key Card, you are the kind of person who can trust your gut feelings, hunches, inner voices, and dreams. When in doubt, you go with your instincts. You may have an uncanny sense of direction. You may even describe yourself as psychic. In general, you will feel your way through life as if you were navigating a familiar stream. The past, present, and future can click together for you, but you may need to strike a balance between body and mind (conscious and subconscious) in order to achieve your full potential.

III The Empress.

Look at your Key Card. This is the card of people who are in touch with their environment. *Empresses have the ability to create and influence the things around them.* If this is your Key Card, things grow, develop, and mature under your careful attention. You are good at parenting, mentoring, coaching, and in other ways of bringing out the skills and talents of others. You may also be rather prolific yourself. You appreciate that there is an ecological balance to be maintained, that everything depends on everything else. In order to achieve your goals, however, you may have to wait a period of time for the things that you desire to come about.

IV The Emperor.

Look at your Key Card. This is the card of people who are natural-born leaders. *Emperors have the ability to control things.* They are decisive and authoritative. And they know how to get to the top. If this is your Key Card, you are the kind of person who likes to live according to the rules (which you help make). And, within this framework, you are extremely capable of making your own decisions. You will also decide things for others. They may respect, honor, and even obey your opinions. You like to rule the roost. But in order to achieve your full potential, you may have to temper your own temper. Learn to respect the opinions of those whose support you depend upon. And be ready to defend your territory.

V The Hierophant.

Look at your Key Card. This is the card of people who have faith. *Hierophants have the ability to believe in things.* If this is your Key Card, your life is knit together by a highly organized system of beliefs. You may hunger after idealistic, patriotic, moral, or religious ideas. You may have a strong sense of standards, ethics, and traditions. You may even require a rigid structure (or hierarchic scheme) in your life. To achieve your full potential, you need to dedicate yourself to pursuits that serve a higher purpose. This card can also indicate that you feel a need for public acceptance. You want to fit in. You want to belong.

VI The Lovers.

Look at your Key Card. This is the card of people who are passionate. *Lovers have the ability to care deeply about things.* They have the ability to care about each other. If this is your Key Card, you are the sort of person who feels hopelessly attracted to someone else. This could mean that infatuations will be a common experience for you, or it could mean that you will have the great fortune to find true love in this life, and it will be "love at first sight." But beware, your true love may not be another person. It may, in fact, strike you as a deep, enduring passion for some kind of work, which you will pursue relentlessly. To achieve your full potential, you must choose something that will love (or reward) you back.

VII The Chariot.
Look at your Key Card. This is the card of people who are heroes. *Charioteers have the ability to conquer things.* They can do the impossible. If this is your Key Card, you will know the thrill of victory in your life, like a surge of adrenaline. You may work long hours and appear to run on high-test, for you thrive on challenging situations and will stay up all night to complete projects. You will take your share of risks. It is not so much the fact that you are fearless (for you may desperately fear failure) but that you are relentless that distinguishes you. You not only keep score but you like to overcome great odds, playing things right down to the wire. To achieve your full potential in this life, you need to strike a balance between self-confidence and winning strategies.

VIII Justice.
Look at your Key Card. This is the card of people who are good critics. *Justices have the ability to evaluate things.* They can cut through the crap of this world and get to the point. They can see what is written between the lines. If this is your Key Card, you are a very insightful person, fair-minded, even-tempered, and a good listener. You want to hear both sides of a story before coming to your own conclusions. But with such a capacity for insight comes an obligation, too. To achieve your full potential you may need to learn how to be forgiving.

IX The Hermit.
Look at your Key Card. This is the card of people who have grown wise. *Hermits have the ability to understand things.* They are the loners of this world. If this is your Key Card, you may like to retreat to your study at night or get off to that cabin in the woods—not just to rest, mind you, but to be alone with your thoughts, even to meditate or pray. Your job in life is to hold up a light for others to follow. To achieve your full potential, you must come back from your hermitage eventually to tell others what you have seen, heard, and learned.

X Wheel of Fortune.
Look at your Key Card. This is the card of people who are fortunate. *Wheel of Fortune people have the ability to benefit from change.* If this is your Key Card, you may even feel as if Lady Luck shines on you. When things happen around you, it always seems as if it's for the better. You always seem to not only make it through the bad times

but to come out better off in the end. To achieve your full potential, though, you may need to work on improving your ability to predict and anticipate when things are about to change.

EXTRA CREDIT

Compute the Key Cards for your spouse, lover, children, friends, or relatives to see which cards signify them.

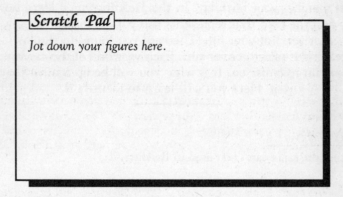

Scratch Pad

Jot down your figures here.

EXTRA EXTRA CREDIT!

What the heck, make a complete family tree, with all of the birth dates and Key Cards of your ancestors.

Go on to the next Reading whenever you are ready to continue.

Reading #2

WHERE AM I?

In the last Reading you learned how to find the Tarot card that matches your birthday. In this Reading you'll learn how to find the card that represents this particular year (or any other year) of your life. The card you found in the last Reading is said to cover you. Each year one of the cards is also said to *cross you*. It is what you will be up against that year. Here you will learn to identify it.

TAROT TOOLS

Just use the same cards you used in Reading #1:

I	*The Magician*
II	*The High Priestess*
III	*The Empress*
IV	*The Emperor*
V	*The Hierophant*
VI	*The Lovers*
VII	*The Chariot*
VIII or XI	*Justice*
IX	*The Hermit*
X	*Wheel of Fortune*

HOW TO

Here you'll do exactly what you did in the previous Reading, except in adding up the numbers in your birth date, use the month, date, and year of your *last* birthday, instead of the year of your birth. (The Tarot years run from birthday to birthday. So if your birthday is not until later this calendar year, you are still living under the influence of last year's card.)

If your birthday is August 29 and this is 1999, you would add:

8 + 29 + 1999 = 2036
which reduces to: 2 + 0 + 3 + 6 = 11
which further reduces to: 1 + 1 = 2

If your birthday adds up exactly to 10, or reduces exactly to 10 at any point in the calculation, reduce it again to 1 if the current year ends in an odd digit, but leave it as 10 if the current year ends in an even digit.

The number you end up with corresponds to a card, which will indicate which Tarot card crosses you this year. It will tell you what kind of Tarot year you are having.

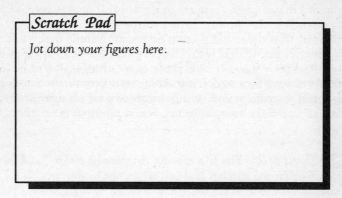

Scratch Pad

Jot down your figures here.

Now take out the card from your deck that *crosses you* this year. Look at it for a minute, then look up your answer in the following Answer section.

For additional information on any card, consult the Quick Reference Guide.

THE ANSWERS

I The Magician. This is a time for making things happen. Look at your card. You will feel the winds of change flowing through you. You will feel charged with energy. You have the ability to influence the world around you. Things will change, because you yourself are changing. It is as if you need only point, and things will happen. The world is at your fingertips. You are in charge of your own destiny. Build things. Take matters into your own hands. Plant the seeds of your own future. Take command. Soak in the warmth of the sun.

II The High Priestess. This is a time when things come together. Look at your card. The past adds up. There is the present. And it is flowing off into the future in a continuous stream. You feel as if you are a part of things. You feel connected. Part of the web. Part of the fabric. You see the picture emerge on the tapestry of your life. You may even feel "at one with the universe." What you do now changes everything. Flow with the currents. Launch projects when the time is right. Sail with the winds. Pay attention to your dreams. Go with your hunches. Roll with the punches. And when you don't know which way to turn, take a hot bath. Watch for the changing phases of the moon.

III **The Empress.** *This is a time for cultivating things.* Look at your card. It is as if things are in no hurry to get finished up this year. They are like crops that you hear growing little by little in the sleepless night. You wait and worry over them. But there is no forcing a thing that is not ready to come into its own. Watch, wait, and persevere this year. Hang in there. Carry on. And carry through with plans. Some things have to be raised. Some things have to be reared. If something resists coming about, don't be in such a rush. Be patient and giving. Incubate your ideas by sleeping on things before you make your decisions. For inspiration, get outside. Look at the stars.

IV **The Emperor.** *This is a time for determining things.* Look at your card. Batten down the hatches and full steam ahead this year. It's a cold, hard, cruel, dog-eat-dog world out there. The air is charged with politics, and power is the name of the game. But it's all subject to which way the wind blows. So look out for changing weather conditions. And at all times remember you are in charge of your own life! As things take shape around you, get a foothold if you can. Focus on creating a semblance of order. Think in terms of plans and strategies. Anticipate the future moves of others. Make decisions. Sense danger. For inspiration, watch a good thunderstorm.

V **The Hierophant.** *This is a time for living up to things.* Look at your card. You may start to feel as if you have to walk on water this year. The standards are extremely high, the challenges great, and nobody is satisfied with the results. Whatever is done must be done better than ever before. Whatever is assessed will be found missing something. But count your blessings. Self-righteousness may rule the scene, but few practice what they preach. When the public turns its critical eye on you, you must be sure to live up to the scrutiny. Take advantage of the chance to prove your own worth. Pay attention to details. Follow guidelines. Serve others with dedication and enthusiasm. If you sense the intervention of a power outside yourself, consider it a sign. Get into the spirit of things. For inspiration, take a sauna, gaze into a fire, or just sit in the dark. Escape into things above and beyond yourself.

VI **The Lovers.** *This is a time for finding things out.* Look at your card. The look of love is in your eyes this year. And you drink in the world around you. Sparks fly. In business, look for mergers and acquisitions. Consider a change in careers. The year will find you attracted by someone or something . . . to the point of distraction. Infatuations and love affairs run rampant in the woods. Things feel "predestined," even allurements and temptations. Some will test the waters of existing relationships and find them tepid. You may switch partners, alter positions, or change roles. Whatever you do, it will make you feel young again, new again, vital and alive (maybe for the first time). Keep an eye out for the signs that indicate things are about to change. Read the look in others' eyes. Discover your own sensuality. Return to nature. If you have trouble getting in touch with your own feelings, don't be afraid to take your clothes off.

VII The Chariot. This is a time for overcoming things. And the odds may be great! Look at your card. Challenging, testing, and proving are all in the picture this year. And crises have a way of popping up. There will be plenty of fires to put out. The environment may even seem unstable at times. Yet it's a time when rising stars tend to shine. Stay on top of things. Turn inward and muster up your courage. Know that you can do it! Grasp the reigns of your own life and pull your own strings. Heroic efforts will pay off suddenly in sure, swift, thrilling victories. To clear your mind of distractions, get some good strenuous physical exercise. Pump some iron. This is a year that runs on a mixture of sweat and adrenaline.

VIII Justice. This is a time for evening things out. Look at your card. Steady does it this year. It is a time that calls for sacrifice. And if you believe in karma, this is about as close as it gets. This is the year when you will find out what your past adds up to. You may even question its worth. And you may have to give up something. But hang in there, will you? This is a time of transition, a critical turning point. However you emerge from this, make it be for the better. This is a time when rewards and punishments are handed out—not randomly, mind you, but with equity and fairness. You will get your just reward! If your life seems to hang suspended in the balance, don't be surprised. You cannot go forward just yet; you can only look back—with nostalgia or regret—on the past. It is a time of steady nerves and preparations. For help with your problems, try yoga or other forms of peaceful meditation. Hang on to the moment. These are the good old days.

IX The Hermit. This is the time for understanding things. Look at your card. It is a time for hiding and seeking, when you will look for (and find) the answers to perplexing problems. It's also a year when you will be drawn into the silence of yourself. It's a good time for giving and taking professional advice. It is a good time to get off by yourself. Take a break from the mundane. Escape the rat race and the routine. The time is right for correcting old habits and resolving long-standing differences. A light goes on. A voice cries from the wilderness. Suddenly the answers come . . . often from a small voice within yourself. Take notice! To relax, take a few deep breaths. Drink tea. Cook with herbs. Touch stones. Watch the birds fly home to their nests. Hold up a candle in the dark.

X Wheel of Fortune. This is the time when things happen. Look at your card. This is a year when being at the right place at the right time counts. It's a time when you can simply luck out in life. You might get a big break or some once-in-a-lifetime opportunity from out of the blue. But beware! Your luck can as easily change in the opposite direction. Either way, this is a year when you are the subject of things that are happening totally outside of your control. Fate rules! Some rise. Some fall. The weather changes suddenly. But for those who like to spin the wheel and take their chances—and it's all in the odds—this is a year for riding out your luck. Some long shots will pay off big. But in general, it's how you play your cards that counts. Whatever happens to you this year, good luck. If it makes you feel any better, be sure to wear your lucky underwear.

EXTRA CREDIT

Compute the Tarot cards for last year and next year. Just change the years when you add things up.

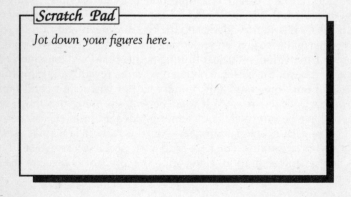

Scratch Pad

Jot down your figures here.

Reading #2

EXTRA EXTRA CREDIT!

What the heck, compute your Tarot card for every year of your life and look for recurring patterns in the events that took place as different cards cycled up.

Go on to the next Reading whenever you are ready to continue.

Reading #3

WHAT'S NEXT?

Readings #1 and #2 showed you how to use numerology to determine the cards that cover you and cross you this year. In this Reading you will shuffle the cards to find the ones that cover and cross you at this moment. By interpreting the specific combination of cards that you deal up, this Reading will give you some advice on what you should do next.

TAROT TOOLS

Use the same cards you used in Readings #1 and #2:

I	The Magician
II	The High Priestess
III	The Empress
IV	The Emperor
V	The Hierophant
VI	The Lovers
VII	The Chariot
VIII or XI	Justice
IX	The Hermit
X	Wheel of Fortune

HOW TO

Using these 10 cards, simply shuffle.

Shuffle the cards any way you choose. (It is absolutely impossible for you to shuffle them wrong.) As you shuffle, ask your question, which for this Reading is: **What do I need to do next?** Or, if you want to get more specific, you can ask: **What should I do about _____?** Fill in the blank with one of your concerns, like "this project," "my love life," "my financial situation," etc.

Keep shuffling until the cards are done. The cards are done when they just don't want to be shuffled anymore. Your cards are also done if, as you shuffle, one leaps out of the deck.

Deal up the top card (or use the leaper) and lay it faceup in front of you.

This card *covers you*. It represents who you are today (or in some specific situation that you want to name).

Note: If you ever turn up a card that's upside down, turn it around so it's right side up, and don't worry about it. You can learn how to read the cards in reversal later.

Across this first card, place the second card (the one now on top of the deck, or the one that leaps out of the deck with subsequent shuffling). This card *crosses you*, representing the situation you face.

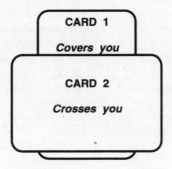

Take a moment to look at the two cards you have dealt up, then consult the Answer section of this Reading. Your answer will suggest a course of action for you to take.

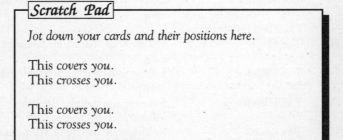

Scratch Pad

Jot down your cards and their positions here.

This *covers you*.
This *crosses you*.

This *covers you*.
This *crosses you*.

For additional information on any card, consult the Quick Reference Guide.

THE ANSWERS

I The Magician

When crossed by . . .		This indicates you will want to . . .
I	The Magician	....
II	The High Priestess	act according to your conscience. Be open.
III	The Empress	act according to your needs. Be natural.
IV	The Emperor	act according to others' wishes. Be loyal.
V	The Hierophant	act according to the rules. Be moral.
VI	The Lovers	act according to your desires. Be romantic.
VII	The Chariot	act according to your skills. Be brave.
VIII	Justice	act according to what is fair. Be honest.
IX	The Hermit	act in your own best interest. Be yourself.
X	Wheel of Fortune	be ready to act on a "sure thing." Take a risk.

II The High Priestess

When crossed by . . .		This indicates you must . . .
I	The Magician	follow your own routine. Remain cool.
II	The High Priestess	....
III	The Empress	follow your intuition. Remain calm.
IV	The Emperor	follow your gut feelings. Remain in control.
V	The Hierophant	follow your beliefs. Remain diligent.
VI	The Lovers	follow your instincts. Remain true.
VII	The Chariot	follow your urges. Remain on guard.
VIII	Justice	follow your conscience. Remain convicted.

II The High Priestess (cont.)

When crossed by . . .		This indicates you must . . .
IX	The Hermit	follow your own inner call. Remain on course.
X	Wheel of Fortune	be ready for a winning streak. Look into all possibilities.

III The Empress

When crossed by . . .		This indicates you will need to . . .
I	The Magician	tend to your own business. Mind your ambitions.
II	The High Priestess	tend to your inner needs. Mind your intuition.
III	The Empress	....
IV	The Emperor	tend to the wishes of others. Mind your constituencies.
V	The Hierophant	tend to the things others expect. Mind your public image.
VI	The Lovers	tend to your heart's desire. Mind your feelings.
VII	The Chariot	tend to the advances of others. Mind your duties.
VIII	Justice	tend to the letter of the law. Mind your resolutions.
IX	The Hermit	tend to those who depend on you. Mind your conscience.
X	Wheel of Fortune	be ready for whatever happens. Consider the odds.

IV The Emperor

When crossed by . . .		This indicates you have to . . .
I	The Magician	control and direct your energy. Rule your own actions.
II	The High Priestess	control and direct your thoughts. Rule your subconscious urges.
III	The Empress	control and direct work in progress. Rule your personal development.

IV The Emperor *(cont.)*

When crossed by . . .		This indicates you have to . . .
IV	The Emperor	. . . .
V	The Hierophant	control and direct others. Rule your own behavior.
VI	The Lovers	control and direct your desires. Rule your own body.
VII	The Chariot	control and direct your temper. Rule your own reactions.
VIII	Justice	control and direct your criticism. Rule over your own decisions.
IX	The Hermit	control and direct your destiny. Make your own rules.
X	Wheel of Fortune	be ready to defend your territory. Weigh the options.

V The Hierophant

When crossed by . . .		This indicates you should . . .
I	The Magician	refrain from self-indulgence. Practice self-control.
II	The High Priestess	refrain from speaking out of turn. Practice self-restraint.
III	The Empress	refrain from worrying about tomorrow. Practice faith.
IV	The Emperor	refrain from lording it over others. Practice humility.
V	The Hierophant	. . . .
VI	The Lovers	refrain from sex. Practice abstinence.
VII	The Chariot	refrain from acts of violence. Practice peaceful coexistence.
VIII	Justice	refrain from criticizing others. Practice toleration.
IX	The Hermit	refrain from public contact. Practice meditation.
X	Wheel of Fortune	be ready when the time comes. Get your act together.

VI The Lovers

When crossed by . . .		This indicates you need to . . .
I	The Magician	know what's up. Check out the action.
II	The High Priestess	know what's been happening. Check out the situation.
III	The Empress	know what can be expected. Check out the current status.
IV	The Emperor	know what the rules are. Check out the facts.
V	The Hierophant	know what's expected of you. Check out the arrangements.
VI	The Lovers	. . . .
VII	The Chariot	know what to look out for. Check out the signals.
VIII	Justice	know what the consequences are. Check out the past.
IX	The Hermit	know the truth. Check out your own feelings.
X	Wheel of Fortune	be ready to make a commitment. Take a chance.

VII The Chariot

When crossed by . . .		This indicates you will have to . . .
I	The Magician	prove what you can do. Take the initiative.
II	The High Priestess	prove which side you are on. Take a stand.
III	The Empress	prove you have endurance. Take whatever time it takes.
IV	The Emperor	prove your leadership. Take the responsibility.
V	The Hierophant	prove your loyalty. Take the first move.
VI	The Lovers	prove your intentions. Take heart.
VII	The Chariot	. . . .
VIII	Justice	prove you can be trusted. Take the oath.
IX	The Hermit	prove yourself. Take the test.
X	Wheel of Fortune	get ready to receive recognition. Hold out hope.

VIII Justice

When crossed by . . .		This indicates you must . . .
I	The Magician	decide things for yourself. Consider cause and effect.
II	The High Priestess	decide what you should do next. Consider the possibilities.
III	The Empress	decide when the time is right. Consider the circumstances.
IV	The Emperor	decide what's necessary. Consider what's fair.
V	The Hierophant	decide what should be done. Consider the consequences.
VI	The Lovers	decide who and what you love. Consider the implications.
VII	The Chariot	decide to do your very best. Consider the alternatives.
VIII	Justice	....
IX	The Hermit	decide what's right for you. Consider how far you will go.
X	Wheel of Fortune	be ready to pay the price, or reap the rewards, of your actions.

IX The Hermit

When crossed by . . .		This indicates you need to . . .
I	The Magician	learn how to direct your energy. Focus on your goals.
II	The High Priestess	learn how to use your time. Focus on what's most important now.
III	The Empress	learn how to nourish others. Focus on meeting individual needs.
IV	The Emperor	learn how to manage others. Focus on developing strengths.
V	The Hierophant	learn how to inspire others. Focus on high ideals.
VI	The Lovers	learn how to care about others. Focus on mutual interests.
VII	The Chariot	learn how to protect others. Focus on overcoming your own fears.

IX The Hermit (*cont.*)

When crossed by . . .		This indicates you need to . . .
VIII	Justice	learn how to accept the truth. Focus on what to do about it.
IX	The Hermit	....
X	Wheel of Fortune	get ready to step into the spotlight. Make the most of your good fortune.

X Wheel of Fortune

When crossed by . . .		This indicates you will have . . .
I	The Magician	the chance to redirect yourself. Change your focus.
II	The High Priestess	the chance to fulfill your destiny. Change your own course.
III	The Empress	the chance to grow and mature. Change your environment.
IV	The Emperor	the chance to lead others. Change your position.
V	The Hierophant	the chance to influence the masses. Change your mission.
VI	The Lovers	the chance to change your life. Change partners.
VII	The Chariot	the chance to overcome the odds. Change your strategy.
VIII	Justice	the chance to decide things once and for all. Change your opinion.
IX	The Hermit	the chance to lead others. Change your outlook.
X	Wheel of Fortune	....

EXTRA CREDIT

For a more detailed Reading, shuffle and deal as before, but keep dealing out cards until no cards are left. Read them all.

┌─**Scratch Pad**─────────────────────────

Jot down your cards and their positions here.

Cover/Cross
Cover/Cross
Cover/Cross
Cover/Cross
Cover/Cross
Cover/Cross
Cover/Cross
Cover/Cross
Cover/Cross
Cover/Cross

EXTRA EXTRA CREDIT!

What the heck, shuffle and deal your cards; then turn to Reading #1, which will describe the card that *covers you* (who you are in this situation). Turn to Reading #2, which will describe the card that *crosses you* (giving you a hint at the situation you face). Then draw your own conclusions.

Go on to the next Reading whenever you are ready to continue.

Reading #4

WHEN WILL I KNOW?

In your first three Readings you have used the Tarot to help
you find the answers to some important questions about
yourself. In the process, you have learned how to do a very
basic and reliable Tarot layout (or spread), a two-card
"Cover and Cross" Reading. Now you'll learn how to do a
three-card Reading. In this Reading we will be using a basic
three-card spread to pinpoint events in time.

TAROT TOOLS
Use the same cards you have been using:

I	*The Magician*
II	*The High Priestess*
III	*The Empress*
IV	*The Emperor*
V	*The Hierophant*
VI	*The Lovers*
VII	*The Chariot*
VIII *or* XI	*Justice*
IX	*The Hermit*
X	*Wheel of Fortune*

HOW TO
Shuffle the cards, and ask: **When will I know about _____?**

As always, the cards will be done when one leaps from the deck, or when
the cards simply don't want to go into one another, or when you just know
they're done. In any case, stop shuffling and turn up the top card . . . place
this first card faceup in front of you—but don't put the cards down just
yet.

Place the second card in the pile to the right of the first card you dealt
up before. Place the third card faceup to the right of the second card.

Look up the answers to each of the three cards in the order in which
you turned them up. The three separate charts in the Answer section tell
you what each card means in each of the three positions. When strung

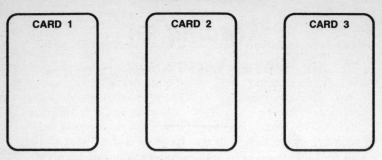

| CARD 1 | CARD 2 | CARD 3 |

together, your "three" answers from these charts will form a single, complete sentence, which represents your total Reading.

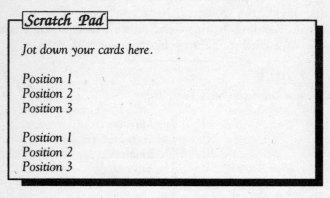

Scratch Pad

Jot down your cards here.

Position 1
Position 2
Position 3

Position 1
Position 2
Position 3

HINT: If the answer you get on your first Reading doesn't make perfect sense to you, write it down to see if the meaning will become clear in time. Until then, repeat the Reading as often as you choose. Sometimes it takes several readings to get a complete message. Be sure to record your answers.

For additional information on any card, consult the Quick Reference Guide.

THE ANSWERS

Position 1

(Read for the card you turned up first.)

When in first position. . .	The message of this card is. . .
I The Magician	That which matters most. . .
II The High Priestess	The prospects for the future . . .

Position 1 (cont.)

When in first position...		The message of this card is...
III	The Empress	The outcome of past efforts...
IV	The Emperor	What you need to know...
V	The Hierophant	The appropriate response to give...
VI	The Lovers	The issue that confronts you...
VII	The Chariot	The strategy that must be followed...
VIII	Justice	The decision that must be reached...
IX	The Hermit	The choices that are presented...
X	Wheel of Fortune	The amount of risk to take...

Position 2

(Read for the card you turned up second.)

When in second position...		The message of this card is...
I	The Magician	will be influenced by you...
II	The High Priestess	could be revealed to you...
III	The Empress	may reach its natural conclusion...
IV	The Emperor	might be settled without question...
V	The Hierophant	shall be realized...
VI	The Lovers	will be colored by emotion...
VII	The Chariot	could be challenged...
VIII	Justice	must be judged...
IX	The Hermit	may finally be understood...
X	Wheel of Fortune	will probably be changed for the better...

Position 3

(Read for the card you turned up third.)

When in third position...		The message of this card is...
I	The Magician	by the New Moon.
II	The High Priestess	by the Crescent Moon.
III	The Empress	by the Full Moon.
IV	The Emperor	by the Quarter Moon.
V	The Hierophant	by the Winter Solstice.
VI	The Lovers	by the Spring Equinox.

Position 3 (*cont.*)

When in third position. . .		The message of this card is . . .
VII	*The Chariot*	by the Summer Solstice.
VIII	*Justice*	by the Fall Equinox.
IX	*The Hermit*	in a matter of days.
X	*Wheel of Fortune*	within the year.

EXTRA CREDIT

To get a quick-and-dirty timeframe for any type of question you need to ask, just shuffle the 10 Trump cards while you ask your time-dependent question. Turn up a single card when the deck is done. In this case, skip the first two tables in the Answer section, and read the card as if it were in position 3.

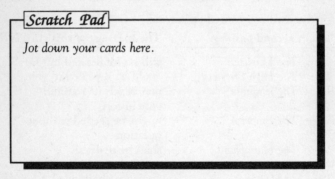

Scratch Pad

Jot down your cards here.

EXTRA EXTRA CREDIT!

What the heck, to sharpen your skills, keep a log book of your Readings about when things are supposed to happen. Every once in a while, compute your batting average.

Go on to the next Reading whenever you are ready to continue.

Reading #5

WHAT SHOULD I BE (WHEN I GROW UP)?

So far you have been using the first 10 Tarot Trumps to ask
questions about who you are and where you're going in
general. Now you'll be using the Tarot Wands—roughly
equivalent to Clubs in regular card decks—to ask work-
related questions. *Wands are about the things we do for a living.*
In this Reading you will learn how to use the first 10 Wands
in order to select the type of work that suits you best.

TAROT TOOLS

Set aside the 10 cards you have been using for the previous four Readings.
(But don't put them too far out of reach, for we'll be needing them again
shortly.)

In this Reading all you need is the Ace through 10 of Wands from your
Tarot deck:

Ace   of Wands
2   of Wands
3   of Wands
4   of Wands
5   of Wands
6   of Wands
7   of Wands
8   of Wands
9   of Wands
10   of Wands

HOW TO

To select your card for this Reading, we will be using a numerological
method, as we did in Readings #1 and #2. The question we will be asking
is: **What kind of work would I be good at?**

To select your card, add up the letters of your *first initial* plus your *last name*:

A	1	J	10	S	19
B	2	K	11	T	20
C	3	L	12	U	21
D	4	M	13	V	22
E	5	N	14	W	23
F	6	O	15	X	24
G	7	P	16	Y	25
H	8	Q	17	Z	26
I	9	R	18		

Let's say your name is T. Cox. You would "add up" your name as follows:

$$(T = 20) + (C = 3) + (O = 15) + (X = 24) = 62$$
$$20 + 3 + 15 + 24 = 62$$

Now add up the result: $6 + 2 = 8$. If "T. Cox" is your name, the 8 of Wands is your card. The object is to get to a number that is between 1 and 10. If you still have a bigger number after adding twice, add a third time.

If your name adds up exactly to 10, reduce it again to 1 only if the first letter of your first name is equal to an odd number. If the first letter is equal to an even number, leave it as 10.

Look up your number in the Answer section.

Scratch Pad

Do your math here.

HINT: Ladies, if you have chosen to take your husband's name, you might want to try this Reading for your maiden name too. Men, try your mother's maiden name.

For additional information on any card, consult the Quick Reference Guide.

<u>THE ANSWERS</u>

Ace of Wands. For a living, consider the line of work your parents do, for this is a card that involves a legacy of some kind—something that is handed over to you to manage or carry on, like a torch passed on in a relay race. *Look at your card.* You will be happiest doing something entrepreneurial, experimental, or even speculative in nature, though it might take an investment of time and money for your bright ideas to become commercial successes. When in doubt, choose an occupation that involves the use of your hands—which are known for their ability to work wonders—or dabble in the written word. For best results, remember, everything that happens around you should be viewed as an opportunity. Keep your eyes (and mind) open to new ideas. Making the most of the things that come along will be the key to your success. *When you draw the Ace of Wands, you can expect an important break to come your way. If your Key Card in Reading #1 was Wheel of Fortune, you will be especially lucky in your upcoming professional pursuits.*

2 of Wands. You will either want a job that gives you the opportunity to get on in the world, or you will want to do something that takes you to far shores and distant lands, for this is the card of those who are smitten with wanderlust; and when it comes, they must heed the call of the horizon. *Look at your card.* You may be inclined to change jobs, positions, or your mind as frequently as the wind changes directions, at least until you discover what you really want to do with your life. But it will come to you eventually, and—for you—looking for it is half the fun anyway. You will especially enjoy anything that involves long-range planning or dealing with associates at a distance. Getting away from it all to mull things over is the key to your success. *When you draw the 2 of Wands, you will want to watch for some important news from abroad. If your Key Card in Reading #1 was The Hermit, you should consider going on a retreat, taking a continuing education or self-improvement course, or going to a seminar.*

3 of Wands. You ought to be in wholesale or anything involving the movement of goods and commodities across state lines or international borders. *Look at your card.* An importing or exporting business would suit you to a T, for this is a card about maintaining a balance of trade. Shipping and expediting are good fields for you. Most certainly, your chosen line of work will involve keeping inventories, taking orders, juggling cash flows, or writing up a balance sheet. Taking the time on a routine basis to study the general economic situation and review market needs is the secret to your financial success. Also, be sure to routinely review the progress you are making toward your goals. *When you draw the 3 of Wands, watch for* changes in the work climate. *If your Key Card in Reading #1 was Justice, you should take time ASAP to review your assets and liabilities.*

4 of Wands. You would prefer to work in a service industry or in a white-collar government job, but you aren't really interested in pushing paper or punching numbers into a computer. *Look at your card.* It's the people contact that you crave. In fact, you get your energy by going out and being with others. You would be happiest in a position that puts you in constant contact with the public and involves at least an occasional party or social event, especially if it's a gala, for this is a card that has something to do with celebrations. Personality, poise, tact, character, and clothes are the main factors that enter into your success. *When you draw the 4 of Wands, you can expect successful performance at work. If The Chariot was your Key Card in Reading #1, you will be a guest of honor at an upcoming event.*

5 of Wands. You thrive (and survive!) in an environment where the competition is stiff and the stakes are high. *Look at your card.* Since you work (and play) well with others, you have a good sense of what it takes to master and direct your energies to the cause at hand. Discipline and endurance are your hallmarks. Since you want to see the big action, you will do best in a Fortune 500 company, or in any position where performance counts. Opt for a wage structure that includes a healthy commission, a bonus program, or an incentive plan based on results or quotas. *If you draw the 5 of Wands, make sure you understand the playing field and the basic rules of the game before you begin. If The Lovers was your Key Card in Reading #1, watch out for conflicts of interest, and always make sure you can deliver what you promise.*

6 of Wands. To be happy in your chosen line of work, you will need a job that involves a just cause to crusade for, or a noble purpose. *Look at your card.* Jobs where you can do something to change the world, advance civilization, snuff out vices, or right wrongs have a particular appeal to you, especially if the job calls for fund-raising or canvassing door to door. You would enjoy being involved in public works projects, environmental programs, civil rights movements, or activism of any kind. *When you draw the 6 of Wands, consider devoting some of your free time to volunteer efforts of a worthwhile nature. If your Key Card from Reading #1 was The Hierophant, you are a peacemaker by nature.*

7 of Wands. You are the sort of person who gravitates toward positions of leadership or even political office. *Look at your card.* Your popular position on the issues gives you a good chance of succeeding if you do choose to throw your hat into the political arena. (If elected, just be sure to keep your promises and take the high ground in everything you do.) If you don't opt for public service, look for a job that has a lot of office politics or requires you to adopt a position to get ahead. Image is the key to your success. *When you draw the 7 of Wands, you will have the opportunity to prove what you can do. If in Reading #1 The Emperor was your Key Card, your work has come to the attention of someone in a position of power.*

8 of Wands. This card is about messages and communications of all kinds speeding toward their destination. *Look at your card.* You will enjoy jobs in which lots of data change hands or in which computers talk to one another long distance. But more important, you will thrive on anything that needs to absolutely, positively get there overnight or in any job that requires you to work under a time pressure while maintaining high quality or professional standards. In looking for work, seek openings that require you to perform well on tight deadlines, to meet schedules, or to perform on cue, for meeting deadlines is your key to success. *If you draw the 8 of Wands, review schedules. If your Key Card in Reading #1 was The Empress, the project you are working on is nearing completion.*

9 of Wands. You will find yourself in positions where you need to hold down the fort, for your claim to fame is that you are particularly good at keeping watch over things that need to be guarded. Consequently you are often entrusted with trade secrets. *Look at your card.* You will want to look for work that involves continual concentration and attentiveness to detail, which are the hallmarks of your success. Wherever you work, you serve as a good example of dedication and commitment. *When you draw the 9 of Wands, you will need to keep up your defenses in the weeks ahead. If The High Priestess was your Key Card in Reading #1, seek environments that reward corporate loyalty and continual diligence, consistency, and dependability.*

10 of Wands. Any job that requires you to carry your own weight will appeal to you. Be careful, thoughtful, about taking on more than you can do or taking on the work of others—both of which you are inclined to do—for this is the card of perfectionists bordering on workaholics. *Look at your card.* To the extent you are rewarded by it, you will like a job that requires you to take your work home with you, especially if the work involves something of a challenging nature. Consistent, tireless, outstanding performance is your key to success, along with the fact that you insist on living up to your own high standards for yourself. *When you draw the 10 of Wands, you are taking your work too seriously. If in Reading #1 The Magician was your Key Card, you will master the challenges that face you.*

EXTRA CREDIT

For a quick assessment of your current job, shuffle the cards and ask: **What does the future hold for me at work?** When the cards are done, deal up the top one. For this question, just read the portion of the answers printed in *italics*.

If you're in the mood, complete this same Reading for those you know and love.

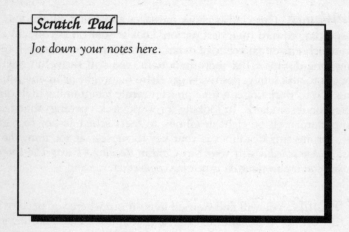

Scratch Pad

Jot down your notes here.

EXTRA EXTRA CREDIT!

What the heck, do these Readings for everybody at work to see what you're up against.

Go on to the next Reading whenever you are ready to continue.

Reading #6

WHAT IS THE WORK CLIMATE?

As in Reading #5, we will continue to ask specific work-related questions of the cards, using the suit of Wands. But since the 10 Trump cards we used earlier also work for any question related to worldly matters, we're going to use them along with the 10 Wands for a two-card Cover and Cross Reading. The Answer section will show you how to read each pair of cards in combination.

TAROT TOOLS

You will need the same 10 suit cards you used in Reading #5: the Ace through 10 of Wands. Plus, you will need the 10 Trump cards you used in Readings #1 through #4:

I	The Magician
II	The High Priestess
III	The Empress
IV	The Emperor
V	The Hierophant
VI	The Lovers
VII	The Chariot
VIII or XI	Justice
IX	The Hermit
X	Wheel of Fortune

Keep these cards in separate stacks.

HOW TO

This will be the same kind of Cover and Cross Reading that you did in Reading #3. (See the Quick Reference Guide for an illustration of this layout.)

Shuffle the 10 Wands, while you ask this question: **What changes can I look for at work?**

You can also use this Reading to answer specific questions about a particular project, assignment, or decision that you have to make at work: **What should I do next about _____?**

When the cards are done being shuffled, deal up the top Wand and lay it faceup in front of you. *This card covers you.* It represents the current situation you are in at work.

Now pick up and shuffle the 10 Trumps as you repeat the question. When these cards are done, deal up the top Trump and place it faceup, crosswise over the card already dealt. *This card crosses you.* It represents the challenge that you face at work.

To see what your cards mean in combination, consult the answers. Your answer will sum up the situation and suggest a course of action for you to take.

|Scratch Pad|

Jot down your cards here.

Cover/Cross

Cover/Cross

HINT: Answers that don't make sense to you now may become clear in a day or so. Write them down for future reference.

For additional information on any card, consult the Quick Reference Guide.

THE ANSWERS

Ace of Wands

When crossed by . . .	This indicates . . .
I The Magician	action plans are initiated. Your career advances.
II The High Priestess	new forecasts are required. An opportunity is given to you.

Ace of Wands *(cont.)*

When crossed by . . .		This indicates . . .
III	The Empress	past plans are reviewed. You are given a chance to improve.
IV	The Emperor	the competition is studied. You are offered a better position.
V	The Hierophant	new incentive plans are announced. You are encouraged to shine.
VI	The Lovers	new methods are proposed. You are given a couple of options.
VII	The Chariot	top performers are rewarded. You are recognized in some way.
VIII	Justice	results are reported. You get your just reward.
IX	The Hermit	a consultant is brought in. You are offered some good advice.
X	Wheel of Fortune	risks and opportunities are assessed. This is the chance of a lifetime.

2 of Wands

When crossed by . . .		This indicates . . .
I	The Magician	expansion is planned. Expand your own horizons.
II	The High Priestess	the way things are done is altered. Go along with the new direction.
III	The Empress	higher profits are sought. Focus on your own productivity.
IV	The Emperor	acquisitions command management attention. Carry out all your assignments in confidence.
V	The Hierophant	new plans meet with approval. Live up to high expectations.
VI	The Lovers	opportunities are vigorously pursued. It is time to pursue your own interests.
VII	The Chariot	alternative aims cause conflict. Make an effort to stay out of the fray.
VIII	Justice	extreme measures are deemed justifiable. Weigh your own alternatives.

2 of Wands (*cont.*)

When crossed by . . .		This indicates . . .
IX	The Hermit	outreach efforts are strongly advised. Base decisions on your own experiences.
X	Wheel of Fortune	changes are definitely in the offing. You will write your own ticket.

3 of Wands

When crossed by . . .		This indicates . . .
I	The Magician	current assets are divested. Somebody wants to trade with you.
II	The High Priestess	offices are moved. You are transferred or relocated.
III	The Empress	new work flows yield improved results. Trade the short term for the long haul.
IV	The Emperor	tighter supervision is enforced. A business trip is in the offing.
V	The Hierophant	public relations is involved. You need to communicate with someone at a distance.
VI	The Lovers	joint ventures are explored. There is a love interest at work.
VII	The Chariot	the troops are addressed. You will be given new marching orders.
VIII	Justice	trade-offs will be made. You have to weigh your options.
IX	The Hermit	higher goals will be set. Demonstrate your leadership skills.
X	Wheel of Fortune	some risks will be taken. Climb out on a limb.

4 of Wands

When crossed by . . .		This indicates . . .
I	The Magician	cooperative efforts are the current direction. You will seal a deal.
II	The High Priestess	things are running their course. Your time is coming.

4 of Wands *(cont.)*

When crossed by . . .		This indicates . . .
III	The Empress	partnerships will presently pay off. You will come out ahead.
IV	The Emperor	deals are being negotiated. You will strike a bargain.
V	The Hierophant	proposals are in the process of being blessed. You put in a public appearance.
VI	The Lovers	joint ventures will soon be consummated. You reach a meeting of the minds.
VII	The Chariot	drafts are subject to comment. You need to follow orders.
VIII	Justice	contracts are being reviewed by legal counsel. You need to sign on the dotted line.
IX	The Hermit	the news is about to be announced. You need to take a stand.
X	Wheel of Fortune	everything is up for grabs. Negotiate a new arrangement.

5 of Wands

When crossed by . . .		This indicates . . .
I	The Magician	efforts are being redirected. Compete for your rightful place.
II	The High Priestess	new competitors emerge. Jockey for position.
III	The Empress	things get in the way of progress. Stick to your knitting.
IV	The Emperor	management takes the hard line. Tough it out.
V	The Hierophant	sacrifices have to be made. Tighten your belt.
VI	The Lovers	somebody moves in on your territory. Stand your ground.
VII	The Chariot	entrepreneurs emerge. Defend your turf.
VIII	Justice	the market fluctuates. Hedge your bets.

5 of Wands (*cont.*)

When crossed by . . .		This indicates . . .
IX	The Hermit	it's difficult to reach high goals. The end result is worth the struggle.
X	Wheel of Fortune	conflicts cannot be avoided. Strive to come out on top.

6 of Wands

When crossed by . . .		This indicates . . .
I	The Magician	high goals are set. Reach for the brass ring.
II	The High Priestess	a phase-in approach is considered. Take one hurdle at a time.
III	The Empress	progress will be closely monitored. You pass the initial test.
IV	The Emperor	authority must be delegated. You deserve more responsibility.
V	The Hierophant	someone is held up as an example. If the shoe fits, wear it.
VI	The Lovers	proposals must be made in advance. Submit your best ideas.
VII	The Chariot	a good leader must be chosen. Apply for the job.
VIII	Justice	a trial period is considered. You pass with flying colors.
IX	The Hermit	new information comes to light. Forge your own path to the top.
X	Wheel of Fortune	just recognition is given. Enjoy the moment of victory.

7 of Wands

When crossed by . . .		This indicates you must . . .
I	The Magician	demonstrate that you are in control. Assume a firm stance.
II	The High Priestess	concentrate as hard as you can. Look them in the eye.

7 of Wands (*cont.*)

When crossed by . . .		This indicates you must . . .
III	The Empress	survey the situation. Bluff your way out of it.
IV	The Emperor	remain firm in your position. Hold the line.
V	The Hierophant	give something up. But hang on to what really matters.
VI	The Lovers	do not reveal your true intentions. Conceal your soft spots.
VII	The Chariot	steer clear of the conflict. Take the high ground.
VIII	Justice	voice a dissenting opinion. Stick up for your rights.
IX	The Hermit	make the calls as you see them. Signal for a time-out.
X	Wheel of Fortune	be ready for a hasty retreat. Stick it out as long as you can.

8 of Wands

When crossed by . . .		This indicates . . .
I	The Magician	a lot of things are up in the air. Juggle your work load.
II	The High Priestess	you have a lot of ideas. Incubate them before you shoot your mouth off.
III	The Empress	there are plenty of irons in the fire. Keep everything moving right along.
IV	The Emperor	many things come at you at once. Put out one fire at a time.
V	The Hierophant	many things compete for attention. Watch out for errors.
VI	The Lovers	there are many distractions. Be careful of miscalculations.
VII	The Chariot	there are a lot of instructions to follow. Mind you carry them all out.
VIII	Justice	there are plenty of decisions reached. Follow through on all of them.

8 of Wands *(cont.)*

When crossed by . . .		This indicates . . .
IX	The Hermit	many things vie for your time. Aim for the light at the end of the tunnel.
X	Wheel of Fortune	there are limitless possibilities. Give it your best shot.

9 of Wands

When crossed by . . .		This indicates you must . . .
I	The Magician	continue to do what you do best. Keep up the good work.
II	The High Priestess	watch for the tide to turn. Keep up appearances.
III	The Empress	do what you need to, to survive. Hang in there.
IV	The Emperor	stay on your guard. Hold down the fort.
V	The Hierophant	protect your way of life. Keep the faith.
VI	The Lovers	protect your interests. Remain diligent.
VII	The Chariot	dig in for the duration. Keep the peace.
VIII	Justice	be willing to perform double duty. Serve your time.
IX	The Hermit	work your way up. Remain true to yourself.
X	Wheel of Fortune	take everything in stride. Play the cards you're dealt.

10 of Wands

When crossed by . . .		This indicates . . .
I	The Magician	you are trying to do too much. Lighten up on yourself.
II	The High Priestess	you are taking it all too seriously. Go with the flow for a while.
III	The Empress	you are overachieving. Take a cold shower.

10 of Wands *(cont.)*

When crossed by . . .		**This indicates . . .**
IV	The Emperor	you are uptight. Sweat it out in the sauna or bath.
V	The Hierophant	you are working too hard. Take every seventh day off.
VI	The Lovers	you are tense and frustrated. Release some romantic energy.
VII	The Chariot	you are stressed out. Get some strenuous exercise.
VIII	Justice	you are hung up. Reassess your priorities.
IX	The Hermit	you are in up to your neck. Seek help.
X	Wheel of Fortune	you are feeling down and out. Take some time off.

EXTRA CREDIT

For a more detailed Reading, deal out additional Cover and Cross pairs, Wands crossed by Trumps, and look up the answer for each pair. You may find the answers are in chronological order. You can keep dealing until you run out of cards or until you're satisfied with the answer.

Scratch Pad

Jot down your cards and conclusions here.

Cover/Cross
Cover/Cross
Cover/Cross
Cover/Cross
Cover/Cross
Cover/Cross
Cover/Cross
Cover/Cross
Cover/Cross
Cover/Cross

EXTRA EXTRA CREDIT!

What the heck, do a month-by-month or week-by-week analysis of any given situation over any given period of time. Just do one Cover and Cross Reading for each period you want to assess.

Go on to the next Reading whenever you are ready to continue.

Reading #7

WHAT IS THE BUSINESS OUTLOOK?

In Reading #7 we will be combining all of the cards we have used so far to get a reading of what's in store for you in the employment arena.

TAROT TOOLS

You will need all of the cards you used in Reading # 6—the Ace through 10 of Wands, and Trumps I–X:

I	The Magician
II	The High Priestess
III	The Empress
IV	The Emperor
V	The Hierophant
VI	The Lovers
VII	The Chariot
VIII or XI	Justice
IX	The Hermit
X	Wheel of Fortune

Sort them out if need be and keep them in separate stacks.

HOW TO

This is a three-card Reading that starts by shuffling the Ace through 10 of Wands as you ask your question: **What do I need to know about my employment situation?**

When the cards are done, deal up the top Wand and place it faceup in front of you. Occupying *position 1* in the Reading, this card talks about the past.

Repeat your question as you shuffle the first 10 Tarot Trumps. When the cards are done, deal up the top Trump and place it faceup to the right of the Wand you turned over earlier. Occupying *position 2* in the Reading, this card represents the present.

Now shuffle the nine remaining Wands again, while repeating your question a third time. When the cards are done, deal up the top Wand and place it faceup to the right of the Trump card. This card occupies *position 3* in the Reading, thus representing the future. (See the Quick Reference Guide for an illustration of this layout.)

When you have done all of this, set the rest of your cards aside, and look up your answer.

Scratch Pad

Jot down your cards here.

Position 1 (past)
Position 2 (present)
Position 3 (future)

Position 1 (past)
Position 2 (present)
Position 3 (future)

For additional information on any card, consult the Quick Reference Guide.

THE ANSWERS

Position 1

When in first position...	In the past...
Ace of Wands	The first impression that you left...
2 of Wands	Something in your background...
3 of Wands	The fact that you distanced yourself...
4 of Wands	The promise that you made...
5 of Wands	The battle that you fought...
6 of Wands	The victory that you had...
7 of Wands	The resistance that you put up...
8 of Wands	The message you sent...
9 of Wands	The time you have spent...
10 of Wands	The extra burden you took on ...

Position 2

When in second position...		Now...
I	The Magician	affects what you are able to get done, and...
II	The High Priestess	determines how far you can go, but...
III	The Empress	creates certain expectations, but...
IV	The Emperor	determines what you can do, and...
V	The Hierophant	keeps you from doing what you want, but...
VI	The Lovers	attracts the attention of others, and...
VII	The Chariot	determines your level of recognition, but...
VIII	Justice	is the element that tips the scales, and...
IX	The Hermit	comes to light, and...
X	Wheel of Fortune	permits all the options to be kept open, but...

Position 3

When in third position...	In the future...
Ace of Wands	there are new developments to report.
2 of Wands	changes come from higher up.
3 of Wands	conditions are altered, to your advantage.
4 of Wands	you benefit from a proposition.
5 of Wands	the odds are about fifty-fifty that things will improve.
6 of Wands	you surmount your difficulties.
7 of Wands	a standoff looms.
8 of Wands	things speed to their obvious conclusion.
9 of Wands	you are able to hold on to your current position.
10 of Wands	you will need to put in some long hours.

EXTRA CREDIT

For an interesting twist, read all of the cards you dealt for this Reading in reverse order, from right to left (so the card on your right is now in position 1). Or shuffle again but deal from right to left. You can decide which direction works better for you.

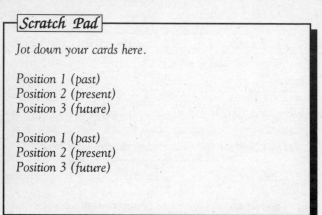

Scratch Pad

Jot down your cards here.

Position 1 (past)
Position 2 (present)
Position 3 (future)

Position 1 (past)
Position 2 (present)
Position 3 (future)

EXTRA EXTRA CREDIT!

What the heck, shuffle the Wands and ask: **What can I expect at work tomorrow?** When the cards are done, deal up the top one and consult the answers for position 3.

Go on to the next Reading whenever you are ready to continue.

Reading #8

HOW AM I DOING AT WORK?

In this Reading you will combine all of the cards you have
handled so far, in order to get a reading on how your work
life is going or how your studies will turn out. The method
you will be using is the most famous way of reading the
cards—the Celtic Cross. It will tell you about your
situation—past, present, and future—and give you
an idea of how you can expect things to go.

TAROT TOOLS

You will need all of the cards you used in Reading #7—the Ace through
10 of Wands, and Trumps I–X:

I	The Magician
II	The High Priestess
III	The Empress
IV	The Emperor
V	The Hierophant
VI	The Lovers
VII	The Chariot
VIII or XI	Justice
IX	The Hermit
X	Wheel of Fortune

Keep them in separate stacks for now.

HOW TO

First, shuffle the 10 Trumps together, as you ask your question: **How
am I doing at work?** or **What are my career prospects with regard
to _____?**

Shuffle until the cards are done, then deal up the top two cards and
place them in a Cover and Cross formation.

Next shuffle the 10 Wands together as you ask your question again: **How
am I doing at work?**

Shuffle until the Wands are done, then deal up the top four cards and place them in positions 3 through 6, around the first two Trumps you have already dealt.

Finally, shuffle the remaining Trumps and Wands together, as you ask your question one last time: **How am I doing at work?**

Shuffle until the cards are done, then deal up the top four cards and place them in positions 7 through 10 to the right of the cards you have already dealt:

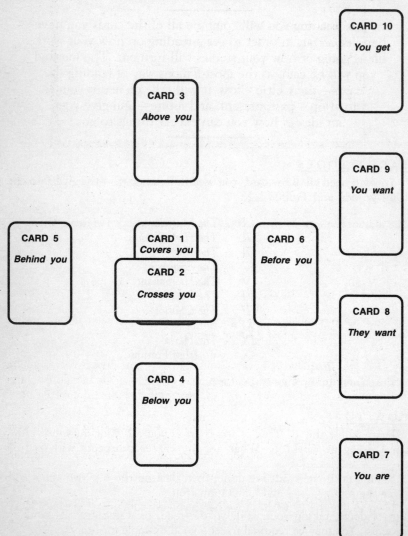

CARD 10

You get

CARD 3

Above you

CARD 9

You want

CARD 5

Behind you

CARD 1
Covers you

CARD 2

Crosses you

CARD 6

Before you

CARD 8

They want

CARD 4

Below you

CARD 7

You are

Scratch Pad

Note your cards and answers here.

Covers you

Crosses you

Above you

Below you

Behind you

Before you

You are

They want

You want

You get

Look up your cards by their position in the layout (1 through 10) in the Answer section.

For additional information on any card, consult the Quick Reference Guide.

THE ANSWERS

Position 1–This covers you.

The card in position 1 shows the current situation you are in with regard to the question you asked. *Look at your card.*

I The Magician. The work you are doing right now involves public contact, standing on your own two feet, retaining your composure, and performing in a certain way. You may be required to take the initiative.

II The High Priestess. The work you are doing right now involves long hours of sitting, more than a few late nights, and a fair share of mind reading. Despite the stress of your work load, you may be required to remain calm.

III The Empress. The work you are doing right now involves working out of doors, taking your work on the road, or watching over work in progress. You may be required to set a good example for others.

IV The Emperor. The work you are doing right now involves strong personalities, high expectations, and power plays of various kinds. You may be required to be tough on the outside and firm in your inner resolve.

V The Hierophant. The work you are doing right now involves many rules and regulations, established ways of doing things, or generally accepted practices. You may be required to live up to stringent standards.

VI The Lovers. The work you are doing right now involves something you love—or even adore—doing or somehow mixes business with pleasure. (Perhaps there is even a love interest on the work scene.) At any rate, you may be required to make some important choices soon.

VII The Chariot. The work you are doing involves feats of physical strength, tests of your athletic abilities, or heroic efforts of some kind. You may be required to take decisive, immediate action soon.

VIII Justice. The work you are doing involves weighing and balancing things, considering options and possible outcomes, or making difficult decisions. You may be required soon to make up your own mind regarding the truth of a matter or to decide whose side you are on.

IX The Hermit. The work you are doing right now involves long hours alone, self-sacrifice of some kind, or the courage to express your own opinion. Soon you may be required to seek someone else's advice or tell what you have learned.

X Wheel of Fortune. The work you are doing right now involves climbing the ladder of success, competing for your proper place in the ranks, or adapting to a change. You may soon be required to take a risk.

Position 2–This crosses you.

The card in position 2 shows the challenge that you will need to confront and overcome to reach your goal. *Look at your card.*

I The Magician. Your work requires you to adapt to a period of rapid changes and new developments in the environment, market, or workplace itself. The challenge is to keep up with everything that's going on.

II The High Priestess. Your work requires you to go through a period of relative stability or temporary slowdown. Time may seem to be passing slowly. The challenge is to find enough to keep you busy.

Reading #8

III The Empress. Your work requires you to deal with something dated, time-sensitive, or due on a deadline. The challenge is to keep up with the work load.

IV The Emperor. You are required to have your work reviewed or inspected by someone else. The challenge is to do everything your bosses want in the way they want it done.

V The Hierophant. Your work requires your performance to measure up to some pretty high standards. The challenge is to live up to the high expectations that others have of you.

VI The Lovers. Your work requires you to be trustworthy, loyal, and diligent, even though it may well be a love/hate relationship of temporary duration. The challenge is to keep your priorities in the right order.

VII The Chariot. Your work requires you to be standing by so that you are ready to spring into action when you're needed. The challenge is to be ready, willing, and able at all times.

VIII Justice. Your work requires you to make your own decisions and choices. The challenge is to establish the correct priorities and then apply yourself.

IX The Hermit. Your work requires you to schedule your time carefully and maintain your own schedule. The challenge is to fit everything you need to do into the hours of the day.

X Wheel of Fortune. Your work requires you to roll with the punches and take advantage of the opportunities that come along. The challenge to survive the changes that take place outside your own control.

Position 3—This is above you.

The card in position 3 is said to be "above you." It represents the best you can hope for, given the current conditions. *Look at your card.*

Ace of Wands. There promises to be an opportunity that comes at you from left field.

2 of Wands. There promises to be an opportunity for expanding your horizons.

Position 3 *(cont.)*

3 of Wands. There promises to be an opportunity to succeed in a joint undertaking.

4 of Wands. There promises to be an opportunity to win the heart of another.

5 of Wands. There promises to be an opportunity to go after what you want.

6 of Wands. There promises to be an opportunity to prove yourself.

7 of Wands. There promises to be an opportunity to motivate others.

8 of Wands. There promises to be an opportunity to be on the receiving end of the stick.

9 of Wands. There promises to be an opportunity to be entrusted with a secret.

10 of Wands. There promises to be an opportunity for moving on to bigger and better things.

Position 4—This is below you.

The card in position 4 is said to be "below you." Cards in the fourth position show the past foundation that needs to be considered with regard to your specific question. *Look at your card.*

Ace of Wands. Your current success depends upon specific actions you have taken in the past, breaks you have gotten, or your overall record of achievement.

2 of Wands. Your current success depends upon plans you have already completed, methods you followed successfully in the past, or things that have taken place at a distance.

3 of Wands. Your current success depends upon a course of action you took in the past, a course of study you completed, or past accomplishments of various kinds.

4 of Wands. Your current success depends upon your ability to live up to the promises you have made in the past, to meet past commitments, or to call upon old contacts.

Position 4 *(cont.)*

5 of Wands. Your current success depends upon your ability to resolve past conflicts, to overcome existing obstacles, or to beat the odds.

6 of Wands. Your current success depends upon your ability to live up to your reputation, to outdo your past level of achievement, or to figure out what to do for an encore.

7 of Wands. Your current success depends upon the level of grass-roots support you have successfully mustered in the past, the size and loyalty of your constituency, or the approval of family and friends.

8 of Wands. Your current success depends upon the things you have set in motion in the past, the contacts you have already made, or the actions you have already taken.

9 of Wands. Your current success depends upon the assumptions you have made in the past, the secrets you have kept, and the loyalties you have developed.

10 of Wands. Your current success depends upon your ability to overcome past defeats, to get out from under the things that oppress you, or to throw off the things that seem to burden you.

Position 5—This is behind you.
Position 6—This is before you.

The card in position 5 is said to be "behind you." Cards in the fifth position point out something that just happened that has a bearing on your question. *Look at your card.*

The card in position 6 is said to be "before you." Cards in the sixth position reveal something that's just about to happen. *Look at your card.*

This same table will give you the Readings for cards in either position 5 or position 6.

In position 5 the cards should be read as *Just recently . . .*

In position 6 the cards should be read as *Just coming up . . .*

Ace of Wands	I see an opportunity coming at you from out of the blue.
2 of Wands	I see you holding the world in your hands.
3 of Wands	I see you making some trade-offs.
4 of Wands	I see you cementing a deal.
5 of Wands	I see you demonstrating your skills.

Positions 5 and 6 *(cont.)*

6 *of Wands*	I see you being successful in your efforts.
7 *of Wands*	I see you being called to action.
8 *of Wands*	I see you winding up loose ends.
9 *of Wands*	I see you holding down the fort.
10 *of Wands*	I see you taking your work home.

Position 7–This is who you are at work. Position 8–This is who they want you to be at work.

The card in position 7 is said to represent you, yourself. Cards in the seventh position show "who you are" with regard to the situation you have asked about. *Look at your card.*

The card in position 8 is said to represent all the people around you. Cards in the eighth position show what others want for you. *Look at your card.*

This same table will give you the Readings for cards in either position 7 or position 8.

In position 7 the cards should be read as **In this situation, you are . . .**

In position 8 the cards should be read as **In this situation, others want you to be . . .**

I	*The Magician*	the one who is out in front of the others; someone who works wonders.
II	*The High Priestess*	the one who supplies the input; someone who reads minds.
III	*The Empress*	the one who produces the output; someone who is production-oriented.
IV	*The Emperor*	the one who causes things to happen; someone who is forceful and aggressive.
V	*The Hierophant*	the one who acts in the corporate interest; someone who plays by the rules.
VI	*The Lovers*	the one who makes the first move; someone who "gets into bed with them."

Positions 7 and 8 (*cont.*)

VII	The Chariot	the one who drives the effort; someone who takes the bull by the horns.
VIII	Justice	the one who is accountable; someone who can straighten things out.
IX	The Hermit	the one behind the scenes; someone who can be depended on in a crisis.
X	Wheel of Fortune	the one who takes the risk; someone who works around the clock.

Ace of Wands	the one there when opportunity knocks; someone who accepts an offer.
2 of Wands	the one who's brought in from outside; someone who is farsighted.
3 of Wands	the one who minds the store; someone who can deliver things on time.
4 of Wands	the one who makes the advances; someone who is anxious to climb on board.
5 of Wands	the one who's on the front line; someone who demonstrates good skills.
6 of Wands	the one who deserves the credit; someone who gets the honors.
7 of Wands	the one who is with the program; someone who knows how to motivate others.
8 of Wands	the one who speeds things along; someone who comes on strong.
9 of Wands	the one who waits patiently; someone who is loyal.
10 of Wands	the one who takes the job home; someone who delivers the goods.

Position 9—This is what you want.

The card in position 9 is said to be your wishes in regard to the matter you have asked about. *Look at your card.*

I The Magician. You want to be a star performer.

II The High Priestess. You want to be personally fulfilled.

Position 9 *(cont.)*

III The Empress. You want to be rewarded for your efforts.

IV The Emperor. You want to be given more authority.

V The Hierophant. You want to be given more status.

VI The Lovers. You want to be wanted.

VII The Chariot. You want to be recognized in some way.

VIII Justice. You want to be evaluated fairly.

IX The Hermit. You want to be understood.

X Wheel of Fortune. You want to be well paid.

Ace of Wands. You want to take advantage of a new opportunity.

2 of Wands. You want to go on to bigger and better things.

3 of Wands. You want to change your place of employment.

4 of Wands. You want to pursue mutual interests.

5 of Wands. You want to take on a new challenge.

6 of Wands. You want to climb the ladder of success.

7 of Wands. You want to hang on to your current position.

8 of Wands. You want to forge straight ahead.

9 of Wands. You want to keep things as they are.

10 of Wands. You want to make your big move.

Position 10—This is what you get.

The card in position 10 is said to be the end result, the culmination of all the other cards, and the answer to your question. *Look at your card.*

Position 10 (*cont.*)

I The Magician. You have the ability to write your own ticket.

II The High Priestess. You have the ability to know your own mind.

III The Empress. You have the ability to finish what you have started.

IV The Emperor. You have the ability to take charge of your life.

V The Hierophant. You have the ability to rise above your problems.

VI The Lovers. You have the ability to discover your niche.

VII The Chariot. You have the ability to ride off into the sunset.

VIII Justice. You have the ability to decide things for yourself.

IX The Hermit. You have the ability to share what you have learned.

X Wheel of Fortune. You have the ability to turn minuses into pluses.

Ace of Wands. You have the chance to receive a big break.

2 of Wands. You have the opportunity to see the world.

3 of Wands. You have the possibility of a new assignment.

4 of Wands. You have the opportunity to celebrate something.

5 of Wands. You have the chance to take on a greater challenge.

6 of Wands. You have the opportunity for career advancement.

7 of Wands. You have the chance to show what you're made of.

8 of Wands. You have the opportunity to be on the receiving end.

9 of Wands. You have the chance to defend your honor.

10 of Wands. You have the opportunity to take something out of the experience.

EXTRA CREDIT

For a quick Reading of what your job holds for you this week, shuffle the 10 Trumps until done, then deal up one, and consult the answers for Card 1.

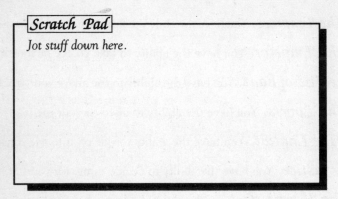

Scratch Pad

Jot stuff down here.

EXTRA EXTRA CREDIT!

What the heck, perform Readings for everybody you know at school or everyone you work with to see what's happening to whom and to get a general picture of your entire work climate.

Go on to the next Reading whenever you are ready to continue.

Reading #9

HOW DO I GET ALONG WITH OTHERS?

So far you've been playing around with the first 10 Tarot Trumps and the first 10 Tarot Wands to find out about yourself and your work. In this Reading the tables will turn a bit as you start to explore your personal relationships with others. The cards you will be using are the Cups, which equate to Hearts in a standard card deck. Cups represent the things that are near and dear to us. They represent the things of the heart.

TAROT TOOLS

You will need to separate the Ace through 10 of Cups from your deck:

Ace	of Cups
2	of Cups
3	of Cups
4	of Cups
5	of Cups
6	of Cups
7	of Cups
8	of Cups
9	of Cups
10	of Cups

HOW TO

To select your card for this Reading, we will be using a numerological method, in which you "add up" the letters in your first name to answer the question: **How am I doing in my personal relationships?**

To identify your card, look up the letters in your *first* name in the following table and add them up. (You might want to get out your pocket calculator for this one.)

A	1		J	10		S	19
B	2		K	11		T	20
C	3		L	12		U	21
D	4		M	13		V	22
E	5		N	14		W	23
F	6		O	15		X	24
G	7		P	16		Y	25
H	8		Q	17		Z	26
I	9		R	18			

For example, if your first name is Victoria, you would add up the letters:

$$(V = 22) + (I = 9) + (C = 3) + (T = 20) +$$
$$(O = 15) + (R = 18) + (I = 9) + (A = 1) = 97$$
$$22 + 9 + 3 + 20 + 15 + 18 + 9 + 1 = 97$$

When you get done adding, add up the digits in the total. If your name is Victoria: $9 + 7 = 16$.

Then add up the total again. For Victoria: $1 + 6 = 7$. The 7 of Cups is Victoria's card for this Reading.

The object is to get to a number between 1 and 10. So keep adding up your totals until you get there.

When the letters of your first name add up exactly to 10, reduce the number again to 1 if the first letter in your first name equals an odd number; otherwise keep the number as 10.

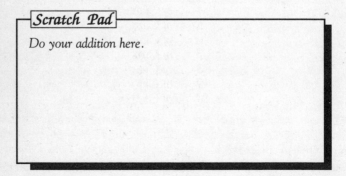

Scratch Pad

Do your addition here.

Find the Cup card of the same number as your name. Then look up your card in the Answer section.

For additional information on any card, consult the Quick Reference Guide.

THE ANSWERS

Ace of Cups. If the Ace of Cups is your card, you tend to get involved in loving relationships of an enduring nature. *Look at your card.* Your best relationships tend to restore themselves continually, like a stream of water pouring from a secret source. As you put energy into relationships at work, personal friendships, or love affairs, your energy level not only remains undepleted, but it actually grows! The Ace of Cups implies a deep, enduring love based on **mutual respect.** As a result, your deepest relationships are likely to include a spiritual dimension. With such depths of emotions involved, however, you will want to be sure to place your trust in others carefully. If things go sour, you will find the way out by looking inside yourself and listening to the truth your own heart reveals to you. *When you draw the Ace of Cups, your future involves an outpouring of affection. Look shortly for a message from a dear friend. If your Key Card in Reading #1 was The Magician, you should not hesitate to make the first move.*

2 of Cups. If the 2 of Cups is your card, you tend to get involved in serious relationships built on intense feelings. *Look at your card.* Your best relationships will involve both a physical and an emotional component. At work, home, school, or play, you will be attracted to members of the opposite sex and to people with whom you share similar physical attributes or interests. Your most successful relationships will feature equal partnerships, based on some kind of **mutual agreement.** But since you may—at the outset at least—be inclined to judge a book by its cover, be careful that something of lasting value exists below the surface. If you doubt your would-be partner's true intentions, you will know the truth by looking deeply into the other's eyes. *When you draw the 2 of Cups, your future involves the cementing of long-term relationships. In the weeks ahead, you can expect to discover someone's true intentions. If in Reading #1 The High Priestess was your Key Card, you should prepare for a meeting of the minds.*

3 of Cups. If the 3 of Cups is your card, you tend to get involved in truly genuine relationships based on close physical proximity and a shared experience. *Look at your card.* Your best relationships often involve a sense of family, which makes you inclined to feel "near and dear" to those you work with, live with, or are otherwise involved with. Your strongest relationships will be based upon **mutual participation** and a strong sense of belonging. Your sisters may be extremely important to you. Or, in general, your female friends may be "like sisters" to you. Such siblings and peers will play a big part in your life. But since you are inclined to hang out with members of your own "gang" or clan, you will want to be careful about getting involved with the wrong crowd. When in doubt about a relationship, examine your own roots and size up your past experience. *When you draw the 3 of Cups, your future involves some kind of networking. In the near term, you can expect an invitation to exchange secrets. If in Reading #1 The Empress was your Key Card, be sure to seek the advice of someone who knows best.*

4 of Cups.

If the 4 of Cups is your card, you tend to get involved in quiet relationships of a strong mental or physical nature. *Look at your card.* You are the "strong, silent type." You are inclined to form rather loose-knit bonds with others, allowing you to keep a safe distance and giving you plenty of breathing space. You get along best with those who present you with a physical test or mental challenge or those with whom you can establish a loose web of **mutual affiliation.** Your brothers may be a strong influence in your life. Or, in general, you may find that you relate to men as if they were your brothers. Since you are inclined to be influenced greatly by those you admire, or by a mentor or someone who serves you as a role model, you will want to choose your heroes carefully. When relationships get rocky, sort out your own thoughts and make an effort to understand and express your own feelings. *When you draw the 4 of Cups, your future involves psyching yourself up for something. Soon you will be put to a mental or physical challenge. If in Reading #1 The Emperor was your Key Card, you should always pay attention to your gut feelings.*

5 of Cups.

If the 5 of Cups is your card, you tend to get involved in intense, caring relationships of an empathetic or understanding nature. *Look at your card.* You are the "sympathetic type." You get along best in an environment where sensitivity to the personal feelings of others counts, or where there needs to be a strong shoulder to lean on. As a result, you tend to gravitate toward the people who "need" you. Your best relationships will be based on **mutual understanding,** accompanied by implicit trust. Religious figures or those who share a common set of beliefs may well be among your best friends and associates. Since you may be overly inclined to accept the kindness of strangers, be careful about getting sucked into deceptive schemes. Though others may disappoint you from time to time— and you may have your fair share of personal regrets—all will be well as long as your heart remains in the right place. When things build up inside you, seek catharsis. *When you draw the 5 of Cups, your future involves an intensely emotional situation. Soon you will feel the need to help someone out of a jam. If in Reading #1 The Hierophant was your Key Card, you should confess your innermost feelings.*

6 of Cups.

If the 6 of Cups is your card, you tend to get involved in pure, honestly affectionate relationships of a giving nature. *Look at your card.* You are the "hopeless romantic" type. You get along best in a civilized environment where common courtesy prevails and where the rules of eti-quette and courtship apply. In love, you want to be wooed. At work, you wanted to be courted. But in the end, your best relationships will be based on some kind of **mutual exchange,** in which you can "return the favor." Children in general or those you have known since childhood could well be among your best friends, for you have a strong sense of continuity. Since you are inclined to be a bit naive, you can't avoid getting hurt once in a while. But the good will most surely outweigh the bad in your life. If you want some advice, seek it from an old and trusted friend. *When you draw the 6 of Cups, your future involves something from out of your past. Soon you will find yourself reminiscing about the good old days. If in Reading #1 The Lovers was your Key Card, you should send flowers to the one whom you adore.*

7 of Cups.

If the 7 of Cups is your card, you tend to get involved in high-powered, stimulating relationships of an enriching nature. *Look at your card.* You get along best in situations that allow you to work on im-proving the standard of living for yourself and those around you. But you will not be happy for long in relationships that do not allow you to simul-taneously pursue your own, perhaps diverse, interests or to develop your own potential. For this reason, your best relationships will prove to be **mutually beneficial.** Your best friends will perhaps be few and far between, but many more look up to you. (It is difficult to get close.) Dream big! But bring yourself down from the clouds for a reality check once in a while. *When you draw the 7 of Cups, your future involves the fulfillment of your wildest dreams. Soon you will get the opportunity to live out a fantasy. If in Reading #1 The Chariot was your Key Card, reach for the golden ring.*

8 of Cups.

If the 8 of Cups is your card, you tend to get involved in fairly structured relationships of an open-ended nature. *Look at your card.* In your dealings with others, you like an environment that provides a solid framework for your interactions but allows you to speak your own mind and maybe even occasionally depart from the norm. As a result, your best relationships will involve **mutual discretion.** Your best friends are likely to be those who see things your way or who agree with your often precedent-setting approaches. Since you have a tendency to bend the rules, you may want to put some upper limits upon how far you are willing to go. If you feel you're getting into a rut, try something new. *When you draw the 8 of Cups, your future involves making a departure of some sort. Soon you will travel to see someone at a distance. If in Reading #1 Justice was your Key Card, whatever you do, be careful not to get caught.*

9 of Cups.

If the 9 of Cups is your card, you tend to get involved in high-spirited, cordial relationships of an outgoing nature. *Look at your card.* You prefer an environment that puts you at ease with yourself and in which you are allowed to be who you are. For this reason, your best relationships depend upon a spirit of **mutual acceptance.** Your best friends are likely to run the gamut of personality types, for you are generally easy to get along with. Since you are inclined to be lighthearted, you might not be taken seriously sometimes, and others may, from time to time, attempt to abuse your good nature. If you feel you're being backed into a corner, you will get out okay if you rely on your instincts. *When you draw the 9 of Cups, your future involves the need to practice public relations. Soon you will have the opportunity to show your hospitality. If in Reading #1 The Hermit was your Key Card, you will be held up as a good example.*

10 of Cups. If the 10 of Cups is your card, you tend to get involved in unpredictable but harmonious relationships that, being of a perfect nature, have their moments. *Look at your card.* You prefer an environment where things go okay in general, despite the cyclical highs and lows and ups and downs of this world. And lo and behold! Every once in a while—from out of nowhere—a rainbow appears as your reward. Your best relationships are based on caring, sharing, and **mutual fulfillment.** And for reasons perhaps not clearly obvious to you (or to anybody else for that matter) things tend to work out for you. You are one of the very fortunate people who enjoy the simple pleasures of life. I can give you no further advice than to keep doing what you're doing. *When you draw the 10 of Cups, your future involves feeling the earth move. Soon you will have a very pleasant experience. If in Reading #1 Wheel of Fortune was your Key Card, you are lucky at love.*

EXTRA CREDIT

If you want to be more specific, ask a question like: **What's my future with _____?** (This week? This month?) In this case, shuffle the cards, and deal up the top Cup. To get your answer, look up your card in the Answer section, but focus on the portion of the answer printed in *italics*.

┌─ *Scratch Pad* ─

Jot down your notes here.

Reading #9

EXTRA EXTRA CREDIT!

What the heck, go ahead and add up the numbers of your nickname, find your card, and read the answer. Which name gives you the more accurate Reading?

Go on to the next Reading whenever you are ready to continue.

Reading #10

HOW'S MY LOVE LIFE?

In this Reading we'll be using the first 10 Cups and the first 10 Trumps to do a barometric reading on the state of our love affairs. The Cups are "divinely" suited for this type of Reading, since they relate to the heart's desire.

TAROT TOOLS

You will need the same cards you used in Reading #9—the Ace through 10 of Cups, plus Trumps I–X:

I	The Magician
II	The High Priestess
III	The Empress
IV	The Emperor
V	The Hierophant
VI	The Lovers
VII	The Chariot
VIII or XI	Justice
IX	The Hermit
X	Wheel of Fortune

Keep the two groups of cards in separate stacks.

HOW TO

This will be the same kind of Cover and Cross Reading that you did in Reading #6. (See the Quick Reference Guide for an illustration of this layout.)

Shuffle the 10 Cups as you ask your question: **How am I doing in my love life?** or **How am I doing in my love relationship with _____?** Clearly you'll want to fill in the name of a current or would-be love interest in the blank provided.

Keep shuffling and repeating your question until the Cups are done. Then deal up the top Cup and lay it faceup in front of you. *This card covers you.*

Repeat the operation with the 10 Trumps. Shuffle the Trumps while you ask your question. When the Trumps are done, deal up the top Trump and place it crosswise on your Cup. *This card crosses you.*

Then look up your answers. Your answer will sum up your current situation.

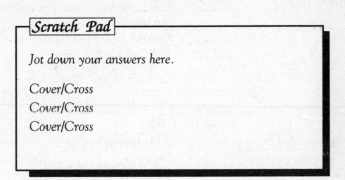

Scratch Pad

Jot down your answers here.

Cover/Cross
Cover/Cross
Cover/Cross

For additional information on any card, consult the Quick Reference Guide.

THE ANSWERS

Ace of Cups

When crossed by...		This indicates...
I	The Magician	there is a physical attraction. Sparks fly; looks count.
II	The High Priestess	there are shared feelings. This is an emotional relationship.
III	The Empress	romantic developments occur suddenly. But feelings evolve over time.
IV	The Emperor	this is a sensual relationship. It is sultry and steamy.
V	The Hierophant	there are moral considerations. Public appearances must be kept up.
VI	The Lovers	there are romantic propositions. Courtship occurs.

Ace of Cups *(cont.)*

When crossed by . . .		This indicates . . .
VII	The Chariot	there are sexual advances. Conquest comes into play.
VIII	Justice	this is a serious step. Big decisions are involved.
IX	The Hermit	this is a transforming relationship. Personal growth occurs.
X	Wheel of Fortune	there are chance meetings and turning points. This is fate.

2 of Cups

When crossed by . . .		This indicates . . .
I	The Magician	this is a purely physical relationship. Appearance and performance are all that count.
II	The High Priestess	this is a purely platonic relationship. Just being together is enough.
III	The Empress	this is a female-dominated relationship. A mother figure is involved.
IV	The Emperor	this is a male-dominated relationship. A father figure is involved.
V	The Hierophant	this is a socially acceptable relationship. You keep up public appearances.
VI	The Lovers	this is a passionate love affair. Mutual consent defines the playing field.
VII	The Chariot	this is a one-night stand. You have a common understanding of the ground rules.
VIII	Justice	this is a fifty-fifty relationship. You are equal among equals.
IX	The Hermit	this is a solitary matter. You go your separate ways.
X	Wheel of Fortune	let this relationship run its course. You will have to wait and see how it turns out.

3 of Cups

When crossed by . . .		This indicates . . .
I	The Magician	you make a date. Be ready to party.
II	The High Priestess	your paths cross. Be there.
III	The Empress	you get together periodically. Things time out right.
IV	The Emperor	you meet by appointment. Make yourself available.
V	The Hierophant	your activities overlap. Make a standing date.
VI	The Lovers	the spirit moves you. Come as you are.
VII	The Chariot	the opportunity presents itself. Cut in.
VIII	Justice	you come to a mutual agreement. Raise your hand if you're sure.
IX	The Hermit	you meet at the appointed hour. Stay out late.
X	Wheel of Fortune	as fate would have it, you ring in a new year together. Or celebrate an anniversary.

4 of Cups

When crossed by . . .		This indicates . . .
I	The Magician	you wonder what you should do next. You wish for a miracle.
II	The High Priestess	you wonder whether you can go on this way. You wish for a change of pace.
III	The Empress	you wonder what the outcome will be. You wish for a sign.
IV	The Emperor	you wonder how others would handle it. You wish for a diplomatic solution.
V	The Hierophant	you wonder if you are doing something wrong. You want to do the right thing.

4 of Cups *(cont.)*

When crossed by . . .		This indicates . . .
VI	*The Lovers*	you wonder if it's the real thing. You want to feel the earth move.
VII	*The Chariot*	you wonder if you can go through with it. You wish it would work itself out.
VIII	*Justice*	you wonder if you can get away with it. You worry you will get caught.
IX	*The Hermit*	you wonder if you should seek some advice. You are looking for something.
X	*Wheel of Fortune*	you wonder if you want to risk it. You can't live with them, you can't live without them.

5 of Cups

When crossed by . . .		This indicates . . .
I	*The Magician*	a rash action is regretted. Pick up the pieces.
II	*The High Priestess*	someone regrets the involvement. Put the past behind you.
III	*The Empress*	someone regrets starting something he or she can't finish. Time wounds and heals.
IV	*The Emperor*	someone regrets taking a firm stand. Live and learn.
V	*The Hierophant*	someone regrets not thinking about the consequences. Repentance comes into play.
VI	*The Lovers*	someone regrets not saying how he or she really feels. Kiss and make up.
VII	*The Chariot*	someone regrets taking advantage of the situation. Do better next time.
VIII	*Justice*	someone regrets having to pay the price now. Do the honorable thing.

5 of Cups *(cont.)*

When crossed by . . .		This indicates . . .
IX	The Hermit	someone regrets not seeing the light sooner. It's never too late.
X	Wheel of Fortune	someone regrets things turned out as they did. So it goes. Make the best of it.

6 of Cups

When crossed by . . .		This indicates . . .
I	The Magician	you feel sexy. Someone charms you.
II	The High Priestess	you feel calm. Someone accepts you for who you are.
III	The Empress	you feel good about the prospects. Someone takes care of you.
IV	The Emperor	you feel secure in your position. Someone flatters you.
V	The Hierophant	you feel right about the situation. Someone comforts you.
VI	The Lovers	you feel serious in your intentions. Someone flirts with you.
VII	The Chariot	you feel aggressive in your behavior. Someone comes on to you.
VIII	Justice	you feel justified in your own feelings. Someone apologizes to you.
IX	The Hermit	you feel as if you suddenly know the truth. Someone confides in you.
X	Wheel of Fortune	you feel that things are going in your favor. Someone cheers you up.

7 of Cups

When crossed by . . .		This indicates . . .
I	The Magician	fantasies are acted out. Virility is involved.

7 of Cups *(cont.)*

When crossed by . . .		This indicates . . .
II	The High Priestess	sensual dreams occur. A mysterious stranger comes into the picture.
III	The Empress	daydreaming goes on. Feminine charms play a part.
IV	The Emperor	control over a situation is desired. Macho games are involved.
V	The Hierophant	it is hoped that desires can be controlled. You swear off love for a while.
VI	The Lovers	infatuation occurs. The naked truth becomes known.
VII	The Chariot	conquests are counted up. There are casualties on both sides.
VIII	Justice	it is hoped things will even out in the end. Decide what counts.
IX	The Hermit	someone pretends to be steadfast. Old habits are hard to break.
X	Wheel of Fortune	someone wishes it could be both ways. A fantasy is lived out.

8 of Cups

When crossed by . . .		This indicates . . .
I	The Magician	there is a return to something started earlier. A prior relationship is revived.
II	The High Priestess	there is a need to feel at peace with yourself. Go somewhere to sort things out.
III	The Empress	someone wants to return to the womb. Seek comfort at home.
IV	The Emperor	something is restored to more solid ground. Someone comes to his or her senses.
V	The Hierophant	there is a return to the fold. Forgive the one who has strayed.
VI	The Lovers	someone wants to return to the one he or she truly loves. Pick up where you left off.

8 of Cups (cont.)

When crossed by . . .		This indicates . . .
VII	The Chariot	there is a desire to play the field again. Brush up on dating skills.
VIII	Justice	things are returned to a more even keel. Change a few of your ways.
IX	The Hermit	someone wants to retreat to the wilderness. You separate for a while.
X	Wheel of Fortune	the good old days are sought again. Adjust to the fact that things have changed.

9 of Cups

When crossed by . . .		This indicates . . .
I	The Magician	there are lots of hormones to deal with. Be comfortable with your body.
II	The High Priestess	plenty of idle time exists. Be content with your feelings.
III	The Empress	there are many things to worry about. Enjoy yourself once in a while.
IV	The Emperor	someone is very experienced in such matters. Draw from your own knowledge.
V	The Hierophant	there are many things to confess. But count your blessings.
VI	The Lovers	you have much love to keep you satisfied. Appreciate a good thing.
VII	The Chariot	there are numerous diversions. Take stock of the experience.
VIII	Justice	someone has second thoughts on the matter. Add up the pros and cons.
IX	The Hermit	plenty of advice is available on the subject. Make up your own mind.
X	Wheel of Fortune	there are lots of opportunities to pursue. Choose among competing interests.

10 of Cups

When crossed by . . .		This indicates . . .
I	The Magician	someone wishes to find a mate. Settle down and have some kids.
II	The High Priestess	someone wishes to retain his or her virginity. Keep your independence for a while longer.
III	The Empress	someone wishes to become a parent. Lead a family life.
IV	The Emperor	someone wishes to be the head of the household. Rule the roost.
V	The Hierophant	someone wishes to be married. Have an official ceremony.
VI	The Lovers	someone wishes to live together . . . forever.
VII	The Chariot	someone wishes to have a little something on the side. Take care.
VIII	Justice	someone wishes to make your relationship legal. Tie the knot.
IX	The Hermit	someone wishes to take the necessary precautions. Protect the ones you love.
X	Wheel of Fortune	someone wishes your luck will hold out. You want to live happily ever after.

EXTRA CREDIT

To trace the development of a relationship over time, shuffle the Cups and ask: **How is my relationship with _____ progressing?** Deal up the top three Cups. Then repeat this process with the Trumps, laying the top three crosswise over the Cups. You will end up with three Cover and Cross pairs, describing the relationship's past, present, and future. (See the Quick Reference Guide for an illustration of this layout.)

Look up your answers.

┌─*Scratch Pad*─────────────────────────────┐

Jot down your figures here.

Cover/Cross
Cover/Cross
Cover/Cross

└──┘

EXTRA EXTRA CREDIT!

What the heck, conduct this Reading for each and every love relationship you've known in your life to see if there are any patterns.

Go on to the next Reading whenever you are ready to continue.

Reading #11

HOW WILL THIS RELATIONSHIP TURN OUT?

In this Reading we will continue to explore our personal relationships with others, by using the first 10 Cups in combination with the first 10 Trumps. Reading #10 gave us a quick way of assessing the progress of a potential, developing, or ongoing love interest and a way of sorting out past relationships. Reading #11 uses a more thorough method to provide an in-depth analysis of any given personal relationship—past, present, and future.

TAROT TOOLS

You will need the same cards you used in Reading #10—the Ace through 10 of Cups, and Trumps I–X:

I	*The Magician*
II	*The High Priestess*
III	*The Empress*
IV	*The Emperor*
V	*The Hierophant*
VI	*The Lovers*
VII	*The Chariot*
VIII or XI	*Justice*
IX	*The Hermit*
X	*Wheel of Fortune*

Keep the two groups of cards in separate stacks.

HOW TO

This Reading will use the same Celtic Cross layout used in Reading #8. (See the Quick Reference Guide for an illustration of this layout.)

Dealing out the cards involves a three-step process.

First, shuffle the 10 Trumps together, as you ask your question: **How will my relationship with _____ turn out?** Fill in the blank with the name of the person or people involved.

Shuffle until the Trumps are done, then deal up the top Trump and place it faceup in front of you. *This covers you.* Then deal up the second Trump and place it crosswise on the card you have already dealt. *This crosses you.*

Now shuffle the 10 Cups together, as you ask your question again: **How will my relationship with _____ turn out?**

Shuffle until the Cups are done, then deal up the top four cards and place them in positions 3 through 6 around the first two Trumps you have already dealt:

> 3—*This is above you*
> 4—*This is below you*
> 5—*This is behind you*
> 6—*This is before you*

Finally, shuffle the remaining Trumps and Cups together, as you ask your question one last time: **How will my relationship with _____ turn out?**

Shuffle until the cards are done, then deal up the top four cards and place them in positions 7 through 10 to the right of the cards you have already dealt:

> 7—*This is who you are*
> 8—*This is who they want you to be*
> 9—*This is what you want*
> 10—*And this is what you get*

Look up your cards by their position in the layout (1 through 10) in the Answer section.

Scratch Pad

Note your cards and answers here.

Covers you
Crosses you
Above you
Below you
Behind you
Before you
You are
They want
You want
You get

HINT: You may find that sometimes the cards will answer a different question from the one you asked. If your cards don't seem to answer the question, think about what question they might be answering. What's really on your mind?

For additional information on any card, consult the Quick Reference Guide.

THE ANSWERS

Position 1—This covers you.

I The Magician. This relationship involves: a young, virile, talented, ambitious, and energetic young man; a magic moment; and a strong desire to control the outcome of things. *Some kind of deliberate action is taking place right now.*

II The High Priestess. This relationship involves: a mysterious woman; something that is silent, hidden, unseen, or otherwise unapparent to the eye; a rite of passage; and a calm willingness to allow things to go their natural course. *Right now nothing is happening behind the scenes.*

III The Empress. This relationship involves: a mature woman who cares deeply about the welfare of others; a mother, mother-to-be, or mother-in-law; a long-awaited event; and the investment of time. *Right now some new development is in the works.*

IV The Emperor. This relationship involves: a father figure or powerful male influence of some kind; a guy who is the strong, silent type; a favor to ask of a trusted friend, and an obligation in return. *Right now things are going on right in front of your eyes.*

V The Hierophant. This relationship involves: a person of high stature, rank, or authority; a plea for help or a request for forgiveness; dependence upon the kindness of strangers; and mercy extended to others. *Right now someone is interceding on your behalf.*

VI The Lovers. This relationship involves: a passionate, loving, or adoring person; the object of your affection, love, admiration, and desire; love at first sight; and a statement of true intentions. *Right now someone is planning what to say to you.*

VII The Chariot. This relationship involves: a man with a healthy libido, ego, and physique; a split decision or unavoidable action; and a little

Position 1 (*cont.*)

something going on the side. *Right now something is happening behind your back.*

VIII Justice. This relationship involves: an intelligent, understanding, insightful, and demanding woman; a decision of great importance; and the need to separate fact from fiction. *Right now a judgment is being made.*

IX The Hermit. This relationship involves: a learned, wise, or holy man who keeps his distance in general; a departure or separation of some duration; and a return to the things that matter. *Right now a journey of some kind is coming to its end.*

X Wheel of Fortune. This relationship involves: things outside of your control; fate; destiny; the luck of the draw; change without notice; and things that fluctuate up and down. *Right now things are happening more or less on their own.*

Position 2–This crosses you.

I The Magician. This relationship requires a lot of energy and determination to make it work. You need to decide whether the outcome is worth the investment of your time.

II The High Priestess. This relationship requires intuitive thought. You need to trust your own instincts and do what feels right to you at the moment.

III The Empress. This relationship requires the passage of a period of time. You need to let things run their natural course, for better or worse, if you hope to realize this relationship's full potential.

IV The Emperor. This relationship requires a strong sense of dedication and loyalty. You need to honor the wishes of those you admire in order to incur their favor.

V The Hierophant. This relationship requires a firm commitment on your part. You need to play by the rules if you hope to sustain a long-term and lasting relationship.

VI The Lovers. This relationship requires an open statement of your intentions. You need to learn to express your feelings, if you ever hope to get to first base.

Position 2 *(cont.)*

VII The Chariot. This relationship requires you to make a bold move. You will have to be the aggressor if you hope to come out a winner in the end.

VIII Justice. This relationship requires honesty. You will have to tell the truth, the whole truth, and nothing but the truth if you ever hope to gain the confidence of the person you care about.

IX The Hermit. This relationship requires vigilance. You need to get to the bottom of things if you ever hope to come out on top.

X Wheel of Fortune. This relationship requires a certain amount of risk taking. You will need to take your chances if you want to find out where this relationship is headed.

Position 3—This is above you.

Ace of Cups. You can expect that this relationship will have its moments, at least at first. You might even feel a little overwhelmed at times.

2 of Cups. This relationship promises to be mutually beneficial, especially if it involves a pact, contract, or formal agreement of some kind.

3 of Cups. This relationship can be high-spirited. It has a carefree, happy-go-lucky feeling about it. Enjoy it for as long as it lasts.

4 of Cups. This relationship may come up a bit wanting of your highest expectations. Perhaps your standards are too high.

5 of Cups. You may live to regret this relationship. You stand the risk of losing more than you might possibly gain.

6 of Cups. This relationship promises romantic moments. It provides you with the opportunity to complete something you began in the past.

7 of Cups. This relationship has the potential to help you realize a fantasy or two. Be careful what you wish for. It may come true.

8 of Cups. This relationship is fairly good, all in all, but you will be tempted to walk away from it at times . . . only to return.

9 of Cups. This relationship has the ability to fulfill your needs. Indeed, it will pay you back measure for measure.

Position 3 (*cont.*)

10 of Cups. This relationship has great, almost limitless potential for all involved. This one is definitely worth pursuing.

Position 4–This is below you.

Ace of Cups. This relationship happened rather spontaneously. The sky opened. Sparks flew. The earth moved. And the rest is history.

2 of Cups. This relationship is based on a negotiation process. A short period of courtship was possibly involved.

3 of Cups. This relationship is based on some kind of shared experience. Perhaps you met through a mutual acquaintance or at some public place.

4 of Cups. This relationship is based on a feeling that something was missing from your life. Perhaps you made a deliberate attempt to go out and find it.

5 of Cups. This relationship is based on some earlier rejection. Perhaps you were on the rebound from an earlier affair that ended suddenly.

6 of Cups. This relationship is based on something that happened in the past. Perhaps it involves someone from out of your childhood.

7 of Cups. This relationship is based upon a flight of your imagination. Perhaps it involves a long-standing secret fantasy of yours.

8 of Cups. This relationship is based on having taken a trip or having turned your back on the past. Perhaps you were running away from something.

9 of Cups. This relationship is based on many similar experiences. Perhaps you should be the one giving the advice.

10 of Cups. This relationship is based on the right stuff. Perhaps you have just now started to appreciate what you had in the past.

Position 5–This is behind you.
Position 6–This is before you.

This same table will give you the Readings for cards in either position 5 or position 6.

Positions 5 and 6 *(cont.)*

In position 5 the cards should be read as *Just recently . . .*
In position 6 the cards should be read as *Just coming up . . .*

Ace of Cups	I see a proposition or self-fulfilling prophecy.
2 of Cups	I see an agreement or mutual decision.
3 of Cups	I see a reunion or gathering of some sort.
4 of Cups	I see a message from an inner voice.
5 of Cups	I see an emotional experience that can't be avoided.
6 of Cups	I see a token of affection.
7 of Cups	I see an illusion or preoccupation.
8 of Cups	I see a departure of some sort, a retreat or a return.
9 of Cups	I see contentment with the way things are.
10 of Cups	I see time taken to smell the roses.

Position 7–This is who you are.
Position 8–This is what they want.

This same table will give you the readings for cards in either position 7 or position 8.

In position 7 the cards should be read as *In this relationship, you are . . .*

In position 8 the cards should be read as *In this relationship, others want you to be . . .*

I	*The Magician*	the one who makes things happen.
II	*The High Priestess*	the one who lets things happen.
III	*The Empress*	the one who waits for things to develop.
IV	*The Emperor*	the one who controls the situation.
V	*The Hierophant*	the one who keeps the faith.
VI	*The Lovers*	the one who is enamored.
VII	*The Chariot*	the one who puts on the moves.
VIII	*Justice*	the one who decides what's right.
IX	*The Hermit*	the one who speaks the truth.
X	*Wheel of Fortune*	the one who takes the risks.
Ace of Cups		the one who gushes over.
2 of Cups		the one who agrees.
3 of Cups		the one who participates.
4 of Cups		the one who doubts.
5 of Cups		the one who gets hurt.

Positions 7 and 8 (*cont.*)

6 *of Cups*	the one who is the hopeless romantic.
7 *of Cups*	the one who fantasizes.
8 *of Cups*	the one who goes back and forth.
9 *of Cups*	the one who is content.
10 *of Cups*	the one who is perfectly happy.

Position 9—This is what you want.

I The Magician. You want it to be special. You want it to be magical. You want to feel the sparks fly.

II The High Priestess. You want it to be eternal. You want it to feel as if it's right. You want it to be what you know in your heart is meant to be.

III The Empress. You want it to stir you, move you, crash over you like the wind and the water. You want it to transform you.

IV The Emperor. You want it be permanent, the way it always was, is, and ever shall be.

V The Hierophant. You want it to be better than it already is. You want it to be the way it is supposed to be; if not now, then in the end.

VI The Lovers. You want it to be the real thing, true, eternal, and beyond every reasonable shadow of a doubt.

VII The Chariot. You want it to overpower you. You want it to ride in and sweep you off your feet. You want it to carry you away with it and have its way with you.

VIII Justice. You want it to be fair and evenhanded. You want the good and the bad to balance out. You want it to give back to you what it takes out of you.

IX The Hermit. You want it to be your light in the darkness. You want it to survive the test of time. You want it to serve as an example for others to shoot for.

X Wheel of Fortune. You want to risk it, even if it goes bad in the end. You want to ride it out for now, if only to see what happens.

Position 9 (*cont.*)

Ace of Cups. You want it to descend upon you. You want it to overwhelm you, engulf you, fulfill you, release you.

2 of Cups. You want it to bind you, join you, connect you, make you whole.

3 of Cups. You want it to uplift you, honor you, comfort you, support you, touch you.

4 of Cups. You want it to quench your thirst, end your search, and satisfy you completely.

5 of Cups. You want it to live up to all that, at its very best, it held out hope to be. You want it to be what it could have been.

6 of Cups. You want it to be once again what it once was. You want to recapture the moment and live it all over again.

7 of Cups. You want it to be everything you could ever hope to have . . . and more than it can ever hope to be.

8 of Cups. You want it to still be there when you return from wherever it is that you are temporarily going.

9 of Cups. You want it to fill you up, empty you, and fill you up again. You can not get enough of it. You want each moment to be as good as the moment before.

10 of Cups. You want it to remain the way it is forever. You want to stop time in its tracks. You want this moment to linger.

Position 10–This is what you get.

I The Magician. This relationship responds to your cues. You can have your way with it. You can make it happen if that is your will. Or you can keep it from happening. You are responsible for your own actions in this matter. You will get out of it what you put into it.

II The High Priestess. This relationship has a way of its own. It tends to rise and swell and ebb and flow with the changing tides. You need to go with the flow. Seek the answers from the silence within you. You will get out of this relationship what is meant to be.

Reading #11

III The Empress. This relationship takes time to reach its full potential. You need to help it grow and develop. You need to tend to it and encourage it along. In the end you will reap what you have sown.

IV The Emperor. This relationship is rather demanding. It commands your full time and attention. It will either hold up well under the pressure, or it will collapse into itself. It teaches you stamina and endurance.

V The Hierophant. This relationship demands dedication and devotion and gives you a means of support in return. For now, it tends to get you through some hard times, and there's a promise it will grow into something even better in the long run.

VI The Lovers. This relationship would seem to be made in heaven. As such, it is beyond your poor power to control, resist, or deny. You cannot say no to this one. You have no choice but to pursue it, for better or worse.

VII The Chariot. This relationship takes daring and courage. It tends to pull you in opposite directions. It may even threaten to pull you apart! But if you keep your guard up, you may emerge from it unbowed.

VIII Justice. This relationship requires sound judgment. You need to consider the pros and cons and separate fact from fiction. You also need to be forgiving and understanding. (You may even need to be forgiven and understood yourself.) Hold out for the respect you deserve.

IX The Hermit. This relationship requires you to keep a safe distance. It challenges you to figure things out, but mostly it teaches you to know yourself.

X Wheel of Fortune. This relationship takes you up and down and round and round with it—and it runs the gamut—for this is a real, honest-to-goodness, full-fledged relationship. You get out of it what you make of it.

Ace of Cups. This relationship requires you to count your blessings. It returns to you, measure for measure, what you invest in it.

2 of Cups. This relationship is about sharing. It takes open communication and an equal footing to make it work. Since it tends to occur in a set context, watch out it doesn't become too routine.

3 of Cups. This relationship cheers you up when you're blue and shares equally in your moments of joy. It accepts, recognizes, and appreciates you.

4 of Cups. This relationship confuses you. It is not what you expected, and yet it sustains you and even promises to complete you, if you hang in there long enough.

5 of Cups. This relationship tugs at your heartstrings. But it teaches you how to pick up the pieces and start all over again.

6 of Cups. This relationship flatters you and makes you feel young again. It can even give you a new lease on life.

7 of Cups. This relationship distracts you, lures you, pulls you in with promises, and will probably spit you back out in the end. Make sure the bait is real before you bite.

8 of Cups. This relationship takes you away from the things you know for a while. But it can be a learning experience, even if, in the end, you find yourself back where you started.

9 of Cups. This relationship fills you up to the brim—and even over the brim! It lives up to its claims and rewards you handsomely.

10 of Cups. This relationship never ceases to amaze you. It is full of pleasant surprises. And it will never have a dull moment.

EXTRA CREDIT

To find out what's going to happen in your relationship this week, shuffle the 10 Trumps together as you ask your question. Deal up the top Trump and look up the answer in the *italic* portion of the answer for position 1.

Scratch Pad
Jot down your card here.

EXTRA EXTRA CREDIT!

What the heck, do a full Reading for last week, this week, and next week to see if there's a pattern developing in your love life.

Go on to the next Reading whenever you are ready to continue.

Reading #12

How Do Others See Me?

Way back in Reading #1 you learned how to identify your Key Card, which revealed a little bit about who you "really are" deep down inside. In this Reading you will learn how you appear to others. For this purpose we will be working with a special selection of cards, including the Kings and Queens of the Tarot suits, since these face cards are good at telling us about the various types of people whom we encounter in life. In this Reading you will be encountering yourself—but from a slightly different perspective than you are used to. You will be looking at yourself from the outside in. Think of it as your "mirror image."

TAROT TOOLS

You will need the following cards from among the suits:

King of Wands
Queen of Wands

King of Cups
Queen of Cups

King of Coins
Queen of Coins

King of Swords
Queen of Swords

Plus, you will need the following two Trumps you have not met before:

Card 0   The Fool
Card XXI The World

These are the first and last cards of the deck, respectively. So what are they doing all mixed in with these Kings and Queens? If this inconsistency bothers you, for the purposes of this Reading, you can think of The Fool as being the "King of the Hill"; and you can think of The World as being the "Queen of the Universe." Or, what the heck, you can just play along.

HOW TO

Find the card that corresponds to your Key Card from Reading #1 in the following table. Then look up your card in the Answer section.

If you skipped Reading #1, go back now and learn how to add up the numbers in your birth date. (You might want to go back at this point and read your earlier description again anyway.)

Your Key Card in Reading #1		Your card in Reading #12
I	The Magician	0 The Fool
II	The High Priestess	Queen of Wands
III	The Empress	Queen of Cups
IV	The Emperor	King of Coins
V	The Hierophant	King of Cups
VI	The Lovers	Queen of Coins
VII	The Chariot	Queen of Swords
VIII	Justice	King of Swords
IX	The Hermit	King of Wands
X	Wheel of Fortune	XXI The World

Scratch Pad

Jot down your card here.

For additional information on any card, consult the Quick Reference Guide.

THE ANSWERS

0 The Fool. If your Key Card in Reading #1 was The Magician, your mirror image is The Fool. *Look at your card.* The Fool is always pursuing something in the distance. And you—as The Magician—are always pursuing some ambitious goal. Still, others can't always see it so brightly and clearly as you, that idea that stretches out in front of you. Others will shake their heads and say, "Oh, no, he's off on one of his 'things' again," or "Oh, boy, there she goes again." You are inclined, my friend, to flit from place to place, from job to job, from lover to lover, from car to car. You just can't seem to settle down in any one place for any length of time. It is the spirit that moves you. And when it calls, you have no choice but to go. People will either fear or admire you for your wanderlust and personal freedom. One thing is certain: Your life will never be dull. Hang in there. You may come upon your true vision yet. *You tend to measure time in moments.*

Queen of Wands. If your Key Card in Reading #1 was The High Priestess, your mirror image is the Queen of Wands. *Look at your card.* From your perspective as a High Priestess type, most everything in your world is intuitively obvious. So it may come as somewhat of a surprise that you actually appear to others to be a bit flighty. Still, your laid-back approach will serve you well in this life, and others will implicitly trust you. People say about you, "She really adjusts well to change," or "That guy can really roll with the punches." The truth is, you are simply "going with the flow," in the true sense of the expression. It's not that you are oblivious to what's going on in your life—with all its ups and downs—but that you seem to take life in your stride. People come to hear your stories, for you speak a gentle truth. And when you choose to give advice, you are right 90 percent of the time. Though you, my friend, may cherish your quiet times alone with your calm thoughts, you will never be at a loss for companionship in this life. May life be good to you. *You tend to measure time by the phases of the moon.*

Queen of Cups. If in Reading #1 The Empress was your Key Card, your mirror image is the Queen of Cups. *Look at your card.* As an Empress type, the plan you are following is always stretched out neatly in front of your mind's eye like a road map. And as the Queen of Cups, you appear to others to be the kind of person who is always prepared—for anything and everything—as if you knew in advance what was going to happen next. Your life seems to be a never-ending series of cyclical events . . . and countless contingency plans. People say to you, "What do we do now, Mom?" Or they say of you, "Now, what would Dad do if this happened to him?" You appear to remain unharried by matters that call upon you to make split-second decisions. But sometimes, my friend, you feel like you're running on empty. How can you see all, be all, and know all, so much of the time? Whatever they say of you—and children can be cruel—your life unfolds to be a rich series of interesting events marked by great feasts. May you always have plenty to eat. *You tend to measure time by the passing of the seasons.*

King of Coins. If in Reading #1 The Emperor was your Key Card, your mirror image is the King of Coins. *Look at your card.* You are possessed of a commanding presence, graceful and charismatic. A golden aura surrounds you. And when you enter a room, by golly, people sense it, feel it, know it. Heads turn. Eyes gaze at you from afar. People move a step backward for you to pass by. Even if you do not end up possessing material wealth in this life, you have an imperial quality that sets you apart. People will say of you, "Now, there goes a man," or "What a woman!" Your aggressive self-confidence impresses some, frightens many, and attracts its own breed of follower. And oh, my friend, sometimes they threaten to crush in around you until you have no space to call your own, no room to breathe. It will be difficult at times to tell who your real friends are in this life. But as a whole, the world will be good to you. May you return the favor. *You tend to measure time from sunrise to sunset.*

King of Cups. If in Reading #1 The Hierophant was your Key Card, your mirror image is the King of Cups. *Look at your card.* You're the sort of person who can walk on water, or at least that's your reputation. You can do no wrong. (And if you do, it was just something that temporarily possessed you—some bad influence from outside you—and which you overcame in the end.) They call you "Miss Goody Two-shoes" and say, "He's too good to be true." But the truth is, you are one of the good guys in this world. You seem to always be in the right place at the right time, always coming to the rescue of others. If there is a just cause to defend, you are up on your soapbox. If there is a prayer to be said, you have already bowed your head. But oh, my friend, if that deep, dark secret of yours ever gets out, others will show you no mercy. Still, you have such an admirable sense of what is right and what is wrong that you will always come out on top in the end. May others show you the respect that you deserve. *You tend to measure time by the calendar.*

Queen of Coins. If in Reading #1 The Lovers was your Key Card, your mirror image is the Queen of Coins. *Look at your card.* You may well be a late bloomer, but bloom you will, just the same. For you are the sort of person who brings things together—if not now, then in the end, like so many dots that at last are connected into a picture that just needs to be colored in. People say of you, "She's in love again," or "He's on the rebound." But even the brokenhearted mend. For you, my friend, the future is always full of tall, dark strangers, and every time you fall in love, it always feels like the first time, and it always seems to be the "real thing." Though you will have your share of pining after those who never come around—or those who stray when your back is turned—your life will be rich with the pulse of life itself, for you belong to the Universe. May you find the one true love you seek in this life. *You tend to measure time in biorhythms.*

Queen of Swords. If in Reading #1 The Chariot was your Key Card, your mirror image is the Queen of Swords. *Look at your card.* You are the sort of person who knows how to get what you want when you want it. And you generally don't take no for an answer, though it may involve being cold—even heartless or conniving—and ruthless. They say of you, "He's a real hard case," or "You'd better watch your step with her." The truth is, my friend, you like things to be exactly your way, but nine times out of ten your bark is worse than your bite. For below your iron-plated surface beats a soft heart that can be won over rather easily. No one has ever asked for a more loyal friend. And in your professional life, you have even been known to be magnanimous. You can do much good in this world if you set your sights high enough and compete hard enough. One thing is for sure: You will have plenty of diversions and distractions in this life (and as many one-night stands as you can handle). May you have plenty of opportunities. *You tend to measure time by changes in the weather.*

King of Swords. If in Reading #1 Justice was your Key Card, your mirror image is the King of Swords. *Look at your card.* You are one tough cookie and a difficult nut to crack. And once you make up your mind, that's that. They say of you, "He can really cut through the crap," or "She seems to have eyes in the back of her head," for what you do not know as fact, you quickly pick up on. Your mind is sharp as a knife, your wit keen, and your words can cut clean to the bone when you choose. You are a reader of what is written between the lines or in the fine print and an expert interpreter of what has happened in the past. But oh, my friend, you are a magnet for the troubled and those in trouble, who seek out the protection of your inner strength and your steadfast endurance. It can be a hard row to hoe, and you may well feel the burden of life as a great weight upon your shoulders. But you will never suffer for a lack of perspective. What you do not experience for yourself in this life, you will draw from the collective experiences of others. May you always have plenty of books to read, and at least a few good friends. *You tend to measure time in years.*

King of Wands. If in Reading #1 The Hermit was your Key Card, your mirror image is the King of Wands. *Look at your card.* You are the rather studious sort, in the sense that you tend to study everything around you . . . almost to the death—usually from a safe distance. You look out at the world with your powers of concentration turned on high beam. You survey all that passes in front of you. You assess. You observe. You sum up. You take things apart and put them back together. They say of you, "If you ask him, he'll be able to fix you up," or "Go ask her what she thinks." But oh, my friend, the line at your door can get awfully long; and once in a while even a guru needs to get away from it all. Your life will be full of departures from the ordinary, followed by returns from the wilderness. One thing is for certain: You will never be at a loss for things to write home about. May the truth you seek, seek you out. *You tend to measure time in decades.*

XXI *The World.* If Wheel of Fortune was your Key Card in Reading #1, your mirror image is The World. *Look at your card.* No matter how deep the snow stacks up in the dead of winter or how humid the windless dog days of summer, you are out there drinking it all in and dancing the dance of life. You lucky stiff! The world always seems to go your way. And ain't life grand? They say of you, "He doesn't have a care in the world," or "She never lets it get to her." And oh, my friend, it's true. No one ever had to convince you to keep a stiff upper lip. You are simply in step with the times. You are always in tune with the beat of the drum. You are "at one." You are "connected." You hear the music of the spheres in your head, and in this you will always be ageless. May you grow to be old. *You tend to measure time in centuries.*

EXTRA CREDIT

Perform this Reading for everyone in your immediate family, your close friends and associates (if they will admit what year they were born), and anyone else you can think of. In addition to what's written here, make your own observations.

Scratch Pad

Jot down your notes here.

EXTRA EXTRA CREDIT!

What the heck, read through all these answers (as well as the answers in Reading #1) to see if you can guess what cards belong to people whose birth dates you don't know.

Go on to the next Reading whenever you are ready to continue.

Reading #13

WHERE DO I BELONG?

In this Reading you will learn how to use the Tarot to get
some advice about where you might be happiest living,
working, or playing. You can also use the technique in this
Reading to think about where you'd like to go on vacation,
to pinpoint the location of something that concerns you but
is happening at a distance, or to think about anything
occurring outside your immediate sphere of influence.

TAROT TOOLS

You will need the same cards you used in Reading #12:

> *King of Wands*
> *Queen of Wands*
>
> *King of Cups*
> *Queen of Cups*
>
> *King of Coins*
> *Queen of Coins*
>
> *King of Swords*
> *Queen of Swords*
>
> *Card 0   The Fool*
> *Card XXI The World*

HOW TO

Just shuffle the cards as you ask your question: **Where will I be happiest
living?** or **Where should I go on** _____? (vacation? business? my
honeymoon?)

You get the idea. Shuffle the cards until done, then deal up the top card
and place it faceup in front of you. Keep dealing cards out in a line until
you come to either The Fool or The World. Then stop.

Look up your answers in the order in which your cards came up. For this Reading, your answers will read as a continuous thought, with the first card giving you the main idea, and each additional card adding detail.

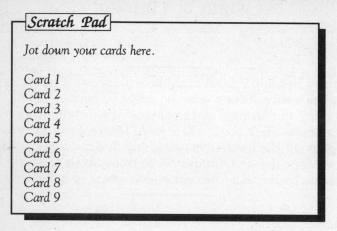

For additional information on any card, consult the **Quick Reference Guide.**

THE ANSWERS

First Card

0 The Fool	You must go where your spirit leads you.
King of Wands	You need to go back where you came from.
Queen of Wands	You need to go visit family.
King of Cups	You need to cross water to get where you are going.
Queen of Cups	You could use a little time at the shore.
King of Coins	You need to go where the byways are crowded.
Queen of Coins	You need to get off in the hills.
King of Swords	You need to go where you can fly free.
Queen of Swords	You need to go where the wind blows you.
XXI The World	Wherever you wind up, you will be happy.

Second Card

0 The Fool	Go someplace you have never been before.
King of Wands	Go someplace where the air is fresh.
Queen of Wands	Go someplace where the sun always shines.

Second Card (*cont.*)

King of Cups	Go someplace where no one can reach you.
Queen of Cups	Go someplace where you can remain in touch.
King of Coins	Go someplace in the heart of a great city.
Queen of Coins	Go someplace that backs up to nature.
King of Swords	Go someplace rather barren and rocky.
Queen of Swords	Go someplace relatively flat and unobstructed.
XXI The World	Go someplace where it's always summer.

Third Card

0 The Fool	Consider getting in your car and seeing where the winding road leads.
King of Wands	Consider heading back East.
Queen of Wands	Consider going to the Midwest.
King of Cups	Consider going overseas.
Queen of Cups	Consider going to the coast.
King of Coins	Consider heading to the Northeast.
Queen of Coins	Consider heading to the Southwest.
King of Swords	Consider going due south.
Queen of Swords	Consider going due north.
XXI The World	Consider flying from place to place to see where you like best.

Fourth Card

0 The Fool	I can see you living up on a hill or in a high-rise.
King of Wands	I can see you living in a flat that's easily accessible.
Queen of Wands	I can see you living in a plain but cozy place.
King of Cups	I can see you living in a remote and isolated spot.
Queen of Cups	I can see you living in a weather-beaten place.
King of Coins	I can see you living in overcrowded conditions.
Queen of Coins	I can see you living in a great, open space.
King of Swords	I can see you living in a sweaty place.
Queen of Swords	I can see you living in a drafty place.
XXI The World	I can see you living in the place of your dreams.

Fifth Card

0 *The Fool*	You should like the Rockies, Cascades, High Sierras—Denver, Wyoming, Montana, Washington State, Oregon, or California.
King of Wands	You should like the Appalachians—New England, upstate New York, Pennsylvania, the Ohio River Valley—the Virginias, the Carolinas, Kentucky, or Tennessee.
Queen of Wands	You should like the Midwest—Ohio, Indiana, Illinois, Iowa, Kansas, Missouri—especially Cincinnati or St. Louis, anywhere on riverbanks.
King of Cups	You should like places off the coast—perhaps the Outer Banks, the Bahamas, or the Florida Keys—but especially Nantucket, Kitty Hawk, or Hilton Head.
Queen of Cups	You should like the eastern shore or Pacific coast—maybe even the Great Lakes—but especially Cape Cod; Seattle; Portland, Oregon; or Portland, Maine.
King of Coins	You should like New York City, Philadelphia, D.C., Boston, and all points in between on the Eastern Corridor—or maybe Chicago at the outside.
Queen of Coins	You should like Palm Springs, Phoenix (especially Scottsdale), Las Vegas, Reno, Denver, or L.A.—you might even take in a few natural wonders on the way.
King of Swords	You should like the deep South—Atlanta, Little Rock, New Orleans; Arkansas, Mississippi, Tennessee, Oklahoma, Texas—even south of the border into Mexico.
Queen of Swords	You should like the North Country—Minnesota, the Dakotas, Montana, Wyoming, Maine—or even across the border into Canada.
XXI The World	You should like going everywhere and seeing it all—perhaps drive cross-country or go abroad.

Sixth Card

0 The Fool	You dream of going to the Alps; or someplace with crags and cliffs.
King of Wands	You dream of going to Athens; or someplace with a strong cultural tradition.
Queen of Wands	You dream of going to Egypt; or someplace having to do with an ancient civilization.
King of Cups	You dream of going to Venice or Rome; or someplace with either canals or cathedrals.
Queen of Cups	You dream of going to the French Riviera; or anyplace where you can sunbathe in the buff.
King of Coins	You dream of going to London or Paris; or someplace at the center of fashion and money.
Queen of Coins	You dream of going to the Far East; or some such mystical and exotic place.
King of Swords	You dream of going down the Amazon; or anyplace where the hunting is good.
Queen of Swords	You dream of going to the land of the Midnight Sun; or anywhere to the far north.
XXI The World	You dream of going to the ends of the earth.

Seventh Card

0 The Fool	Plan to be away at New Moon.
King of Wands	Plan to be away during the waxing Quarter Moon.
Queen of Wands	Plan to be away at Full Moon.
King of Cups	Plan to be away during the waning Quarter Moon.
Queen of Cups	Plan to be away at Crescent Moon.
King of Coins	Plan to go during the summer.
Queen of Coins	Plan to go during the fall.
King of Swords	Plan to go during the winter.
Queen of Swords	Plan to go during the spring.
XXI The World	Plan to go when the seasons change.

Eighth Card

0 The Fool	Take along only what you need. Pack light.
King of Wands	Take something to do on the trip.

Queen of Wands	Check to make sure they take pets.
King of Cups	Take your rubbers, just in case.
Queen of Cups	Pack a swimsuit.
King of Coins	Carry your credit cards in a safe place.
Queen of Coins	Get out some extra cash from the bank.
King of Swords	Be sure to pack your sports gear and sweats.
Queen of Swords	Don't forget to check the weather forecast.
XXI The World	Take something you can wear to a dance.

Ninth Card

0 The Fool	Plan to return on or before New Moon.
King of Wands	Plan to return at or before the first Quarter Moon.
Queen of Wands	Plan to return a day or two before Full Moon.
King of Cups	Plan to return after the third Quarter Moon.
Queen of Cups	Plan to return when you see the Crescent Moon at dusk.
King of Coins	Plan to return when you see the Crescent Moon at dawn.
Queen of Coins	Plan to return during the waxing moon.
King of Swords	Plan to return a day or two after Full Moon.
Queen of Swords	Plan to return during the waning moon.
XXI The World	Plan to return on or after New Moon.

Wild Card

0 The Fool	You would enjoy camping out overnight; or a little mountain climbing.
King of Wands	You would enjoy getting to see the natural wonders; or going to your cabin in the woods.
Queen of Wands	You would enjoy getting to see your family; or going to see a play.
King of Cups	You would enjoy seeing a cathedral or shrine; or finding a great seafood place.
Queen of Cups	You would enjoy eating out at a good spot; or going to the boardwalk.
King of Coins	You would enjoy getting to see some historic sites; or going on a tour of a winery.

Wild Card *(cont.)*

Queen of Coins	You would enjoy doing a little shopping; or having your fortune told.
King of Swords	You would enjoy getting to see an ancient battlefield; or attending a good ball game.
Queen of Swords	You would enjoy going to an amusement park; or being stranded by a big storm.
XXI The World	You would enjoy a night on the town; or dancing until dawn.

EXTRA CREDIT

To plan your weekend, shuffle the cards and ask, **What would I enjoy doing this weekend?** Then deal up a couple of cards and consult the "Wild Card" portion of the Answer section. Take your pick among the possibilities you draw.

Scratch Pad

Jot down your card here.

EXTRA EXTRA CREDIT!

What the heck, to find out when you should plan to be away, shuffle, deal up three cards, and read your answers in the Seventh Card, Eighth Card, and Ninth Card portions of the Answer section.

Go on to the next Reading whenever you are ready to continue.

Reading #14

WILL I BE A RICH MAN?

So far in this book, we have explored what the cards have to say about our personality, our professional interests, and our relationships with others. Now, in the next couple of Readings, we will turn our attention to money and the things that money buys. For this Reading, we will be using cards from the Tarot suit of Coins, since these cards are especially good at answering questions about money matters. The Coins—which may be called Pentacles or Discs in your deck—have become the Diamonds in our standard playing cards.

TAROT TOOLS

You will need the following cards from your deck:

Ace	of Coins
2	of Coins
3	of Coins
4	of Coins
5	of Coins
6	of Coins
7	of Coins
8	of Coins
9	of Coins
10	of Coins

HOW TO

In this Reading we will be answering the question: **What role does money play in my life?**

To select your card for this Reading, we will be using numerology again, as we did in Readings #5 and #9.

In Reading #5 you used your first initial and the letters in your last name to learn about career matters. In Reading #9 you added up letters in your first name to learn about relationships. Now, to find out about money, just add up the letters in both your first and last names, using the following table:

A	1	J	10	S	19
B	2	K	11	T	20
C	3	L	12	U	21
D	4	M	13	V	22
E	5	N	14	W	23
F	6	O	15	X	24
G	7	P	16	Y	25
H	8	Q	17	Z	26
I	9	R	18		

Be sure to add your first and last names separately.

Let's say your name is Adaline Resak. First, add up your first name:

$$(A=1) + (D=4) + (A=1) + (L=12) + (I=9) + (N=14) + (E=5) = 46$$
$$1 + 4 + 1 + 12 + 9 + 14 + 5 = 46$$

Reduce this number to a number between 1 and 10 by adding it up again. If your name is Adaline: $4 + 6 = 10$. If you end up with a number here of 11 or higher, add again.

Now add up your last name. If your last name is Resak:

$$(R = 18) + (E = 5) + (S = 19) + (A = 1) + (K = 11) = 54$$
$$18 + 5 + 19 + 1 + 11 = 54$$

Reduce by adding: $5 + 4 = 9$. Reduce again, if you need to, to get a number between 1 and 10.

Then add up your two numbers for your first and last names. If your name is Adaline Resak, you would add up $10 + 9 = 19$, then reduce $1 + 9 = 10$. Look up this number in the answers.

If the letters of your names add up to exactly 10, as in this example, reduce the number again if your middle initial is equal to an odd number; otherwise keep the answer as 10.

Scratch Pad

Do your math here.

HINT: Also try your maiden (or mother's maiden) name. And if you go by any nicknames, you should check out those variations, too. Have fun. Good luck.

For additional information on any card, consult the Quick Reference Guide.

THE ANSWERS

Ace of Coins. Well now, aren't you the lucky one? For this, my good buddy, is money from out of the blue. *Look at your card.* Perhaps you are the sort who enters contests and gets lucky. Or inherits a bundle from dear old granddad. At any rate, whatever you get in the way of cold, hard cash in this life seems to be handed to you on a silver platter. Well, if I were you, I wouldn't leave home without my checkbook, because your life will be as full of spending as it is of earning. Easy come, easy go, they say. And this is true of your cash flow. But in the end, you'll have something to show for the money that comes to you, if you play your good fortune well and invest wisely. May your good luck hold out. *If in Reading #1 The Magician was your Key Card, you have an uncanny ability to handle your money.* **Your lucky number,** by the way, **is 10.**

2 of Coins. Well, you'll do your fair share of making ends meet and of juggling your accounts in between, but it looks like you'll come out okay in the end. *Look at your card.* You're the sort who is inclined to let your money manage itself, which is okay as long as you've got plenty of it. Otherwise you tend to run out. And most banks want you to at least make the minimum payment every month. If you know what I mean, don't feel bad; but do try to keep your checkbook balanced, and try to live within your means. (Then again, what the heck, you only go around once in this world; and what's a credit line for anyway?) Good luck in your travels. *If in Reading #1 The High Priestess was your Key Card, you have a "way with money" that defies the odds.* **Your lucky number is 9.**

3 of Coins. You will probably depend on others for your financial support in this life, but no one can ever accuse you of not earning your keep. *Look at your card.* Your line of work may require you to find people to fund your projects or ideas. You may find yourself living on stipends, allowances, fellowships, or grants. Or you may simply be "kept" financially by your parents, a spouse, or a patron of some sort. But even though your living tends to come from something other than a paycheck, you will work very hard at what you do just the same. It is, in fact, the quality of life that you provide to others that keeps you on their "bankroll." Good luck with your artistic pursuits. *If in Reading #1 The Empress was your Key Card, you are into creative financing.* **Your lucky number is 8.**

4 of Coins. Whatever money comes to you in this life, you are inclined to want to hold on to it. *Look at your card.* You are the rather frugal sort who tends to pinch a few pennies now and then. You may spend your time cutting out coupons, shopping for bargains, or comparing the prices on the gas pumps (which are not bad ideas). Or you may be inclined to save everything that comes into your possession or to hoard up canned goods in case of nuclear holocaust. Your bank accounts (if you choose to trust a bank with your money) are probably healthier than you think . . . and that's not counting the cash (even gold and silver?) you've got stashed around the house. Good luck with the interest rates. *If in Reading #1 The Emperor was your Key Card, you will surely amass more than you will ever need in this life.* **Your lucky number is 7.**

5 of Coins. I'm sorry to see that money is a struggle for you, but then again, the absence of cash tends to inspire spiritual wealth, and in this respect you will always be well off. *Look at your card.* This is a card about people who "grew up in the Great Depression" or people who have been turned out in the cold at some time in their lives. When it comes to money matters, you will, at one time or another, have to fend for yourself. But this is also a card about people who pull themselves up by their bootstraps. It's possible that yours can be a rags-to-riches story in the end, for the poor have a way of overcoming adversity in a big way. If you do strike it rich someday, always remember where you came from (and the people who made it all possible for you). Best wishes for a speedy economic recovery. *If in Reading #1 The Hierophant was your Key Card, you will spend considerable time and money helping others.* **Your lucky number is 6.**

6 of Coins. No matter how much money you have, you will always have a little bit left over to come to the aid of others *Look at your card.* You are the generous, philanthropic sort who perhaps does a lot of volunteer work. And it's a funny thing, but like a boomerang, the money you give tends to come back to you again. What you lend is paid back. What you give is returned in kind. Or cash just comes flowing in to replenish your charitable contributions fund. Your money would seem to come from your own good works (or perhaps you are the recipient of funds from a trust). Either way, you don't ever have to worry about a rainy day. If you get in a real pinch, those you have helped in the past will come gladly to your rescue. Good luck with your fund-raiser. *If in Reading #1 The Lovers was your Key Card, the source of your wealth is likely to be from a good marriage.* **Your lucky number is 5.**

7 of Coins. Your financial condition will depend upon your own diligence and hard work in this life. *Look at your card.* Your funds may take a little while to mature (and there may be a hefty penalty involved for early withdrawal), but if you hang in there, you stand a good chance of reaping the full rewards of your efforts. Your money may come from dabbling in the stock market or dealing in commodities of some sort; whatever it is, it would seem to involve your making an investment. It could be an investment of your time, or money, or both. As any investor knows, it's important to watch changing conditions carefully and know when to sell out. Good luck with your early returns. *If in Reading #1 The Chariot was your Key Card, you have the ability to triumph over money in this life.* **Your lucky number is 4.**

8 of Coins. Your money will come from the mastering of a trade or profession by which you will earn a fairly decent living. *Look at your card.* You will go through life practicing and perfecting your craft, and due to the high quality of your craftsmanship, you will be rewarded fairly (perhaps handsomely) for your labors. Your skills can be equally applied to the "making of money" via even modest savings and conservative investments. You probably have some U.S. savings bonds stashed away in your dresser or a savings account that earns a set rate of interest (and, I would assume, a little insurance). Good luck with your current project. *If in Reading #1 Justice was your Key Card, the quality of your work will earn you a good reputation, which in turn will result in financial rewards.* **Your lucky number is 3.**

9 of Coins. You are the sort of person who likes money for the beauty and gracious life-style that it is capable of buying. *Look at your card.* The quality of life and the nature of your surroundings are especially important to you. You are likely to lead a rather genteel existence, even if you are a person of small means, for you know how to enhance your environment. Your home is no doubt your single largest investment, and you are constantly fixing it up, especially on the outside. I'll even bet you have a garden, if only in a window box. Or you may work out of your home. (If so, make sure you read the tax laws before deducting home office expenses.) At any rate, your home life and livelihood intersect at some point. Good luck with your refurbishing project. *If in Reading #1 The Hermit was your Key Card, you will always have a roof over your head (but you may prefer to camp out under the stars).* **Your lucky number is 2.**

10 of Coins. You come from money. *Look at your card.* Perhaps someone in your family's past lucked out with money. Or perhaps you are the one who will amass and hand down a newfound legacy. Chances are you will do at least as well as your parents, probably better. (And who knows; maybe you will even live to see the "good things in life.") This is the card of those who achieve that old thing we used to call "The American Dream." Though it may have died for some of the rest of us, it still lives on in you. Good luck with your new venture. *If in Reading #1 Wheel of Fortune was your Key Card, you are inclined to be especially lucky with money.* **Your lucky number is 1.**

EXTRA CREDIT

For a quick Reading of your financial situation—past, present, and future—shuffle the 10 Coins until done, then deal up the top three. The first card you deal up will represent your situation in the past; the second card, your present situation; and the last card, your situation in the future. You can read the complete answers for each card to get a feeling for each of the three timeframes. (See the Quick Reference Guide for an illustration of this layout.)

Scratch Pad

Jot down your cards here.

Card 1 (past)
Card 2 (present)
Card 3 (future)

EXTRA EXTRA CREDIT!

What the heck, to find out what your lucky number is today, shuffle the Coins until done and deal up the top Coin. Look up your card and read the **boldfaced** answer.

Go on to the next Reading whenever you are ready to continue.

Reading #15

HOW'S MY MONEY DOING?

In Reading #14 you learned how to use the Tarot to find out a little about your financial inclinations. In this Reading you will continue to use the first 10 Tarot Coins to answer some specific questions about money matters, but you'll add the first 10 Trumps as well.

TAROT TOOLS

You will need the same cards you used in Reading #14—the Ace through 10 of Coins.

Plus, you will need Trumps I–X:

I	*The Magician*
II	*The High Priestess*
III	*The Empress·*
IV	*The Emperor*
V	*The Hierophant*
VI	*The Lovers*
VII	*The Chariot*
VIII *or* XI	*Justice*
IX	*The Hermit*
X	*Wheel of Fortune*

HOW TO

This is a Cover and Cross Reading, like you last did in Reading #10. (See the Quick Reference Guide for an illustration of this layout.)

First, shuffle the 10 Coins while you repeat your question: **How can I expect my money to go this year?** or **How can I expect my money to go when _____?**

In the first case, you can ask about any particular timeframe, a specific month, week, or day. In the second case, you will want to fill in the blank with some specific money matter: "when I get that new job," "when I pay off my creditors," "when I'm on vacation," "when I'm retired"—you get the idea.

Shuffle the Coins until done, then deal out the top Coin and lay it faceup in front of you. *This card covers you.*

Next, shuffle the 10 Trumps, while you repeat your question. When the Trumps are done, turn over the top Trump, laying it crosswise on the Coin you dealt up before. *This card crosses you.* Set your Trumps aside, and keep the Coins and Trumps piles separate.

After you consult your answer for this Cover and Cross pair, continue dealing up Coins and crossing them with Trumps from the shuffled decks in front of you . . . until you get tired or until no cards are left.

Look up each Cover and Cross pair in the Answer section. For this Reading, your answer will read as a continuous thought, with the first Cover and Cross pair giving you the main idea, and each additional Cover and Cross pair adding details.

Scratch Pad

Jot down your cards here.

Cover/Cross
Cover/Cross
Cover/Cross
Cover/Cross
Cover/Cross
Cover/Cross
Cover/Cross
Cover/Cross
Cover/Cross
Cover/Cross

For additional information on any card, consult the Quick Reference Guide.

THE ANSWERS

Ace of Coins

When crossed by . . .

I   The Magician

You will receive . . .

a little extra pay, perhaps from a part-time or summer job.

Ace of Coins *(cont.)*

When crossed by . . .		You will receive . . .
II	The High Priestess	money you have been waiting for, perhaps from a refund.
III	The Empress	more than you expected, perhaps as a result of a seasonal upturn.
IV	The Emperor	what you expect, perhaps as a result of negotiations with your boss.
V	The Hierophant	the money you need, perhaps as the answer to a prayer.
VI	The Lovers	an advance of some kind, perhaps in exchange for agreeing to something.
VII	The Chariot	a monetary reward, perhaps in recognition of your past performance on the job.
VIII	Justice	money that is due you, perhaps as the result of some damages suffered.
IX	The Hermit	a return of some kind, perhaps from a trust or retirement fund.
X	Wheel of Fortune	some unexpected money, perhaps as the result of blind chance.

2 of Coins

When crossed by . . .		To see your way clear . . .
I	The Magician	balance your checking account.
II	The High Priestess	transfer funds to long-term savings.
III	The Empress	take out a cash advance.
IV	The Emperor	develop a budget or financial plan.
V	The Hierophant	sacrifice a few luxuries right now.
VI	The Lovers	soften up on impulse buying.
VII	The Chariot	reign in on shopping sprees.
VIII	Justice	pay down your credit balances.
IX	The Hermit	lighten up on expensive habits.
X	Wheel of Fortune	review your spending history.

3 of Coins

When crossed by . . .		You may need to demonstrate that . . .
I	The Magician	you have enough cash on hand.
II	The High Priestess	you have an ongoing means of support.
III	The Empress	you have money coming in.
IV	The Emperor	you have funds on deposit.
V	The Hierophant	you can meet your obligations.
VI	The Lovers	you can put a little money up front.
VII	The Chariot	you are willing to pay back your debts.
VIII	Justice	you have no outstanding accounts.
IX	The Hermit	you are as good as your word.
X	Wheel of Fortune	you can make ends meet.

4 of Coins

When crossed by . . .		You might put some money aside . . .
I	The Magician	for a real vacation from work.
II	The High Priestess	in order to fulfill a long-time dream of yours.
III	The Empress	to provide for your family's future.
IV	The Emperor	to cover your taxes.
V	The Hierophant	for gift giving at the holidays.
VI	The Lovers	for a romantic weekend alone.
VII	The Chariot	for car repairs and insurance.
VIII	Justice	for repaying long-term debts.
IX	The Hermit	for monthly utility bills.
X	Wheel of Fortune	for seasonal repairs.

5 of Coins

When crossed by . . .		You are in desperate need of . . .
I	The Magician	a raise in pay; or an overall increase in revenue.
II	The High Priestess	steady pay; or better cash flow.

5 of Coins *(cont.)*

When crossed by . . .		You are in desperate need of . . .
III	The Empress	your paycheck; or a review of your expenses.
IV	The Emperor	a tax refund; or a review of your assets.
V	The Hierophant	more discretionary funds; fewer obligations; or a review of your liabilities.
VI	The Lovers	a raise in your allowance; better interest rates; or fewer commitments.
VII	The Chariot	an expense account; incentive plan; or a review of benefits.
VIII	Justice	better accounting procedures; or a speed-up in collecting amounts due.
IX	The Hermit	a good accountant; or some expert financial advice.
X	Wheel of Fortune	an overall improvement in your financial situation.

6 of Coins

When crossed by . . .		You may pay out a little money . . .
I	The Magician	in order to get yourself set up.
II	The High Priestess	in order to buy something on time.
III	The Empress	in order to make money over time.
IV	The Emperor	in order to make the government happy.
V	The Hierophant	in order to feel good about yourself.
VI	The Lovers	in order to fulfill unmet desires.
VII	The Chariot	in order to reward good performance.
VIII	Justice	in order to make up for something.
IX	The Hermit	in order to keep up appearances.
X	Wheel of Fortune	in order to turn things around.

7 of Coins

When crossed by . . .		**You will earn enough . . .**
I	The Magician	to prepare you for the task you face.
II	The High Priestess	to put you a little ahead.
III	The Empress	to keep you going for a while.
IV	The Emperor	to keep you in the style to which you are accustomed.
V	The Hierophant	to keep you in your place.
VI	The Lovers	to encourage you to make the next move.
VII	The Chariot	to give you a leg up.
VIII	Justice	to get what you deserve.
IX	The Hermit	to place you on higher ground.
X	Wheel of Fortune	to make you think you're on top of the world.

8 of Coins

When crossed by . . .		**You may need to . . .**
I	The Magician	manage to the bottom line.
II	The High Priestess	close the books and start all over again.
III	The Empress	add up your receipts.
IV	The Emperor	review your itemized deductions.
V	The Hierophant	assess your net worth.
VI	The Lovers	incorporate or consolidate accounts.
VII	The Chariot	create a profit-and-loss statement.
VIII	Justice	adjust your balance sheet.
IX	The Hermit	rework your end-of-year projections.
X	Wheel of Fortune	revise the bottom line.

9 of Coins

When crossed by . . .		**You will have sufficient funds . . .**
I	The Magician	to take care of your needs.
II	The High Priestess	to fulfill your desires.

9 of Coins (*cont.*)

When crossed by . . .		You will have sufficient funds . . .
III	The Empress	to provide for your family.
IV	The Emperor	to manage your household.
V	The Hierophant	to maintain your standard of living.
VI	The Lovers	to pursue your interests.
VII	The Chariot	to support your life-style.
VIII	Justice	to maintain the status quo.
IX	The Hermit	to see a light at the end of the tunnel.
X	Wheel of Fortune	to cover unexpected bills.

10 of Coins

When crossed by . . .		You have the opportunity to . . .
I	The Magician	put your money to work for you.
II	The High Priestess	see your way free and clear.
III	The Empress	stand on your own two feet.
IV	The Emperor	get in control of your money.
V	The Hierophant	get by on what you've got.
VI	The Lovers	put love above money.
VII	The Chariot	give it your best shot.
VIII	Justice	get what you think you deserve.
IX	The Hermit	get over the hump.
X	Wheel of Fortune	put it all on the line.

EXTRA CREDIT

For a quick Reading of how you can expect your money to go over the next three years, shuffle and turn over three Coins. Then shuffle and cross them with three Trumps to form three Cover and Cross Readings. (See the Quick Reference Guide for an illustration of this layout.)

Scratch Pad

Jot down your cards here.

Cover/Cross
Cover/Cross
Cover/Cross

EXTRA EXTRA CREDIT!

What the heck, keep dealing up Cover and Cross pairs to project your finances for the next decade.

Go on to the next Reading whenever you are ready to continue.

Reading #16

HOW MUCH CAN I EXPECT TO GAIN?

In this Reading you will continue to work with the first 10 Coins and the first 10 Trumps to ask questions related to money. This time you will be mixing the cards together to perform a comprehensive financial review and forecast, using the same Celtic Cross method we used in Reading #11.

TAROT TOOLS

You will need the same cards you used in Reading #15—the Ace through 10 of Coins, and Trumps I–X:

I	The Magician
II	The High Priestess
III	The Empress
IV	The Emperor
V	The Hierophant
VI	The Lovers
VII	The Chariot
VIII or XI	Justice
IX	The Hermit
X	Wheel of Fortune

Keep them in separate stacks for now.

HOW TO

This is a Celtic Cross spread, like the one you last did in Reading #11. (See the Quick Reference Guide for an illustration of this layout.)

First, shuffle the 10 Trumps together, as you ask your question: **How do I stand to profit from _____?**

Fill in the blank with the name of anyone or anything that stands to bring you money. Some ideas are: How do I stand to profit from . . . "my potential marriage," "my current job," "my prospective investment," "my creative idea," "my schooling." You can be just about as specific as you want.

Shuffle until the Trumps are done, then deal up the top Trump and place it faceup in front of you. *This covers you.* Then deal up the second Trump and place it crosswise on the card you have already dealt. *This crosses you.*

Now shuffle the 10 Coins together, as you ask your question again: **How do I stand to profit from _____?**

Shuffle until the Coins are done, then deal up the top four Coins and place them in positions 3 through 6, around the first two Trumps you have already dealt:

> 3—*This is above you*
> 4—*This is below you*
> 5—*This is behind you*
> 6—*This is before you*

Finally, shuffle the remaining Trumps and Coins together, as you ask your question one last time: **How do I stand to profit from _____?**

Shuffle until the cards are done, then deal up the top four cards and place them in positions 7 through 10 to the right of the cards you have already dealt:

> 7—*This is who you are*
> 8—*This is who they want you to be*
> 9—*This is what you want*
> 10—*And this is what you get*

Look up your cards by their position in the layout (1 through 10) in the Answer section.

Scratch Pad

Note your cards and answers here.

Covers you
Crosses you
Above you
Below you
Behind you
Before you
You are
They want
You want
You get

For additional information on any card, consult the Quick Reference Guide.

THE ANSWERS

Position 1–This covers you.

I The Magician. This venture involves money that appears suddenly and disappears just as fast. Though it's a fifty-fifty proposition, there may be a few tricks hidden up somebody's sleeve. *If you don't know what to do, you can always flip a coin, but only you can decide when to believe the result.*

II The High Priestess. This venture involves positioning yourself to be in the right place at just the right moment. Perhaps you are riding on a true undercurrent that could become the next new wave. But nothing about the future is certain. Go with your intuition on this one. *And if you can't decide, sleep on it. You will have your answer by morning.*

III The Empress. This venture involves doing all you can for the time being, and then sitting back to see if anything takes hold. You've planted the seeds of something that might be. But only time will tell whether or not things will materialize as planned. *When in doubt, keep your fingers crossed, and watch out for signs that the weather is about to change. Go with your instincts on this one.*

IV The Emperor. This venture involves doing what you can to retain your current position. You may have to live up to your end of a bargain or honor the promises you have made in the past. There seems to be little room for compromise or concession here. You may even have enemies! *When in doubt, try not to let on. Go with your hunches on this one.*

V The Hierophant. This venture involves holding something up to public scrutiny. Whatever it is you're involved in, make sure that it measures up to current standards, otherwise it will not meet with public acceptance. You may even have to pay a price for your indiscretion! *When in doubt, say a silent prayer. Go with your conscience on this one.*

VI The Lovers. This venture involves a sweet deal. But before making a final commitment, be sure to discuss the division of labor, express your needs, define your responsibilities, and determine the complete benefits and compensation package. *When in doubt, ask questions. But in the end, go with your heart.*

Position 1 *(cont.)*

VII The Chariot. This venture involves an ambitious plan of some kind and some stiff competition. You will want to make sure that you understand the enemy's strategy as well as your own game plan in the ensuing conflict that is sure to erupt. *When in doubt, make contingency plans. Go with your gut feelings on this one.*

VIII Justice. This venture involves listing the pros and cons or adding up the numbers every way you can to see what you can come up with. But, of course, nothing ever exists in black and white, and everything is subject to interpretation. Be that as it may, you will have to make up your own mind. *You may have to give it the benefit of the doubt. Go with what is written between the lines on this one.*

IX The Hermit. This venture involves going where few have gone before. You'll be forging new ground, opening new territory, stepping out on a limb. But if anybody can do it, you can. However, this journey may involve a personal sacrifice of some kind. *When in doubt, meditate. Go with your inner voices on this one.*

X Wheel of Fortune. This venture involves taking a significant risk. You may have to put your money where your mouth is, play the cards you're dealt, or effectively bluff your way out of a situation. You may well be risking everything here, for everything may be at stake. *When in doubt, go for it. Wear your lucky socks for this one.*

Position 2—This crosses you.

When crossed by . . .		This venture now requires you . . .
I	The Magician	to have the Midas touch.
II	The High Priestess	to read minds and predict the future.
III	The Empress	to cool your heels while things develop.
IV	The Emperor	to stay on top of things.
V	The Hierophant	to perform miracles.
VI	The Lovers	to kiss and make up.
VII	The Chariot	to be gung ho.
VIII	Justice	to cut through the crap.
IX	The Hermit	to show some vision.
X	Wheel of Fortune	to take your chances.

Position 3—This is above you.

Ace of Coins. This venture promises to pay off big down the road. But it may require a constant reinvestment of energy, effort, or profits to make it swing.

2 of Coins. This venture promises to offer upward mobility. But there will be as many downturns as upswings along the way. And you may feel at times as if it takes a step backward to get ahead.

3 of Coins. This venture requires a sales effort. You may have to line up a few prospective buyers or investors before you can effectively launch a money-making effort.

4 of Coins. This venture requires keeping something under your hat. You may need to patent or copyright something before you put it on the market. Or you might have to keep your true intentions secret.

5 of Coins. This venture requires you go without for a while. There is likely to be a period of struggling before you achieve your objective. You may have to sacrifice a little at first in order to demonstrate good faith.

6 of Coins. This venture requires you to give something of yourself to those around you. Quite possibly it's money, but it could also be your valuable time.

7 of Coins. This venture requires you to apply some muscle. Blood, sweat, and tears may even be involved. And still, things will not seem to progress as rapidly as you would like them to.

8 of Coins. This venture requires you to put your skills to work. You may need to serve an apprenticeship first or get certified in some way before you can earn up to your full potential.

9 of Coins. This venture requires you to make full, constructive use of the assets available to you. You may be entrusted with the custodianship of another's property; in which case, you will need to mind the store well.

10 of Coins. This venture requires you to play with the high rollers. The chance for great success is here, as well as the risk of flat-out failure. Going for it all is very much like going for broke. Be careful.

Position 4–This is below you.

Ace of Coins. This venture came at you from out of the blue, promising rich rewards, dangling a proposition in your face.

2 of Coins. This venture came in with the tide, soon receded, but would not stay away.

3 of Coins. This venture was instigated or commissioned by someone who knew about you.

4 of Coins. This venture was not entirely aboveboard when it started out; secrets were kept from or by you.

5 of Coins. This venture was begun when you were down on your luck, or perhaps on the rebound from something else that didn't work out.

6 of Coins. This venture was funded by someone with capital to invest in what was perceived to be a worthwhile cause.

7 of Coins. This venture came as the outgrowth of something else, based upon the early successes of prior efforts.

8 of Coins. This venture resulted from past performance and skills well demonstrated on a consistent basis.

9 of Coins. This venture came as the result of having been involved in profitable ventures in the past.

10 of Coins. This venture came as a result of knowing people in high places, or a word having been planted with the right person.

Position 5–This is behind you.
Position 6–This is before you.

This same table will give you the Readings for cards in either position 5 or position 6.

In position 5 the cards should be read as *Just recently . . .*

In position 6 the cards should be read as *Just coming up . . .*

Positions 5 and 6 *(cont.)*

Ace of Coins	money comes in, perhaps unexpectedly.
2 of Coins	money changes hands or is floated.
3 of Coins	money is put up or advanced.
4 of Coins	money is tight or tied up.
5 of Coins	money is turned down or comes with strings attached.
6 of Coins	money is accepted or given.
7 of Coins	money is invested or otherwise put to work.
8 of Coins	money is earned or interest is accrued.
9 of Coins	money is spent, perhaps for improvements.
10 of Coins	money is lavished or squandered.

Position 7—This is who you are.
Position 8—This is what they want.

This same table will give you the Readings for cards in either position 7 or position 8.

In position 7 the cards should be read as **In this venture, you are . . .**

In position 8 the cards should be read as **In this venture, others want you to be . . .**

I	The Magician	the one who does the work.
II	The High Priestess	the one who figures out what needs to be done.
III	The Empress	the one who watches over things.
IV	The Emperor	the one who remains in control.
V	The Hierophant	the one who provides the inspiration.
VI	The Lovers	the one who remains true to the cause.
VII	The Chariot	the one who is on the front line.
VIII	Justice	the one who takes the blame.
IX	The Hermit	the one who puts in the time.
X	Wheel of Fortune	the one who takes the risk.
Ace of Coins		the one who puts up the money.
2 of Coins		the one handles the books.
3 of Coins		the one who creates earnings.
4 of Coins		the one who puts a lid on expenses.
5 of Coins		the one who gets the shaft.
6 of Coins		the one who contributes a fair share.

Positions 7 and 8 *(cont.)*

7 *of Coins*	the one who produces capital gains.
8 *of Coins*	the one who keeps a nose to the grindstone.
9 *of Coins*	the one who is pampered.
10 *of Coins*	the one who cashes in.

Position 9—This is what you want.

I The Magician. You want this venture to give you enough money to satisfy both your whims and caprices.

II The High Priestess. You want this venture to be your destiny calling out to you   but most of all, you want a steady income.

III The Empress. You want this venture to produce strong results, as long as you get to share in the profits that come about.

IV The Emperor. You want this venture to be something that lasts, producing solid returns for as long as it can be made to run.

V The Hierophant. You want this venture to live up to your highest expectations, especially with regard to gaining higher status in the world or public acceptance of your ideas.

VI The Lovers. You want this venture to entice and tempt you with a fabulous offer you can't refuse.

VII The Chariot. You want this venture to ultimately succeed, but not without a contest first—for you desire most the spoils of war and public accolades.

VIII Justice. You want this venture to succeed on its own merits, with your monetary reward directly based on your own performance.

IX The Hermit. You want this venture to be a rags-to-riches story, in which you emerge as a person others look up to.

X Wheel of Fortune. You want this venture to result in a general improvement of your overall financial position.

Ace of Coins. You want this venture to pay off big, with lots of easy money.

2 of Coins. You want this venture to give you the wherewithal to even out your cash flow.

3 of Coins. You want this venture to provide you with a visible means of ongoing support.

4 of Coins. You want this venture to permit you to build up your assets and cash reserves.

5 of Coins. You want this venture to save you from the financial woes that have haunted you in the past.

6 of Coins. You want this venture to support you for a while, until you can stand on your own two feet.

7 of Coins. You want this initial venture to eventually grow into something bigger and better.

8 of Coins. You want this venture to permit you to support yourself by making full use of your skills.

9 of Coins. You want this venture to provide you with the things you need to live in the style to which you are accustomed.

10 of Coins. You want this venture to answer all of your material needs.

Position 10—This is what you get.

I The Magician. The outcome of this matter is entirely in your own hands. How much will you profit? The sky seems the limit. This card implies that, if directed correctly, your efforts will pay off in precisely the way you intend. Good luck, my friend.

II The High Priestess. It's impossible to tell at this time what the outcome of this venture will be. The future is always undetermined, but particularly in this case, for this venture marks a juncture or turning point in your life. The action that you take now will redirect your future course. Choose wisely, my friend.

III The Empress. It looks like you're making good progress in implementing this venture, and things are starting to come along. Still, there are some critical moments ahead of you before the outcome will be determined. Remain vigilant in your endeavors. Hang in there, my friend.

IV The Emperor. This venture is built on a firm foundation, which should improve the odds of success in the long run. But make sure you don't have blinders on. Monitor the environment for changing conditions that might affect your decisions. Track results. Remain steadfast, my friend.

V The Hierophant. This venture may promise more than it can possibly deliver. On the other hand, it offers you a semblance of security for the time being. When it's all said and done, my friend, may you come out on top.

VI The Lovers. This venture promises some immediate thrills and perhaps a long-term, productive relationship that will grow and develop over time, if you play your cards right. Best wishes, my friend.

VII The Chariot. This venture has the ability to provide you with the thrill of victory (or the agony of defeat). It may be a fight to the finish, but this is a glorious opportunity that you may not want to let pass. Go for it, my friend.

VIII Justice. This venture is based more on the past than on the future. This may be the time when your past catches up to you, finally providing the remuneration that you deserve. Congratulations, my friend.

IX The Hermit. This venture may get a little lonely at times, or you may feel as if it takes you away from something that you really wanted to do. But the personal rewards will be great, even if the money ain't. So be it, my friend.

X Wheel of Fortune. This venture is what needs to be at this juncture in your life. And for better or worse, you have made your decision to take the risk. Good luck, my friend.

Ace of Coins. This venture has its rewards, and they could even be greater than you currently project.

2 of Coins. This venture has its ups and downs and ins and outs, and you will have to learn the ropes before it all comes together for you.

3 of Coins. This venture contains a lot of expectations, and you will have to deliver what your backers desire if you want to see your reward.

Position 10 (*cont.*)

4 of Coins. This venture requires putting a lid on spending and driving the bottom line up to the max. Still, you stand to gain if you can deliver according to plan.

5 of Coins. This venture leaves somebody out. Make sure that you don't overlook something critical.

6 of Coins. This venture succeeds with the assistance of somebody who has a bankroll to put up.

7 of Coins. This venture requires constant monitoring and good timing. Wait long enough to reap the full rewards.

8 of Coins. This venture requires diligence and perseverance. Make sure that you produce your quota on time and up to standards, if you want to see a payback.

9 of Coins. This venture requires you to invest some money in your surroundings if you are to enjoy the things that money brings.

10 of Coins. This venture is so successful, you'd better keep an eye out for industrial spies and thieves.

EXTRA CREDIT

To find out if you should make a particular investment, shuffle the Trumps together and ask: **Should I invest in** _____? When the cards are done, deal up the top Trump and read your answer from the *italic* portion of Card 1 in the Answer section.

Scratch Pad

Jot down your card here.

Reading #16

EXTRA EXTRA CREDIT!

What the heck, conduct a Reading for things that happened in the past to see how you have profited from them.

Go on to the next Reading whenever you are ready to continue.

Reading #17

HOW SUCCESSFUL WILL I BE?

So far we have used the Tarot Trumps and cards from three of the four Tarot suits to get indications about career, love, and money matters. In the next several Readings, we will be turning to questions related to power, success, and the inevitable conflict that surrounds such pursuits. For these questions, you will be using the Tarot Swords, which are particularly well suited for helping you think about strategy. As the Spades in modern poker decks, Swords are about the "weapons" and "tools" in our personal arsenal of survival skills.

TAROT TOOLS

Select from your deck the first 10 Swords:

Ace	of Swords
2	of Swords
3	of Swords
4	of Swords
5	of Swords
6	of Swords
7	of Swords
8	of Swords
9	of Swords
10	of Swords

HOW TO

In this Reading, we will be asking the question: **How successful will I be in this life?**

To select your card for this Reading, you will be using the same numerological method you used in Readings #5, #9, and #14. But this time, rather than adding up all the letters in your name, you will be adding up the letters in your monogram—the initials of your first, middle, and last names—to determine your position in the power structure.

To select your card, add up the initials of your name:

A	1	J	10	S	19
B	2	K	11	T	20
C	3	L	12	U	21
D	4	M	13	V	22
E	5	N	14	W	23
F	6	O	15	X	24
G	7	P	16	Y	25
H	8	Q	17	Z	26
I	9	R	18		

If your initials are A. B. K., you would add:

$$(A = 1) + (B = 2) + (K = 11) = 14$$
$$1 + 2 + 11 = 14$$

Then reduce the result by adding the numbers together again. If your initials are A. B. K., you would add 1 + 4, winding up with 5. The 5 of Swords would be A. B. K.'s card for this Reading.

If your initials add up exactly to 10, reduce the number to 1 if your middle initial is an odd number; otherwise keep 10 as your number.

Look up your number in the Answer section.

Scratch Pad

Do your math here.

HINT: If you have married or changed your name for any reason, you might want to add up the initials in both your former name and the name you now use. It's also interesting to check out the answer you get by skipping your middle initial in the equation.

For additional information on any card, consult the Quick Reference Guide.

THE ANSWERS

Ace of Swords. The degree of success you can achieve in this life is largely dependent on forces outside yourself, but it is you who will determine the end result. *Look at your card.* The Ace of Swords is about success that comes on the heels of an unexpected opportunity. You must be willing, ready, and waiting for your big break (and it wouldn't hurt to be in the right place at the right time). But more important, you must be bold enough to accept the challenge when it is handed down. Your greatest successes may well involve a legacy of some kind, but it is your personal initiative that will be the deciding factor in your success—which, with a little luck, will be great. *When you draw the Ace of Swords, you should anticipate a sure, swift, clean, decisive victory . . . and "may the better man win." If your Key Card in Reading #1 was Wheel of Fortune, your claim to fame will come as a result of a change in the power structure.*

2 of Swords. The degree of success you can achieve in this life is largely dependent on prevailing conditions and natural causes—cycles that you can learn to predict. *Look at your card.* The 2 of Swords is about success that comes as a result of figuring out what's going on in the world around you. You must watch, look, and listen for the signs that things are about to change so you can keep one step ahead of the game (or get a foot in the door). Your greatest successes will involve an understanding of past events and a vision of what's about to happen next. (Perhaps at some time you will be tempted to get in on the ground floor of something.) Your greatest challenge will be to overcome your own inertia, but all in all—and with a little inspiration—you stand a good chance of coming out ahead. *When you draw the 2 of Swords, you should anticipate a standoff or stalemate situation. If your Key Card in Reading #1 was The Hermit, your claim to fame will involve an idea that promises to be the next new wave.*

3 of Swords. The degree of success you can achieve in this life is largely dependent upon the circumstances (and predicaments!) you find yourself in, but with a little conviction, you shall overcome. *Look at your card.* The 3 of Swords is about success that comes as a result of living through some kind of stormy weather or temporary adversity in your life. When others fail you or things get you down, you need to bolster up your courage and take heart. (Or perhaps you need to have a change in heart.) Though your greatest success may well involve the severing of a disappointing relationship, with a little diligence—and endurance counts!—you can still come out on top. *When you draw the 3 of Swords, expect a little blood, sweat, and tears; or quite possibly the weather could interfere with your immediate plans. If*

Justice was your Key Card in Reading #1, your claim to fame will involve some kind of fight for the right.

4 of Swords. The degree of success you can achieve in this life is largely dependent upon community standards and established ideals, but you can learn to play by these rules. *Look at your card.* The 4 of Swords is about success that comes as a result of assuming the "proper position" in life. You need to find your niche. You need to determine how you best fit into the established order of things. Your greatest successes will come as a result of performing good deeds. (Or perhaps you need to lay your past to rest and turn over a new leaf.) But, with a little self sacrifice, you stand to earn the enduring respect of others. *When you draw the 4 of Swords, you should prepare yourself for battle. If The Chariot was your Key Card in Reading #1, your claim to fame will involve a courageous undertaking.*

5 of Swords. The degree of success you can achieve in this life is largely dependent upon the strength of your competitors and rivals, but you can learn to stick up for yourself. *Look at your card.* The 5 of Swords is about success that comes as a result of an enemy's surrender. When provoked, you need to maintain your confidence and resolve, even when you are opposed by "strength in numbers" and other incredible odds. You need to learn to defend yourself (and your territory) and be willing to fight for what you believe. Your greatest successes will come as a result of standing up to those who challenge your position. If you remain persistent—and put up a good fight—you will no doubt come out on top, at least when it counts. *When you draw the 5 of Swords, you should expect a rival to emerge from the shadows. If The Lovers was your Key Card in Reading #1, your claim to fame will involve a passionate encounter.*

6 of Swords. The degree of success you can achieve in this life is largely dependent upon events and forces that you cannot fully comprehend; still, you can always find a way out of a difficult situation. *Look at your card.* The 6 of Swords is about success that comes as a result of making a departure of some sort. You need to learn when the time is right to change directions or pick up your roots (possibly bail out of a bad situation). By establishing some distance from the past, you will be able to understand it more completely and make a transition into a better life. Your greatest successes will involve an embarkation, a journey, or a relocation. With a little faith— and a couple of prayers—you stand a good chance of eventually winding up in the place where you can be successful. *When you draw the 6 of Swords, troubled waters will soon need to be forged. If The Hierophant was your Key Card in Reading #1, your claim to fame will involve a spiritual journey.*

7 of Swords. The degree of success you can achieve in this life is largely dependent upon how closely others are paying attention, but you can pretty much figure out what you can get away with. *Look at your card.* The 7 of Swords is about success that comes as a result of cunning and stealth. In order to be successful, you'll need to figure out how to make your competitive moves undetected. Your greatest successes will come as a result of carrying off well-laid master plans (perhaps in broad daylight). All in all— and with a little sense of daring—you stand a good chance of making out well in the end. *When you draw the 7 of Swords, tread softly but carry a big stick. If The Emperor was your Key Card in Reading #1, your claim to fame will involve an appropriation of power.*

8 of Swords. The degree of success you can achieve in this life is largely dependent upon the trials and tribulations that befall you, but you can stand to make a few sacrifices and still come out ahead of the game. *Look at your card.* The 8 of Swords is about success that comes out of desolate, desperate—even tragic—situations. You may feel sometimes as if your hands are tied so tightly, you cannot escape from your current situation. (Or you may be inclined to get hopelessly wrapped up in your endless work.) But your greatest successes will emerge from these times of personal sacrifice. If you can just keep hanging in there, you are sure to escape (or be rescued) in the end. *When you draw the 8 of Swords, you can expect that someone will be singled out to take the blame. If The Empress was your Key Card in Reading #1, your claim to fame will involve a stunning comeback.*

9 of Swords. The degree of success you can achieve in this life is largely dependent upon things that happened to you in the past, but even the things that haunt you can be overcome. *Look at your card.* The 9 of Swords is about success that emerges out of a bad dream . . . or that comes from the sort of realization you have in the dead of night. Perhaps you will need to get out from under the memories that oppress (even possess) you. But if you can get a grip on your fears and anxieties (or learn to deal with your afflictions), success will surely come to you. *When you draw the 9 of Swords, someone will live to regret their own actions. If The High Priestess was your Key Card in Reading #1, your claim to fame will involve a prophetic dream.*

10 of Swords. The degree of success you can achieve in this life is largely dependent upon the way others treat you, but you can always pump up your self-image. *Look at your card.* The 10 of Swords is about success that comes out of being put down. So the first thing you need to do is to quit putting yourself down. You need to put an end to feelings that you are not good enough. You need to build your self-esteem. Your greatest successes will emerge from a reevaluation of who you are—and from a rebirth of sorts that follows this passage. If you keep giving it your best shot, you are sure to become the master of your fate. *When you draw the 10 of Swords, you can expect a little backstabbing to go on. If The Magician was your Key Card in Reading #1, your claim to fame will involve a miraculous recovery.*

EXTRA CREDIT

For a quick Reading of the challenges you will face this week, shuffle the Swords, ask your question, and when the cards are done, turn over the top one. Consult the *italic* portion of the Answer section.

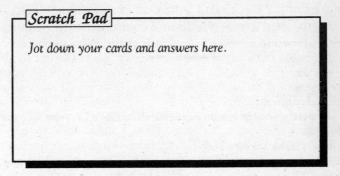

Scratch Pad

Jot down your cards and answers here.

EXTRA EXTRA CREDIT!

What the heck, make a family tree with everybody's initials and associated cards to see if you see any patterns in your bloodline.

Go on to the next Reading whenever you are ready to continue.

Reading #18

HOW'S MY GAME?

Now we will continue working with the first 10 Swords on questions related to power, strategy, and struggles of all kinds, but in this Reading we'll be dealing only with struggles of the fun kind! Contests! Feats of daring! Tests of strength! And games of skill and chance! In this Reading you'll be asking how you're doing in the games you play.

TAROT TOOLS

You will need the same cards you used in Reading #17—the Ace through 10 of Swords.

Plus, you'll need Trumps I–X:

I	The Magician
II	The High Priestess
III	The Empress
IV	The Emperor
V	The Hierophant
VI	The Lovers
VII	The Chariot
VIII or XI	Justice
IX	The Hermit
X	Wheel of Fortune

Keep the two sets of cards in separate stacks for now.

HOW TO

This will be a Cover and Cross Reading with a twist. Instead of dealing up just one Cover and Cross pair, you'll deal up three.

First, shuffle the 10 Swords as you ask your question: **How can I expect my game to go this season?** or **How can I improve my game?**

When the cards are done, deal up the top three Swords faceup in front of you.

Then shuffle the Trumps. Repeat your question. When these cards are done, deal up the top three, and place them crosswise over the three Swords you dealt before:

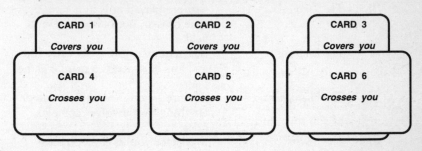

CARD 1	CARD 2	CARD 3
Covers you	Covers you	Covers you
CARD 4	CARD 5	CARD 6
Crosses you	Crosses you	Crosses you

Look up the answers for the resulting pairs of cards. For this Reading, your answers will read as a continuous thought. The first Cover and Cross pair gives you the main idea. The second and third pairs add detail.

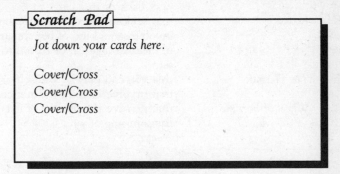

Scratch Pad

Jot down your cards here.

Cover/Cross
Cover/Cross
Cover/Cross

For additional information on any card, consult the Quick Reference Guide.

THE ANSWERS

Ace of Swords

When crossed by . . .

I   *The Magician*

You are best at games . . .

involving the skills you use at cards and anything that involves playing or performing tricks.

Ace of Swords *(cont.)*

II	The High Priestess	involving a set period of time, especially if they're played indoors.
III	The Empress	that are played only at a certain time of year, out of doors or on a field.
IV	The Emperor	that require a strong offensive line and lots of strategy; a map or game plan.
V	The Hierophant	that are sanctioned and officiated; anything that involves complex rules.
VI	The Lovers	that place you in close physical contact, or that involve mixed doubles.
VII	The Chariot	that require a strong defense or that involve something done on horseback or in a car.
VIII	Justice	that seldom end in draws or that involve some kind of benchmark to measure against, or record to set.
IX	The Hermit	that you can play by yourself or that involve crossing a distance.
X	Wheel of Fortune	that involve the placing of bets or the spinning of wheels.

2 of Swords

When crossed by . . .		**You will do okay . . .**
I	The Magician	if you practice enough beforehand.
II	The High Priestess	if you psych up for the big event.
III	The Empress	if you use your remaining time-outs wisely.
IV	The Emperor	if you don't step out of bounds.
V	The Hierophant	if you try a few Hail Marys.
VI	The Lovers	if you abstain the night before.
VII	The Chariot	if you don't get cocky.
VIII	Justice	if you play according to the rules.
IX	The Hermit	if you don't let the crowd get to you.
X	Wheel of Fortune	if you give it your best shot.

3 of Swords

When crossed by . . .	To avoid (further?) injury . . .
I	The Magician	always warm up before your workout.
II	The High Priestess	give your body enough time to recover in between events.
III	The Empress	build up to your peak performance and pace yourself along the way.
IV	The Emperor	go in once in a while for a physical and monitor your pulse.
V	The Hierophant	abstain from your bad habits during training.
VI	The Lovers	always keep your mind on the game.
VII	The Chariot	be sure to wear the proper equipment and keep your gear in good shape.
VIII	Justice	spend some time sitting on the bench or observing things from the stands.
IX	The Hermit	cool down properly afterward.
X	Wheel of Fortune	alternate your routine.

4 of Swords

When crossed by . . .	To prepare for the big game . . .
I	The Magician	gather your strength.
II	The High Priestess	get a good night's sleep.
III	The Empress	eat a good breakfast.
IV	The Emperor	wrap or cover your most vulnerable spots.
V	The Hierophant	say your prayers or keep your fingers crossed.
VI	The Lovers	put on your lucky underwear.
VII	The Chariot	make a strong entrance.
VIII	Justice	imagine the outcome in your favor.
IX	The Hermit	allow the silence to descend upon you; shut out everything else.
X	Wheel of Fortune	take a few deep breaths.

5 of Swords

When crossed by . . .		The outlook for the season ahead . . .
I	The Magician	is favorable, but you can expect it to involve a battle of wills.
II	The High Priestess	is promising, but you can expect it to include a battle of wits.
III	The Empress	is favorable, but it might well feel like a fight for survival.
IV	The Emperor	is solid, but your limits will be tested.
V	The Hierophant	is good, but you might have to spend some time in the penalty box.
VI	The Lovers	is fantastic, but you have to work as a team.
VII	The Chariot	is fabulous, but it involves a stiff fight to the bittersweet end.
VIII	Justice	is about fifty-fifty, due to some close or questionable calls.
IX	The Hermit	is decent, as long as you like underdogs, comebacks, and Cinderella stories.
X	Wheel of Fortune	is pretty much up in the air, if you ask me.

6 of Swords

When crossed by . . .		You ought to consider going to . . .
I	The Magician	the Olympics.
II	The High Priestess	the NBA playoffs.
III	The Empress	the World Series.
IV	The Emperor	the Super Bowl.
V	The Hierophant	the Chess Masters Tournament.
VI	The Lovers	Wimbledon.
VII	The Chariot	the Kentucky Derby.
VIII	Justice	the U.S. Open.
IX	The Hermit	the New York Marathon.
X	Wheel of Fortune	the Indianapolis 500.

7 of Swords

When crossed by . . .		I can see you . . .
I	The Magician	picking up some points.
II	The High Priestess	improving your endurance.
III	The Empress	sliding into home plate.
IV	The Emperor	going out for a forward pass.
V	The Hierophant	making some inspired moves.
VI	The Lovers	working on your technique.
VII	The Chariot	running around the defense.
VIII	Justice	getting out of the sand trap.
IX	The Hermit	leading the field.
X	Wheel of Fortune	crossing the finish line first.

8 of Swords

When crossed by . . .		Your greatest handicap . . .
I	The Magician	can be overcome, if you work like hell on your technique.
II	The High Priestess	can be overcome, if you give it the time it needs.
III	The Empress	can be overcome, if you will be a little more patient.
IV	The Emperor	can be overcome, if you will just get up off your behind.
V	The Hierophant	can be overcome, if you pay attention to the words of an instructor.
VI	The Lovers	can be overcome, if you can avoid distractions.
VII	The Chariot	can be overcome, if you will only be a little more aggressive.
VIII	Justice	can be overcome, if you can learn to be a little more consistent.
IX	The Hermit	can be overcome, if you keep your spirits up and mind focused.
X	Wheel of Fortune	can be overcome, if you believe in miracles.

9 of Swords

When crossed by . . .		To break a losing streak . . .
I	The Magician	first wake up and smell the roses, then purify your body in some way.
II	The High Priestess	first pay attention to your dreams, then meditate to cleanse your mind.
III	The Empress	first place something lucky under your pillow, then do what you can to improve the situation.
IV	The Emperor	first take a sauna or a steamy bath, then shower and shave as you reassess the situation.
V	The Hierophant	first light a few candles, burn some incense, and say a few prayers; then remain celibate until your strength returns.
VI	The Lovers	first take a few cold showers, then get real close to someone, just as soon as you can.
VII	The Chariot	first make a wish over your shoulder at the Crescent Moon; then work at rebuilding your self-confidence.
VIII	Justice	first review the clips from the last game, then reach your own conclusions.
IX	The Hermit	first seek the advice of a trusted friend; then get away by yourself to think things through.
X	Wheel of Fortune	first carry a silver coin in your pocket, then read a book on self-improvement.

10 of Swords

When crossed by . . .		You have the advantage . . .
I	The Magician	of your own experience.
II	The High Priestess	of having put your past behind you.

10 of Swords (*cont.*)

When crossed by . . .		You have the advantage . . .
III	The Empress	of getting to start fresh again.
IV	The Emperor	of having known both victory and defeat.
V	The Hierophant	of being able to rectify your actions.
VI	The Lovers	of being on the rebound.
VII	The Chariot	of being able to make a comeback.
VIII	Justice	of having wiped the slate clean.
IX	The Hermit	of having endured a rite of passage.
X	Wheel of Fortune	of being able to work your way back to the top again.

EXTRA CREDIT

For a more complete Reading, keep dealing up pairs of cards (Swords crossed by Trumps). Be sure to write down all your answers so that you can look at them together. Sometimes this sequence will prove to be in chronological order. Look up your answers just as before.

Scratch Pad

Jot down your cards and answers here.

Cover/Cross
Cover/Cross
Cover/Cross
Cover/Cross
Cover/Cross
Cover/Cross
Cover/Cross
Cover/Cross
Cover/Cross
Cover/Cross

EXTRA EXTRA CREDIT!

What the heck, conduct this Reading for every member of your team to see how you can expect the game to turn out overall.

Go on to the next Reading whenever you are ready to continue.

Reading #19

WHAT'S MY WINNING STRATEGY?

Your work with the Swords continues in this Reading, as you ask questions about the strategy you should follow when handling the individual conflicts, struggles, and contests that occur in your life.

TAROT TOOLS

You will need the same cards you used in Reading #18—the Ace through 10 of Swords, and Trumps I–X:

I	*The Magician*
II	*The High Priestess*
III	*The Empress*
IV	*The Emperor*
V	*The Hierophant*
VI	*The Lovers*
VII	*The Chariot*
VIII or XI	*Justice*
IX	*The Hermit*
X	*Wheel of Fortune*

Keep the two sets of cards in separate stacks for now.

HOW TO

This is a Celtic Cross spread, like the one you last did in Reading #16. (See the Quick Reference Guide for an illustration of this layout.)

First, shuffle the 10 Trumps together as you ask your question: **What should my strategy be with regard to** _____**?** Fill in the blank with the name of anyone or anything that stands to bring you conflict, to present you with a struggle, or to challenge you with a contest.

Shuffle until the Trumps are done, then deal up the top Trump and place it faceup in front of you. *This covers you.* Deal up the second Trump and place it crosswise on the card you have already dealt. *This crosses you.*

Now shuffle the 10 Swords together, as you ask your question again: **What should my strategy be with regard to** _____**?**

Shuffle until the Swords are done, then deal up the top four Swords and place them in positions 3 through 6, around the first two Trumps you have already dealt:

> 3—*This is above you*
> 4—*This is below you*
> 5—*This is behind you*
> 6—*This is before you*

Finally, shuffle the remaining Trumps and Swords together, as you ask your question one last time: **What should my strategy be with regard to _____?**

Shuffle until the cards are done, then deal up the top four cards and place them in positions 7 through 10 to the right of the cards you have already dealt:

> 7—*This is who you are*
> 8—*This is who they want you to be*
> 9—*This is what you want*
> 10—*And this is what you get*

Look up your cards by their position in the layout (1 through 10) in the Answer section.

Scratch Pad

Note your cards and answers here.

Covers you
Crosses you
Above you
Below you
Behind you
Before you
You are
They want
You want
You get

For additional information on any card, consult the Quick Reference Guide.

THE ANSWERS

Position 1—This covers you.

I The Magician. This challenge requires you to pick yourself up, dust yourself off, and start all over again. It's a dog-eat-dog world out there. And in this game, it's "every man for himself." Trust in no one but yourself. Someone would like to see you fall flat on your face, but don't let the person "keep a good man down." You can take a few hits and still get back up again.

II The High Priestess. This challenge requires you to confront the thing that keeps you awake at night. What is the terrible insecurity that haunts you, anyway? In this world of ups and downs and in-betweens, the greatest threat to you right now is fear of failure. Someone would like to throw you off your game, but don't let the person get to you. You will be able to make ends meet somehow.

III The Empress. This challenge requires you to overcome your feelings of hopelessness. Yes, things can look pretty bleak and barren sometimes. But the world helps those who help themselves. You run the risk of digging a hole for yourself. Someone would like to weigh you down, but don't let the person sink you. Take stock of the assets you have left.

IV The Emperor. This challenge requires you to deal with something underhanded or top secret. In this world where the strongest, the fittest, and the keenest tend to make out like bandits, you've got to take a few risks, keep a few cards up your sleeve, or carry an argument in your hip pocket. Someone would like to see you to get away with something, but be careful not to get caught in the act. Borrow what you need to get by for a while.

V The Hierophant. This challenge requires you to deal with something in an aboveboard way. In this world of lies and deceptions, honesty is often the best defense, and let the chips fall where they may. Someone would like to see you remain silent on the subject, but it helps to get the matter off your chest. Perhaps the time has come to quit lying to yourself and move on. Cash in your chips while you're still ahead.

VI The Lovers. This challenge requires you to make up your own mind. In a world where things tend to go wrong about as many times as they work out right, you've got to recognize a good thing when you see it

Reading #19

and sense when it's safe to let your barriers down. Someone would like to court you, but don't be afraid to keep a safe distance. Choose the right time to make a withdrawal.

VII The Chariot. This challenge requires you to strike out on your own. In this world where people have to learn how to stand on their own two feet, you sometimes need to prove something to yourself. Yes, you can make it on your own. There are others out there just as determined to get ahead as you are, but don't let them run all over you. Maintain a little something in reserve.

VIII Justice. This challenge requires you to mend a broken heart, heal old wounds, or make amends. In this world where right and wrong are two sides of the same coin, you can expect a little human suffering along the way. Someone would like to get even with you for something, but don't let yourself be blindsided. Try not to be gullible. Keep something for a rainy day.

IX The Hermit. This challenge requires you to seek new horizons. In this world where the grass is always greener on the other side, you sometimes need to seek the place where you best fit in. Someone would like to see you get ahead, but you may need to depart with your dignity and determination in hand. Choose wisely. Invest carefully.

X Wheel of Fortune. This challenge requires your full attention right now and all the resources you can muster. In this world where the rich get richer, you sometimes need to invest everything you can afford to risk. Someone would like to give you a helping hand. Accept an offer, and don't look a gift horse in the mouth.

Position 2—This crosses you.

When crossed by . . .		Watch out for . . .
I	The Magician	someone who wants to challenge you.
II	The High Priestess	someone who is your equal.
III	The Empress	someone you thought you could trust.
IV	The Emperor	someone who is a sleeping giant.
V	The Hierophant	someone who thinks they have God on their side.

Position 2 *(cont.)*

When crossed by . . .	**Watch out for . . .**
VI The Lovers	someone who knows how to get to first base.
VII The Chariot	someone who knows how to get away with something.
VIII Justice	someone who really knows how to get even.
IX The Hermit	someone who understands everything.
X Wheel of Fortune	someone who wants to see you fail.

Position 3–This is above you.

Ace of Swords. You stand a good chance of emerging from your current challenge victorious. At best, you will make peace with your enemies. At worst, you will simply defeat them.

2 of Swords. Your current challenge is most likely to resolve itself in harmony. At best, it will be a win/win solution. At worst, it will end in stalemate.

3 of Swords. Your current challenge is most likely to result in some kind of personal disappointment. At best, you will be able to throw off your false illusions. At worst, you will suffer disenchantment.

4 of Swords. Your current challenge is most likely to resolve itself quietly, but in your favor. At best, you will receive some personal satisfaction. At worst, your conscience will be cleared.

5 of Swords. Your current challenge will likely work to defend your reputation. At best, you will walk away the clear and obvious winner. At worst, it will be a close decision in your favor.

6 of Swords. Your current challenge will resolve itself with a departure of some sort. At best, you will escape completely from your current situation. At worst, you will overcome some major obstacles.

7 of Swords. Your current challenge will resolve itself in a close brush with destiny. At best, you will be rewarded for your daring. At worst, you will escape without getting caught.

Position 3 (cont.)

8 of Swords. Your current challenge will result in a dilemma that you must ultimately resolve yourself. At best, you will manage to escape from the most fearful consequences. At worst, you will have to face the music.

9 of Swords. Your current challenge resolves itself in a sudden realization. At best, you will realize something important about yourself. At worst, you will learn how to do something better next time.

10 of Swords. Your current challenge resolves itself in a stunning defeat. At best, you will be the undisputed winner. At worst, you will fall flat on your face.

Position 4–This is below you.

When in fourth position . . .	Your current challenge emerges . . .
Ace of Swords	from a long-standing rivalry.
2 of Swords	out of something that was not completely resolved in the past.
3 of Swords	as the outgrowth of something that went wrong in the past.
4 of Swords	as the culmination of a series of events that unfolded in sequence in the past.
5 of Swords	as the result of a past victory.
6 of Swords	from a past (and secret?) life.
7 of Swords	from something you have brought upon yourself.
8 of Swords	from some crisis in the past.
9 of Swords	on the heels of something you are not quite over yet.
10 of Swords	as the result of a past defeat.

Position 5–This is behind you.
Position 6–This is before you.

This same table will give you the Readings for cards in either position 5 or position 6.
In position 5 the cards should be read as *Just recently . . .*
In position 6 the cards should be read as *Just coming up . . .*

Positions 5 and 6 *(cont.)*

Ace of Swords	a significant battle is won.
2 of Swords	a semblance of order is restored.
3 of Swords	a relationship encounters a storm.
4 of Swords	a well-deserved rest is taken.
5 of Swords	a personal conflict is resolved.
6 of Swords	a journey is embarked upon.
7 of Swords	something remains unaccounted for at the end of the day.
8 of Swords	something is all tied up in red tape.
9 of Swords	a bad dream is remembered.
10 of Swords	something is said behind your back.

Position 7—This is who you are.
Position 8—This is what they want.

This same table will give you the Readings for cards in either position 7 or position 8.

In position 7 the cards should be read as **In this conflict, you are . . .**

In position 8 the cards should be read as **In this conflict, others want you to be . . .**

I	The Magician	the one who saves the day.
II	The High Priestess	the one who makes it through the night.
III	The Empress	the one who keeps watch around the clock and reports back.
IV	The Emperor	the one who is reported to.
V	The Hierophant	the one who has a vested interest.
VI	The Lovers	the one who remains loyal.
VII	The Chariot	the one who gets hurt.
VIII	Justice	the one who is guilty.
IX	The Hermit	the one who shoulders the burden.
X	Wheel of Fortune	the one who lucks out.

Ace of Swords	the one who wins out in the end.
2 of Swords	the one who makes the truce.
3 of Swords	the one who loses more than is gained.

Positions 7 and 8 *(cont.)*

4 *of Swords*	the one who lies in wait.
5 *of Swords*	the one who stands guard.
6 *of Swords*	the one who flees.
7 *of Swords*	the one who escapes.
8 *of Swords*	the one who's left behind.
9 *of Swords*	the one who is spared.
10 *of Swords*	the one who is betrayed.

Position 9—This is what you want.

I The Magician. You want this conflict to result in a personal transformation. You want to emerge from it stronger than you were before.

II The High Priestess. You want this conflict to run its course so that you can ultimately continue on your own way forward.

III The Empress. You want this conflict to produce some significant results so that you can profit as a reward for your efforts.

IV The Emperor. You want this conflict to result in an increase in the power your position already commands.

V The Hierophant. You want this conflict to result in something bigger and better than the way of life you already enjoy.

VI The Lovers. You want this conflict to result in personal gratification and the satisfaction of your physical desires.

VII The Chariot. You want this conflict to result in the public recognition of your accomplishments.

VIII Justice. You want this conflict to result in the settling of the matter once and for all.

IX The Hermit. You want this conflict to result in something on the order of a higher attainment.

X Wheel of Fortune. You want this conflict to resolve itself.

Ace of Swords. You want this conflict to be resolved in a swift, decisive way.

Position 9 *(cont.)*

2 *of Swords.* You want this conflict to be resolved in due course, for there is no urgency.

3 *of Swords.* You want this conflict to be resolved with compassion and human understanding as soon as possible.

4 *of Swords.* You want this conflict to be resolved by getting something off your chest first thing in the morning.

5 *of Swords.* You want this conflict to be resolved at any cost by the end of the day.

6 *of Swords.* You want this conflict to be forgotten in the stretch of time and the span of distance.

7 *of Swords.* You want this conflict to be brought out into the open immediately, where it can be quickly resolved.

8 *of Swords.* You want this conflict to result in your eventual liberation and ultimate freedom, but right now you feel that your hands are tied.

9 *of Swords.* You want this conflict to have never taken place—and you rue the day that it sucked you in.

10 *of Swords.* You want this conflict to result in an absolute end to the past, to be followed by a new beginning.

Position 10—This is what you get.

I *The Magician.* Your winning strategy is to focus your energy, attention, and efforts on the things that matter most and are directly within your span of control, talent, and reach. When in doubt, start small and work your way up to bigger and better things. It is your own diligent efforts that will pay you back most in this life. Have a good day every day.

II *The High Priestess.* Your winning strategy is to listen to your inner voices, follow your own instincts, and go with your hunches on all matters of significance. When in doubt, flip a coin but don't even look to see how it lands. Your greatest rewards in this life will come when you fly by the seat of your pants. Have a good time all the time.

III *The Empress.* Your winning strategy is to pay close attention to what's going on around you, to constantly monitor progress against goals,

Position 10 *(cont.)*

and to consistently watch for any signs of changing conditions that might affect performance. When in doubt, overcompensate for things that might go wrong. Your greatest rewards in this life will come from being diligent and prepared. Have a good season.

IV The Emperor. Your winning strategy is to adopt a hard line and stick to it; to carve out a territory and defend it; and to always remember the other people who help make it all possible. When in doubt, err on the side of paranoia. Your greatest rewards in this life will come from correctly second-guessing those who would like to have your job. Have a good quarter.

V The Hierophant. Your winning strategy is to invoke higher powers than your own, to remain humble, and to adopt humanitarian causes that serve the greatest good for the greatest number. When in doubt, network. Your greatest rewards in this life will come from fighting the good fight. Have a good year.

VI The Lovers. Your winning strategy is to romance your way along, to charm the pants off others, to seduce them, and to work your way into their hearts. When in doubt, flirt. Your greatest rewards in this life will come as a result of forming close (even intimate) relationships with others. Have a good night.

VII The Chariot. Your winning strategy is to flex your muscles, sharpen your reflexes, and put on a good show of raw physical strength on command. When in doubt, pump iron. Your greatest rewards in this life will come as a result of athletic contests or other feats of bravery, daring, and competition. Have a good week.

VIII Justice. Your winning strategy is to follow all the rules to the letter, to live up to the highest standards of integrity, and to consistently base your decisions on the interpretation of hard facts. When in doubt, come down on the side of lenience. Your greatest rewards will come in this life from measuring up to common standards and practices. Have a good month.

IX The Hermit. Your winning strategy is to retreat to a quiet place to think things through and mull things over, then—once the inspiration has come—to return with your revelations in hand. When in doubt, meditate. Your greatest successes in this life will come from reaching your own independent conclusions. Have a good weekend.

Position 10 *(cont.)*

X *Wheel of Fortune*.
Your winning strategy is to place a bet on your lucky number, to spin the wheel, and to take your chances. When in doubt, walk away with your winnings. Your greatest successes in this life will come when lady luck rides with you. Have a good life.

Ace of Swords.
Your winning strategy is to strike out boldly after the things you want. To you, success in life is measured by power and conquest. When in doubt, act first and ask permission later. Your greatest successes in this life will come as a result of aggressive campaigns. Good luck in your maneuvers.

2 of Swords.
Your winning strategy is to step into the middle of things, to negotiate a solution, and to arbitrate a compromise. When in doubt, bury the hatchet. Your greatest successes in this life will come as a result of sitting around a conference table. Good luck in your negotiations.

3 of Swords.
Your winning strategy is either to love them and leave them or to forgive and forget—but either way, to never look back. When in doubt, put an end to the affair. Your greatest successes in this life will come as the result of the severing of bad relationships. Good luck in your affairs.

4 of Swords.
Your winning strategy is to take it easy, to not get upset by very much, and to pay attention to your dreams. When in doubt, sleep on it. Your greatest successes in this life will come as a result of things that happen in the dead of night. Good luck with your mental preparations.

5 of Swords.
Your winning strategy is to put up your guard, hold up your dukes, and stick to your ground. But when in doubt, punt. Your greatest successes in this life will come as the result of overcoming the obstacles, hurdles, and enemies in your way. Good luck in holding your ground.

6 of Swords.
Your winning strategy is to know when it's time to retreat, to move on, to seek greener pastures, or to start a new life someplace else. When in doubt, move on. Your greatest successes in this life will come as the result of making a departure from the things you already know. Good luck in your coming passage.

7 of Swords.
Your winning strategy is to proceed with caution, to take the necessary precautions, and to walk on eggshells. When in doubt, play it safe. Your greatest successes in this life will come as the result of keeping your strategies to yourself. Good luck in making your moves.

Position 10 *(cont.)*

8 of Swords. Your winning strategy is to play the role of the martyr, to deny your own needs on the behalf of others, and to get all wrapped up in your responsibilities. When in doubt, feel guilty. Your greatest successes in this life will come as the result of making a personal sacrifice. Good luck in making your escape.

9 of Swords. Your winning strategy is to put in long hours; to eat, breathe, work, and sleep your troubles; and to waken inspired in the dark. When in doubt, worry. Your greatest successes in this life will come as the result of relentless endeavor. Good luck in your nocturnal efforts.

10 of Swords. Your winning strategy is to have eyes in the back of your head, to never trust anybody, and to "beware the ides of March." When in doubt, play dead. Your greatest successes in this life will come as the result of some grave humiliation that befalls you. Good luck in keeping a low profile.

EXTRA CREDIT

For a quicker Reading, shuffle the 10 Swords and the 10 Trumps together while you ask the question. When the cards are done, deal up the top four and place them in a line. Read them in the Answer section as positions 7, 8, 9, and 10.

Scratch Pad

Jot down your cards here.

Position 7

Position 8

Position 9

Position 10

EXTRA EXTRA CREDIT!

What the heck, perform this Reading for the various people you work or play with, to help you develop your overall competitive strategy.

Go on to the next Reading whenever you are ready to continue.

Reading #20

WHAT KIND OF FOOL AM I?

In this Reading you'll learn about your weak spot, your tragic flaw, as it were—your Achilles' heel. For this Reading we'll be using a special selection of cards—including all the Pages and Knights—which I think of collectively as the Tarot Fools.

TAROT TOOLS

From your Tarot deck you will need to select the following cards:

> *Page of Wands*
> *Knight of Wands*
>
> *Page of Cups*
> *Knight of Cups*
>
> *Page of Coins*
> *Knight of Coins*
>
> *Page of Swords*
> *Knight of Swords*

Plus, you will need:

> *Card 0*   *The Fool*
> *Card XXI*   *The World*

HOW TO

Find your Key Card from Reading #1 in the following chart; then consult the Answer section for the card that corresponds to your Key Card.

If you skipped Reading #1, go back now and learn how to add up the numbers in your birth date. (This is a good time to review your answer in Reading #1 anyway.)

Your Key Card in Reading #1	Your card in Reading #20
I The Magician	Card 0 The Fool
II The High Priestess	Page of Cups
III The Empress	Page of Coins
IV The Emperor	Knight of Coins
V The Hierophant	Knight of Cups
VI The Lovers	Page of Wands
VII The Chariot	Knight of Swords
VIII Justice	Page of Swords
IX The Hermit	Knight of Wands
X Wheel of Fortune	Card XXI The World

Scratch Pad

Jot down your card here.

For additional information on any card, consult the Quick Reference Guide.

THE ANSWERS

Card 0 The Fool. If The Magician was your Key Card in Reading #1, you, my friend, are **destiny's fool,** for when destiny calls you, you must go—regardless of the consequences. *Look at your card.* You spark with energy. You sparkle with dreams in the making. You are like new worlds being born. And you worry the people in your life half to death! They say, "So when are you going to slow down, already?" But, my fool on the hill, you love the surge of the fast lane, don't you? You love being in the thick of things and in the midst of where it's all happening. What can I say? Burn out young if you must, then; for no one makes a more beautiful flame in the process. *When you draw The Fool, I see you taking a bold leap into the unknown. Watch out for the first step. . . . It's a doozy.*

Page of Cups. If The High Priestess was your Key Card in Reading #1, you, my friend, are **premonition's fool,** for you read the signs of the future in everything you behold, and it alters your life. *Look at your card.* Oh, déjà vu! There you go again . . . relating the details of your intricate dreams . . . studying the leaves scattered on the walls of your teacup . . . reading innuendo into everything that's said. Somehow it seems your world is disproportionately full of coincidences. And what is this nagging feeling in your bones today? The people in your life are not sure about you sometimes. They say, "So why are you so superstitious?" or "Gee, you're so psychic." What can I say? Let your "funny feelings" rule you, if you must; for no one is more colorful in the process. *When you draw the Page of Cups, I see you getting in over your head. Watch out for the undertow.*

Page of Coins. If The Empress was your Key Card in Reading #1, you, my friend, are a **fool for progress,** and you are always envisioning something better. *Look at your card.* This is Utopia. This is Camelot. This is New Harmony, Pennsylvania. This is the dawning of the new age . . . and you are ushering it in. Oh, brave new world—or so you say. And oh, my gullible fool, you are so easily swept along by the vision—even if it belongs to someone else. You become transfixed, absorbed, engrossed in the creative process. People say to you, "How can you be so utterly taken in by it?" or "How can you be so obsessed and preoccupied?" What more can I add? Turn your back completely on the past, if you must, and live in your dream world; for no one is more alive in the process. *When you draw the Page of Coins, I see you coming up on a pitfall. Watch out you don't lose sight of your goal.*

Knight of Coins. If The Emperor was your Key Card in Reading #1, you, my friend, are a **fool for appearances,** and you are always trying to make a good impression. *Look at your card.* Oh yes, there you are up on your vantage point—dressed to the hilt, dressed fit to kill, dressed for the ultimate success (in basic black perhaps?). And don't you cast a striking image? Don't you make an immediate impression? People say to you, "Great threads," "Nice wheels," and "Where'd you get those shoes?" But behind your back they accuse you of being superficial and shallow. What can I say? Judge the books by their covers if you must, and spend your life in front of a mirror; for no one casts a better reflection or a bigger shadow in the process. *When you draw the Knight of Coins, I see you going downhill. Watch out for slipups.*

Knight of Cups. If The Hierophant was your Key Card in Reading #1, you, my friend, are a **fool for causes,** and you are always out canvassing for something. *Look at your card.* There you are going door to door with your cup extended, asking for handouts (and leaving literature behind). Won't you help out the less fortunate? Won't you help me save humanity (or some other species)? Your contribution is urgently needed. These are the lines you use. In return, people say to you, "No, I gave at the office," or "Oh, well, it sounds like a good cause, but . . ." Sometimes they will simply tell you to drop dead. What can I say? Make others feel guilty if you must; for no one else creates more out of nothing in the process. *When you draw the Knight of Cups, I see you getting set up. Watch out for an ambush.*

Page of Wands. If The Lovers was your Key Card in Reading #1, you, my friend, are a **sentimental fool,** and you are constantly expressing your most intimate feelings. *Look at your card.* There you are up on your soapbox (or under somebody's balcony) baring your soul, proclaiming your intentions for the world to hear . . . and exposing your own behind in the process. People say to you, "Go for it, buddy," and "Right on!" for we have all been love's captive. What more can I say? When in doubt, send long-stemmed roses, and break a few hearts (maybe even your own) if you must along the way; for no one is more involved in the process. *When you draw the Page of Wands, I see you standing on rocky ground. Watch out for sudden moves.*

Knight of Swords. If The Chariot was your Key Card in Reading #1, you, my friend, are a **fool who rushes in,** and there is no stopping you. *Look at your card.* Hoick! Charge! And Tallyho! For there you go. . . . Once again you have hit the ground running. And don't look now, but there goes caution, thrown to the wind—again. People say to you, "Hold your horses for a minute, will you?" But by then it's already too late. You are gone in a cloud of dust. What can I tell you? Be gung ho if you must, and let the chips fall where they may; for the process would stagnate without you. *When you draw the Knight of Swords, I see you running up against an obstacle. Watch out for low-hanging branches.*

Page of Swords. If Justice was your Key Card in Reading #1, you, my friend, are a **fool for the rules,** and when you play, you play for keeps. *Look at your card.* If you're bluffing, you could sure fool me. For it is not just a physical strength you wield, but an undaunting courage that emanates from your deep, inner sense of conviction, as keen and sharp as a knife. What's right is right, and what's wrong must not be abided—or so you swear. People say to you, "Calm down, it's just a game." What can I add? If you must take on the good fight, so be it; for nobody brings more order to the process. *When you draw the Page of Swords, I see you getting involved in an uphill battle. Watch out you don't trip.*

Knight of Wands. If The Hermit was your Key Card in Reading #1, you, my friend, are a **fool for the truth,** and you are constantly hoping to discover it. *Look at your card.* On your marks. Get set . . . But this is one race you will have to run by yourself, with yourself, against yourself, for yourself . . . and with a little luck, you may even come out a winner in the end. People say to you, "What bandwagon are you on this time?" or "Where have you been keeping yourself?" What can I say? Go off to the wilderness and think things through if you must; for nobody gets closer to the process. *When you draw the Knight of Wands, I see you being held back. Watch out for land mines.*

XXI *The World.* If Wheel of Fortune was your Key Card in Reading #1, you, my friend, are a **fool for freedom,** and you are always looking for new ways to try your wings. *Look at your card.* It is the experience itself that matters most to you—the dance of the Universe, if you will—and so you are always seeking the experience, unrestrained and unfettered by anything but the boundaries of the human imagination. People will call you wild and irresponsible—and oh, you do get out of hand sometimes—and some may even say you go crazy. Let them say what they will. You bring art to the world, and nobody but nobody belongs to the process more than you. *When you draw The World, I see you on top of it. Don't worry about anything.*

EXTRA CREDIT

For a quick Reading of what you need to watch out for this week, shuffle the 10 Tarot Fools, ask your specific question, and deal up the top card. Read the *italic* portion of the answers.

┌─ **Scratch Pad** ─────────────────────────┐

Jot down your cards and answers here.

└───┘

EXTRA EXTRA CREDIT!

What the heck, complete this Reading for everybody in the office to see what kinds of fools you're up against in the world.

Go on to the next Reading whenever you are ready to continue.

Reading #21

WHAT'S IN THE MAIL?

In Reading #20 you met the Tarot Knights and Pages (aka
the Tarot Fools), and they told you what you need to watch
out for in your life. The Pages and Knights are also good at
telling you about messages that are coming your way or
about communications that are overdue. Use this Reading to
get a status report.

TAROT TOOLS

You will need the same cards you used in Reading #20:

> *Page of Wands*
> *Knight of Wands*
>
> *Page of Cups* ·
> *Knight of Cups*
>
> *Page of Coins*
> *Knight of Coins*
>
> *Page of Swords*
> *Knight of Swords*
>
> Card 0　　*The Fool*
> Card XXI　*The World*

HOW TO

Just shuffle the cards as you ask your question: **What message will I
receive?**

Shuffle the cards until done. Deal up the top card and place it faceup in
front of you. Keep dealing out cards and placing them in front of you in a
line until you come to either The Fool or The World. Then stop.

Look up your answers in the order in which your cards came up. For this

Reading, your answers will read as a continuous thought, with the first card giving you the main idea, and each additional card adding detail.

> **Scratch Pad**
>
> *Jot down your cards and answers here.*
>
> Card 1
> Card 2
> Card 3
> Card 4
> Card 5
> Card 6
> Card 7
> Card 8
> Card 9

For additional information on any card, consult the Quick Reference Guide.

THE ANSWERS

First Card

0 The Fool	You await news of an adventuresome nature.
Page of Wands	You await news of a romantic nature.
Knight of Wands	You await news of a spirited nature.
Page of Cups	You await news of a prophetic nature.
Knight of Cups	You await news of an official nature.
Page of Coins	You await news of an encouraging nature.
Knight of Coins	You await news of a serious nature.
Page of Swords	You await news of a definite nature.
Knight of Swords	You await news of a swift nature.
XXI The World	You await news of a tremendously exciting nature.

Second Card

0 The Fool	A message comes by electronic means.
Page of Wands	A message is being rehearsed.

Knight of Wands	A message awaits you.
Page of Cups	A message comes by mail.
Knight of Cups	A message is being polished.
Page of Coins	A message comes hand-delivered.
Knight of Coins	A message is being drafted.
Page of Swords	A message is in the mail.
Knight of Swords	A message is being dispatched.
XXI The World	The message is delivered.

Third Card

0 The Fool	The news brings a smile to your face.
Page of Wands	The news brings you back in touch with someone.
Knight of Wands	The news brings you back into action.
Page of Cups	The news brings tears to your eyes.
Knight of Cups	The news brings a sense of relief.
Page of Coins	The news brings a glimmer of hope.
Knight of Coins	The news brings a scowl to your face.
Page of Swords	The news brings you to your feet.
Knight of Swords	The news brings a sense of urgency.
XXI The World	The news brings you back to life.

Fourth Card

0 The Fool	The news concerns something that is happening at a distance.
Page of Wands	The news concerns something that requires a personal response.
Knight of Wands	The news concerns something that delays you.
Page of Cups	The news concerns something that is occurring right now and right under your nose.
Knight of Cups	The news concerns something that requires swift diplomacy.
Page of Coins	The news concerns something that is about to happen relatively close to home.
Knight of Coins	The news concerns something that requires you to take immediate action.
Page of Swords	The news concerns something that comes up.
Knight of Swords	The news concerns something that's running late.
XXI The World	The news concerns something wonderful and big.

Fifth Card

0 The Fool	You can expect to hear from a long-lost relative.
Page of Wands	You can expect to hear from your admirer.
Knight of Wands	You can expect to hear from your buddy.
Page of Cups	You can expect to hear from your subconscious.
Knight of Cups	You can expect to hear from your counselor.
Page of Coins	You can expect to hear from your mother.
Knight of Coins	You can expect to hear from your boss.
Page of Swords	You can expect to hear from your defender.
Knight of Swords	You can expect to hear from your opponent.
XXI The World	You can expect to hear from Mother Nature.

Sixth Card

0 The Fool	You will hear something that amuses you on the radio, perhaps on your way into work.
Page of Wands	You will take notice of something or somebody else, and perhaps exchange a secret glance or pass a note back and forth.
Knight of Wands	You will be asked to stand by in case you're needed, perhaps to be called in at the very last moment.
Page of Cups	You will see something on TV that captures your interest, perhaps late at night.
Knight of Cups	You will serve notice upon someone, or have notice served upon you, but perhaps peace will descend by the end of the day.
Page of Coins	You will be distracted by something during the day, perhaps when you are supposed to be working.
Knight of Coins	You will notice something that has suddenly changed or that suddenly needs to be changed, perhaps at the end of the day.
Page of Swords	You will be asked to think on your feet, perhaps to give an impromptu demonstration, do some fancy footwork, or fast-talk your way out of something.
Knight of Swords	You will be called to the rescue of somebody else, perhaps involving a quick trip or sudden getaway.
XXI The World	You will be called upon to sing and dance.

Seventh Card

0 The Fool	Be sure to stay tuned for late-breaking developments.
Page of Wands	Be sure to speak clearly and say what you mean.
Knight of Wands	Be sure to hold your horses until it's your turn to speak.
Page of Cups	Be sure to read the newspaper before you throw it out.
Knight of Cups	Be sure to read (and follow) the instructions.
Page of Coins	Be sure to pick up your messages.
Knight of Coins	Be sure to check the mail.
Page of Swords	Be sure to review the facts before you jump to a conclusion.
Knight of Swords	Be sure to act first and ask questions later.
XXI The World	Be sure to situate yourself where you can see and hear.

Eighth Card

0 The Fool	The news comes early on, and you are the first to know.
Page of Wands	The news passes by word of mouth.
Knight of Wands	The news is held up awhile in reaching you—you may even be the last to know.
Page of Cups	The news is whispered in advance, and you are privy to it.
Knight of Cups	The news is quickly spread (at a press conference?).
Page of Coins	The news emerges in its own good time, and you help spread it.
Knight of Coins	The news leaks out, but you remain silent.
Page of Swords	The news becomes the center of attention.
Knight of Swords	The news reaches you as it is happening.
XXI The World	You are the news.

Ninth Card

0 The Fool	You send for something frivolous.
Page of Wands	You send for something recorded.
Knight of Wands	You send for something that needs to be returned.
Page of Cups	You send your thoughts.
Knight of Cups	You send for something by special delivery.

Ninth Card *(cont.)*

Page of Coins	You send a token of your affection.
Knight of Coins	You send for something that needs to be assembled.
Page of Swords	You send for something you've been putting off.
Knight of Swords	You send for a backup or replacement.
XXI The World	You send for something from a far-off place.

Wild Card

0 The Fool	You will receive happy news.
Page of Wands	You will receive welcome news.
Knight of Wands	You will receive promising news.
Page of Cups	You will receive mellow news.
Knight of Cups	You will receive good news.
Page of Coins	You will receive sterling news.
Knight of Coins	You will receive spurious news.
Page of Swords	You will receive definitive news.
Knight of Swords	You will receive sudden news.
XXI The World	You will receive wonderful news.

EXTRA CREDIT

For a quicker Reading, ask your question, shuffle, deal up the top card, and read your answer from the "Wild Card" portion of the Answer section.

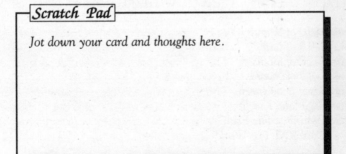

Scratch Pad

Jot down your card and thoughts here.

EXTRA EXTRA CREDIT!

What the heck, go back in time and ask how you received various pieces of important news in the past, just to see how well this Reading works for you.

Go on to the next Reading whenever you are ready to continue.

Reading #22

YES OR NO?

In this Reading you may ask as many yes/no questions as you
like . . . about anything you like.

TAROT TOOLS

You will need *all* of the cards you have used so far in the book. Separate
them into these piles:

I	*The Magician*
II	*The High Priestess*
III	*The Empress*
IV	*The Emperor*
V	*The Hierophant*
VI	*The Lovers*
VII	*The Chariot*
VIII or XI	*Justice*
IX	*The Hermit*
X	*Wheel of Fortune*

Plus: *1–10 of Wands*
Plus: *1–10 of Cups*
Plus: *1–10 of Coins*
Plus: *1–10 of Swords*
Plus: *Kings and Queens*
Plus: *Pages and Knights*
Plus: *Card 0   The Fool*
       Card XXI The World

Keep these eight stacks of cards separated for now.

HOW TO

This will be a Cover and Cross Reading as we've done so many times
before in the book. (See the Quick Reference Guide for an illustration of
this layout.)

Ask any yes/no question you have on your mind. But first select the stack of cards that is "good at" answering the type of question you want to ask.

I–X of Trumps	Questions about specific **individuals.**
1–10 of Wands	Questions about **work.**
1–10 of Cups	Questions about love **relationships.**
1–10 of Coins	Questions about **money.**
1–10 of Swords	Questions about **strategy.**
Kings and Queens	Questions about **places.**
Pages and Knights	Questions about **messages.**

Put the other stacks (except for The Fool and The World) aside.

Repeat the question while you shuffle your cards. When the cards are done shuffling, deal up the top one. *This covers you.*

Next, shuffle Card 0 and Card XXI together, while you repeat your question. When these cards are done, deal up the top one and place it crosswise on the card you dealt before. *This crosses you.*

Look up your answer.

Scratch Pad

Jot down your questions and answers here.

Cover/Cross

Cover/Cross

Cover/Cross

HINT: There's a trick to asking yes/no questions. It's best to ask fairly specific, short questions. If you want more details about something, ask for them one detail at a time, and reshuffle each time. This Reading works for time sequences, too, if you word your question accordingly, for example: Will I get a raise by June? Will I get married next year?

For additional information on any card, consult the Quick Reference Guide.

THE ANSWERS

Trumps I–X–Yes/no questions about specific individuals.

(also makes a good general purpose Reading).

When crossed by . . .		0 The Fool	XXI The World
I	The Magician	Possibly	Absolutely
II	The High Priestess	Could be	Probably
III	The Empress	Maybe	Certainly
IV	The Emperor	Perhaps	Definitely
V	The Hierophant	Hopefully	Assuredly
VI	The Lovers	Not sure	For sure
VII	The Chariot	Potentially	Positively
VIII	Justice	Uncertain	Decidedly
IX	The Hermit	Not yet	Eventually
X	Wheel of Fortune	No	Yes

Wands 1–10–Yes/no questions about work.

When crossed by . . .	0 The Fool	XXI The World
Ace of Wands	Heaven forbid	God willing
2 of Wands	Yeah, sure	Why not
3 of Wands	Go for it	It's a go
4 of Wands	Surely	Truly
5 of Wands	Might be	Will be
6 of Wands	Condolences	Congratulations
7 of Wands	Unsure	No sweat
8 of Wands	It's hit or miss	Bull's-eye
9 of Wands	Take it easy	Proceed with caution
10 of Wands	Maybe later	Maybe sooner

Cups 1–10–Yes/no questions about relationships.

When crossed by...	0 The Fool	XXI The World
Ace of Cups	Looks good	Feels right
2 of Cups	Negative	Positive
3 of Cups	Odds oppose	Odds favor
4 of Cups	Thumbs up	Hands down
5 of Cups	Not ever	Never again
6 of Cups	It's all in the past	It's happening now
7 of Cups	Only in your fantasies	Wishes come true
8 of Cups	Not right now	Once in a blue moon
9 of Cups	Fat chance	Sure bet
10 of Cups	So it goes	So be it

Coins 1–10–Yes/no questions about money.

When crossed by...	0 The Fool	XXI The World
Ace of Coins	You can bet on it	You can count on it
2 of Coins	Plus	Minus
3 of Coins	Favored	Granted
4 of Coins	By no small means	By all means
5 of Coins	Tough luck	Maybe next time
6 of Coins	Good luck	Good enough
7 of Coins	Not quite yet	In good time
8 of Coins	Try it	Keep trying
9 of Coins	All right	Naturally
10 of Coins	Okay already	Very well

Swords 1–10–Yes/no questions about strategy.

When crossed by...	0 The Fool	XXI The World
Ace of Swords	Negative	Affirmative
2 of Swords	It's up in the air	Yes and no
3 of Swords	Too bad	Sorry
4 of Swords	In the end	As it turns out
5 of Swords	Aye	Aye aye

Swords 1–10 *(cont.)*

6 *of Swords*	Come on	Go on
7 *of Swords*	By hook or by crook	By the skin of your teeth
8 *of Swords*	In no small way	In every way
9 *of Swords*	Not even in your dreams	In your dreams
10 *of Swords*	Too soon	Too late

Kings and Queens—Yes/no questions about places.

When crossed by...	0 The Fool	XXI The World
King *of Wands*	Red light	Green light
Queen *of Wands*	Conditions permitting	Come what may
King *of Cups*	Looks rocky	Come hell or high water
Queen *of Cups*	The signs are mixed	The signs are good
Queen *of Coins*	Conceivably	Clearly
King *of Coins*	No problem	On the money
Queen *of Swords*	You may	You can
King *of Swords*	It's a long shot	It's a close call

Pages and Knights—Yes/no questions about messages.

When crossed by...	0 The Fool	XXI The World
Page *of Wands*	Stand by	You're on
Knight *of Wands*	It's held up for now	Things move right along
Page *of Cups*	It looks fishy	It smells okay
Knight *of Cups*	It's in the mail	It's in the bag
Knight *of Coins*	Expect a slight delay	Take one step at a time
Page *of Coins*	The signs are misty	The signs are clear
Knight *of Swords*	What's the rush?	Charge ahead
Page *of Swords*	Play it by ear	Roll with the punches

EXTRA CREDIT

Try shuffling *all* the cards together (except 0 and XXI) while asking your question. Deal up the top card. Then proceed as before, shuffling Cards 0 and XXI together until done and crossing your first card with the top one of these. Look up your answers as before.

Scratch Pad

Jot down your questions and answers here.

Cover/Cross

Cover/Cross

Cover/Cross

EXTRA EXTRA CREDIT!

What the heck: ask yes/no questions about things that happened to you in the past, write down your answers, and compute the cards' batting average. How many times were they right?

Go on to the next Reading whenever you are ready to continue.

Reading #23

WHO AM I DEEP DOWN INSIDE?

We now turn away from our outer, material and physical,
world to our inner, psychological and spiritual, world—for
the Tarot is good at telling us about both aspects of our
lives. In this part of the book, you will be using a set of cards
you haven't used yet: Trumps XI–XX. These are the cards
that deal with the things that go on in our heads. In this
Reading you will be learning about your inner self. You will
be receiving your Spirit Card.

TAROT TOOLS

You will need the following cards from your deck (these are listed backward, because we have "reversed directions" in the Tarot):

XX	Judgement
XIX	The Sun
XVIII	The Moon
XVII	The Star
XVI	The Tower
XV	The Devil
XIV	Temperance
XIII	Death
XII	The Hanged Man
XI or VIII	Strength

HOW TO

Find the card that corresponds to your Key Card from Reading #1 in the
following table. Then look up your card in the Answer section.

If you don't remember your Key Card, go back to the beginning of the
book and read the How To section of Reading #1.

Your Key Card in Reading #1		Your Spirit Card in Reading #23	
I	The Magician	XX	Judgement
II	The High Priestess	XIX	The Sun

Your Key Card in Reading #1		Your Spirit Card in Reading #23	
III	The Empress	XVIII	The Moon
IV	The Emperor	XVII	The Star
V	The Hierophant	XVI	The Tower
VI	The Lovers	XV	The Devil
VII	The Chariot	XIV	Temperance
VIII	Justice	XIII	Death
IX	The Hermit	XII	The Hanged Man
X	Wheel of Fortune	XI	Strength

Scratch Pad

Jot down your card here.

For additional information on any card, consult the Quick Reference Guide.

THE ANSWERS

XX Judgement. You are a person of good intentions. *Look at your card.* As The Magician on the outside and Judgement on the inside, you are the possessor of a **determined spirit.** You are the kind of person who is focused, directed, and motivated by that strong internal drive that some have called the "free will." You are a person of willpower. And that's why you can literally do anything you set your mind to. In addition to the standard senses, you possess an acute sense of cause and effect; and deep down inside you honestly believe that people get (and deserve) what they've got coming to them—for you, at least, this is true.

XIX The Sun. You are a person who lives life to the fullest. *Look at your card.* As The High Priestess on the outside and The Sun on the inside, you are the possessor of a **free and gentle spirit.** You are laid-back, easygoing, good to get along with, and nice-nevertheless-nice—for come what may, you will roll with the punches and come out laughing in the end. In addition to the five typical senses, you have what is commonly known as a sense of humor. Laughter is what gets you through this life and keeps your youthful spirit free.

XVIII The Moon. You are a person who follows a different drummer. *Look at your card.* As The Empress on the outside and The Moon on the inside, you are the possessor of an **impulsive spirit.** You are complex, deep, secretive, difficult to get to know, hard to reach, next to impossible to figure out, and as moody and fickle as they come. But mostly you are mysterious—and that is the secret to your endless, alluring charm. In addition to the senses everybody else has, you are endowed with an uncanny sense of rhythm, and when you dance, it is the dance of life.

XVII The Star. You are a person who doesn't know when to quit. *Look at your card.* As The Emperor on the outside and The Star on the inside, you are the possessor of a **persistent spirit.** You are intense, focused, constant (if not totally consistent), absolutely dedicated, and completely diligent—a real powerhouse, a true workhorse. You can do two things at once. You can do things with one hand tied behind your back. And when you're down and out, you can bet sure money it won't be long until you make your comeback. In addition to the normal human senses, you have a well-developed gut instinct that helps you avoid the snares and snags of life, and nine times out of ten, your "funny feelings" will be right.

XVI The Tower. You are a person with a strong conscience. *Look at your card.* As The Hierophant on the outside and The Tower on the inside, you are the possessor of an **enlightened spirit.** From time to time you literally "see the light"—in revelations, inspirations, sudden realizations, prophetic dreams. Perhaps "inner voices" descend on you, telling you what you ought to do next, informing you of the right thing to do. You are intense, convicted (and convinced that you are right), opinionated, and a bit self-righteous at times. And even though the ends may not always justify your means, your intentions are usually good. In addition to the typical human senses, you have a good sense of drama, which serves you well in expressing the beautiful visions of the possibilities you see.

XV The Devil. You are a person with an overwhelming urge. *Look at your card.* As The Lovers on the outside and The Devil on the inside, you are the possessor of a **captivated spirit.** You are eternally young in your quest for the thing that enamors and beguiles you. You are "hopeless" about it, you are "helpless" about it. You cannot get it off your mind. You cannot get out from under it—for that urge of yours possesses you so completely that you cannot be held accountable for your own behavior sometimes. It is not a question of "just saying no" to you, for it is not a question of saying yes, either. For you, the urge *is*. You have all the same senses that everybody else has, but you have a heightened sense of each of them, which encourages you to want to experience the world more than others ever can—and in this pursuit, no one can doubt but that you will surely succeed.

XIV *Temperance*.

You are a person who just can't hold still. *Look at your card*. As The Chariot on the outside and Temperance on the inside, you are the possessor of a **dynamic spirit**. You are strong of purpose, energetic, untiring, and enthusiastic to a fault—a real gung ho, rah-rah, can-do kind of guy. You feel you can move mountains, walk on water, and take on the entire world single-handedly . . . or at least give it your best shot, even if you have to go down trying. In addition to the common, ordinary senses, you are endowed with a sense of undying confidence that supports (and encourages) you throughout your life of dedicated service.

XIII *Death*.

You are a person who keeps on going. *Look at your card*. As Justice on the outside and Death on the inside, you are the possessor of a **resolute spirit**. You are rigorous, intense, and serious. And everything you do seems to take on overtones of a life work and undertones of a fight to the death. You are earnest, dependable, true, stalwart, indefatigable; and no matter what, you can be counted upon implicitly to come through in the end. In addition to the senses everybody else has, you have a strong sense of resolve. There is "nothing personal" about your more profound decisions and actions, for you are willing to do difficult things in order to keep everything operating as it must—and as it should. You are a great leveler, and this, above all else, is your claim to fame: You bring uncompromising equality and justice to the world.

XII *The Hanged Man*.

You are a driven person. *Look at your card*. As The Hermit on the outside and The Hanged Man on the inside, you are the possessor of an **independent spirit**. You are self-motivated, self-directed, and perhaps a bit self-centered as a result, for you are your own best friend and your most ruthless competitor. You are constantly pitting yourself against yourself, constantly striving to reach new heights, and constantly punishing yourself for even insignificant failures. A perfectionist by nature, you pursue your own truth with a vengeance, discarding what doesn't work and inventing what you think will. In addition to the senses everybody else has, you have an excellent sense of time, timing, and what makes things tick, which helps your sometimes radical ideas find their place in the scheme of things.

XI *Strength*.

You are a person who learns from adversity. *Look at your card*. As Wheel of Fortune on the outside and Strength on the inside, you are the possessor of a **peaceful spirit.** You are both empathetic and sympathetic to the world and the people around you. Kind, understanding, compassionate, and nonviolent by nature, you believe in living and letting live. You practice a gentle tolerance of all living things (and their behaviors and habits), for you understand the physical and emotional pain that others feel, even if you have not walked in their shoes. You go through life encouraging harmony and understanding . . . and you meet with great success in comforting others, who take strength from your seemingly endless reserve. In addition to the five senses that everybody else has, you are capable of "reading minds," for you instinctively know what others are actually feeling below their defensive exteriors. This lets you help and comfort them—and for this reason, you will attract many devoted friends.

EXTRA CREDIT

To explore your emotional state this month, shuffle the Trumps (XI–XX) while you ask this question: **How am I doing emotionally?** When the cards are done, deal up the top Trump and consult the Answer section.

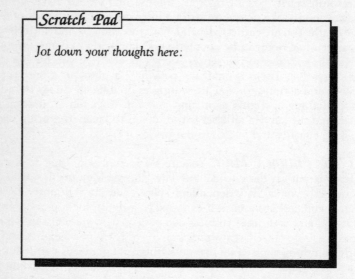

Scratch Pad

Jot down your thoughts here:

EXTRA EXTRA CREDIT!

What the heck, read all the answers and look for yourself in every one of them, for we are each—to a lesser or greater extent—to be found in every Spirit Card in the deck. Who do you think you are?

Go on to the next Reading whenever you are ready to continue.

Reading #24

WHAT ARE MY MOTIVATIONS?

We continue on the path to understanding our inner self in this Reading as we investigate the things that are behind the actions we find ourselves taking in life. In this Reading you will be looking at the reasons for the things you do. You will be looking at your secret, inner motivations by using Trumps I–XX as your guides

---

TAROT TOOLS

You will need the same cards you used in Reading #23:

XX	*Judgement*
XIX	*The Sun*
XVIII	*The Moon*
XVII	*The Star*
XVI	*The Tower*
XV	*The Devil*
XIV	*Temperance*
XIII	*Death*
XII	*The Hanged Man*
XI *or* VIII	*Strength*

Plus, you will need the cards you used in Reading #1:

I	*The Magician*
II	*The High Priestess*
III	*The Empress*
IV	*The Emperor*
V	*The Hierophant*
VI	*The Lovers*
VII	*The Chariot*
VIII *or* XI	*Justice*
IX	*The Hermit*
X	*Wheel of Fortune*

Keep the two stacks of cards separate for now.

HOW TO

This will be a three-pair Cover and Cross Reading. (See the Quick Reference Guide for an illustration of this layout.)

First, shuffle Trumps XI–XX as you ask your question: **What are my basic motivations?** or **What are my motivations with regard to _____?**

When the cards are done, deal up the top three faceup in a line in front of you.

Then shuffle Trumps I–X as you repeat your question. When the cards are done, deal up the top three and lay these crosswise across the first three cards you dealt.

Look up the answer for each pair of cards. For this Reading, your answers will read as a continuous thought, with the first Cover and Cross pair giving you the main idea, and each additional Cover and Cross pair adding detail.

Scratch Pad

Jot down your cards and answers here.

Cover/Cross
Cover/Cross
Cover/Cross

Cover/Cross
Cover/Cross
Cover/Cross

For additional information on any card, consult the Quick Reference Guide.

THE ANSWERS

XX Judgement (What do I aspire to?)

When crossed by . . .		You aspire to . . .
I	The Magician	make something of yourself.
II	The High Priestess	fulfill your "intended" purpose.
III	The Empress	make the most of things.
IV	The Emperor	"greatness" as measured in material terms.

XX Judgement *(cont.)*

When crossed by . . .		**You aspire to . . .**
V	The Hierophant	"greatness" as measured in spiritual terms.
VI	The Lovers	sexual fulfillment or romantic accomplishment.
VII	The Chariot	athletic prowess.
VIII	Justice	equality and fair treatment.
IX	The Hermit	seek your own truth.
X	Wheel of Fortune	fulfill your own destiny.

XIX The Sun (What do I yearn for?)

When crossed by . . .		**You yearn to . . .**
I	The Magician	know what you can really do.
II	The High Priestess	understand where you are headed.
III	The Empress	thrill at the experience.
IV	The Emperor	control the outcome of things.
V	The Hierophant	do what is right.
VI	The Lovers	find somebody right.
VII	The Chariot	be the best that you can be.
VIII	Justice	achieve a certain balance in your life.
IX	The Hermit	know yourself.
X	Wheel of Fortune	live each moment to the fullest.

XVIII The Moon (What do I dream of?)

When crossed by . . .		**You dream of . . .**
I	The Magician	creating something better.
II	The High Priestess	what will be in the future.
III	The Empress	achieving your goals.
IV	The Emperor	expanding your horizons.
V	The Hierophant	having your prayers answered.
VI	The Lovers	feeling the earth move.
VII	The Chariot	getting on top of things.
VIII	Justice	evening the score.
IX	The Hermit	getting off by yourself.
X	Wheel of Fortune	having the best of both worlds.

XVII *The Star (What kind of life-style do I need?)*

When crossed by . . .		You need a life-style that . . .
I	The Magician	puts you in charge.
II	The High Priestess	takes care of itself.
III	The Empress	is free of want.
IV	The Emperor	is free from interference.
V	The Hierophant	is full of purpose.
VI	The Lovers	satisfies your emotional needs.
VII	The Chariot	puts you to the test.
VIII	Justice	gives you your just due.
IX	The Hermit	takes you to the heights.
X	Wheel of Fortune	never has a dull moment.

XVI *The Tower (What am I open to?)*

When crossed by . . .		You are open to . . .
I	The Magician	making the most of the situation.
II	The High Priestess	anything that comes along.
III	The Empress	new experiences.
IV	The Emperor	accepting a favored position.
V	The Hierophant	religious experience.
VI	The Lovers	acting on impulse.
VII	The Chariot	accepting the challenge.
VIII	Justice	weighing the alternatives.
IX	The Hermit	new ideas or advice.
X	Wheel of Fortune	changes of all sorts.

XV *The Devil (What do I need to watch out for?)*

When crossed by . . .		You need to watch out for . . .
I	The Magician	burnout.
II	The High Priestess	inertia.
III	The Empress	overproduction.
IV	The Emperor	abuse of power.
V	The Hierophant	fanaticism.
VI	The Lovers	obsession.
VII	The Chariot	excessive use of force.
VIII	Justice	vindictiveness.
IX	The Hermit	self-deprivation.
X	Wheel of Fortune	fatalism.

XIV Temperance (What am I influenced by?)

When crossed by . . .		You are influenced by . . .
I	The Magician	your ego.
II	The High Priestess	your biorhythms.
III	The Empress	your physical environment.
IV	The Emperor	your political leaders.
V	The Hierophant	your spiritual leaders.
VI	The Lovers	your loved ones.
VII	The Chariot	your hero.
VIII	Justice	your laws.
IX	The Hermit	your values.
X	Wheel of Fortune	your lucky stars.

XIII Death (What am I most resistant to?)

When crossed by . . .		You are most resistant to . . .
I	The Magician	changing your own way of doing things.
II	The High Priestess	the passage of time.
III	The Empress	living within your means.
IV	The Emperor	political rhetoric.
V	The Hierophant	bureaucracy.
VI	The Lovers	sexual advances.
VII	The Chariot	popular opinion.
VIII	Justice	legal restrictions.
IX	The Hermit	taking the advice of others.
X	Wheel of Fortune	change in general.

XII The Hanged Man (What do I feel guilty about?)

When crossed by . . .		You are inclined to feel guilty about . . .
I	The Magician	your own native abilities.
II	The High Priestess	the way your life is going.
III	The Empress	the luxuries you enjoy.
IV	The Emperor	the power that you wield.
V	The Hierophant	falling short of the ideal.

XII The Hanged Man *(cont.)*

When crossed by . . .	**You are inclined to feel guilty about . . .**
VI The Lovers	doing what comes naturally.
VII The Chariot	not meeting expectations.
VIII Justice	expressing your own opinions.
IX The Hermit	spending time by yourself.
X Wheel of Fortune	your own good fortune.

XI Strength *(What do I need to control?)*

When crossed by . . .	**You need to take control of . . .**
I The Magician	yourself.
II The High Priestess	your present situation.
III The Empress	your fate.
IV The Emperor	your destiny.
V The Hierophant	your own behavior.
VI The Lovers	your own desires.
VII The Chariot	your own temper.
VIII Justice	your own actions.
IX The Hermit	your own decisions.
X Wheel of Fortune	your life in general.

EXTRA CREDIT

Ask any of the questions printed in *italics* at the top of each answer set. Shuffle Trumps I–X as you repeat the question, then deal up the top card. Find the answer in the list under the question you chose.

Scratch Pad

Jot down your cards and answers here.

What do I aspire to?
What do I yearn for?
What do I dream of?
What kind of life-style do I need?
What am I open to?
What do I need to watch out for?
What am I influenced by?
What am I most resistant to?
What do I feel guilty about?
What do I need to control?

EXTRA EXTRA CREDIT!

What the heck, conduct this Reading for all of your friends, associates, and business partners in order to understand better where they are coming from.

Go on to the next Reading whenever you are ready to continue.

Reading #25

WHAT DO MY DREAMS MEAN?

In the last two Readings we have been dealing with the things that go on inside our heads, the things that make us tick—our psyches if you want, our souls if you will. In this Reading you will continue to delve deeper into yourself, as you attempt to unravel the message of your dreams, using Trumps I–XX as your guides.

TAROT TOOLS
You will need the same cards you used in the previous Reading:

XX	Judgement
XIX	The Sun
XVIII	The Moon
XVII	The Star
XVI	The Tower
XV	The Devil
XIV	Temperance
XIII	Death
XII	The Hanged Man
XI or VIII	Strength

Plus:

I	The Magician
II	The High Priestess
III	The Empress
IV	The Emperor
V	The Hierophant
VI	The Lovers
VII	The Chariot
VIII or XI	Justice
IX	The Hermit
X	Wheel of Fortune

Keep them in separate stacks for now.

Reading #25

HOW TO

This Reading will use the Celtic Cross method. (See the Quick Reference Guide for an illustration of this layout.)

Dealing out the cards involves a three-step process.

First, shuffle the Trumps I–X together, as you ask your question: **What is my subconscious trying to tell me?** or **What does my dream about _____ mean?** Fill in the blank with the name you have given your recurring dream or a detail from a dream you had recently.

Shuffle until the Trumps (I–X) are done, then deal up the top Trump and place it faceup in front of you. *This covers you.* Deal up the second Trump and place it crosswise on the card you have already dealt. *This crosses you.*

Now shuffle Trumps XI–XX together, as you ask your question again. Shuffle until done, then deal up the top four cards and place them in positions 3 through 6, around the first two Trumps you have already dealt:

3—*This is above you*
4—*This is below you*
5—*This is behind you*
6—*This is before you*

Finally, shuffle all the remaining Trumps (I–XX) together, as you ask your question one last time. Shuffle until the cards are done, then deal up the top four cards and place them in positions 7 through 10 to the right of the cards you have already dealt:

7—*This is who you are*
8—*This is who they want you to be*
9—*This is what you want*
10—*And this is what you get*

Look up your cards by their position in the layout (1 through 10) in the Answer section.

Scratch Pad

Note your cards and answers here.

Covers you
Crosses you
Above you
Below you
Behind you
Before you
You are
They want
You want
You get

For additional information on any card, consult the Quick Reference Guide.

THE ANSWERS

Position 1—This covers you.

*I **The Magician.*** In your waking hours you have been working pretty hard, or you've at least had a lot going on. A few key things seem to remain up in the air.

*II **The High Priestess.*** In your waking hours you have been a bit preoccupied with something—perhaps something you have done has been weighing on your mind. It seems you don't know which way to go.

*III **The Empress.*** In your waking hours you have been waiting for something to materialize. Perhaps something you started in the past is about to pay off. But it seems that there is not much to be done about it right now except to sit tight.

*IV **The Emperor.*** In your waking hours things are pretty much under control at the moment. It is possible, though, that a potential problem,

Position 1 (*cont.*)

recently brought to your attention, threatens the peace. Right now it seems you have a little something to worry about.

V The Hierophant. In your waking hours you believe you are doing the right thing in general. Or perhaps you are making an attempt to clean up your act. At the moment there seem to be a few lingering doubts—or a couple of slipups that you earnestly regret.

VI The Lovers. In your waking hours something has captured your devoted attention. Or perhaps you have been more than a little distracted. It seems that, for some reason, you are hesitating about making the next move.

VII The Chariot. In your waking hours you are in the driver's seat, and things have been going pretty much your way. But perhaps there are a lot of demands on you as a result. It seems that something is attempting to pull you down—or at least in a different direction.

VIII Justice. In your waking hours you have been trying to reach an important decision. Perhaps you have been weighing the pros and cons. It seems that you are not quite sure yet which side to come down on.

IX The Hermit. In your waking hours you have recently learned something that has given you a new perspective on your life. Or perhaps you have found out something that has caused you to stop and rethink your situation. It seems that you are now waiting for the final resolution.

X Wheel of Fortune. In your waking hours you have been running high on a lucky streak lately. Or perhaps your luck has changed for better or worse. It seems that at this time you are waiting for the other shoe to drop.

Position 2–This crosses you.

I The Magician. In your sleep, your subconscious has been trying to help you put the pieces of your life together. In your dreams, you have been attempting to work out your problems.

II The High Priestess. In your sleep, your subconscious has been attempting to help you see past the present moment. In your dreams, you have been trying to get beyond something that blocks your progress.

Position 2 (*cont.*)

III The Empress. In your sleep, your subconscious has been trying to help you gain a better perspective. In your dreams, you have been attempting to see the bigger picture.

IV The Emperor. In your sleep, your subconscious has been attempting to help you conquer your fears. In your dreams, you have been trying to overcome your insecurities.

V The Hierophant. In your sleep, your subconscious has been trying to help you release a burden that you are carrying on your shoulders. In your dreams, you have been attempting to overcome your feelings of guilt.

VI The Lovers. In your sleep, your subconscious has been attempting to help you realize something that you have suppressed. In your dreams, you have been trying to live out your secret desires or forbidden fantasies.

VII The Chariot. In your sleep, your subconscious has been trying to help you cope with your self-image. In your dreams, you have been attempting to mend a wounded ego.

VIII Justice. In your sleep, your subconscious has been attempting to help you reach a conclusion or make a decision. In your dreams, you have been trying to make up your mind about something.

IX The Hermit. In your sleep, your subconscious has been trying to help you find a way out of your current situation. In your dreams, you have been attempting to see the light at the end of the tunnel.

X Wheel of Fortune. In your sleep, your subconscious has been attempting to help you adjust to a recent change in your life. In your dreams, you have been trying to make the most of things.

Position 3—This is above you.

XX Judgement. Someone from a former life will soon appear to you in a dream. If you pay attention, the news they bring will be of earth-shattering importance to you now.

XIX The Sun. Something from out of your childhood will soon crop up in the night and run through your dreams. If you pay attention, you will learn something about yourself.

Position 3 *(cont.)*

XVIII The Moon. Soon you will have a dream in which animals appear to you and perhaps speak. If you pay attention, they will give you some useful advice.

XVII The Star. Soon you will again have a recurring dream in which at least two unrelated things are combined. If you pay attention this time, perhaps you will finally be able to make the connection.

XVI The Tower. Soon you will have a dream in which you catch yourself falling and wake suddenly as a result. If you pay attention, you will have an inspiration the next day.

XV The Devil. Soon you will have a dream in which a stranger or someone you barely know sexually excites you. If you pay attention, you will learn something about your own secret desires.

XIV Temperance. Soon you will have a dream in which your soul takes flight and journeys to a distant place. If you pay attention, you will see a reflection of the things that are possible in your life.

XIII Death. Soon you will have a dream in which something or someone threatens to kill you and in which you either try to escape or fight back. If you pay attention, you will be better able to cope with the changes in your life.

XII The Hanged Man. Soon you will have a dream in which you overcome great odds by some miraculous twist. If you pay attention, you will realize that there is something you must not forget to do.

XI Strength. Soon you will have a dream in which you are transformed into an animal. If you pay attention, you will learn a great deal about why you behave the way you do.

Position 4—This is below you.

XX Judgement. In general, you have been sleeping like the dead and therefore may not remember your dreams upon waking. Nevertheless, you have been dreaming, and your dreams have been at work in your life. If you want to remember them better, try sitting up in bed a few minutes in the morning before getting up.

Position 4 (*cont.*)

XIX The Sun. In general, you have been having your most vivid dreams at dawn. These are the ones that spin in your head when you wake up the next day. Next time, take note of them.

XVIII The Moon. In general, you have been having your most memorable dreams when the moon is full. And on those moonlit nights you awake from them feeling a bit restless. Next time, get up and write them down.

XVII The Star. In general, you go through several dream cycles in a single night, most of which you will not remember the next day. Still, your dreams will never cease to influence what you do. They have been operating in the background of your conscious behavior for some time now.

XVI The Tower. In general, you tend to awaken only from your nightmares, and since these disturbing dreams are the ones you remember best, you may not think very highly of dreaming. But what you may not appreciate is that your dreams have been defusing your pent-up hostilities.

XV The Devil. In general, your spellbinding, captivating dreams have had a way of releasing your frustrations. If you have been waking aroused, don't worry. All in all, it's been relatively safe sex.

XIV Temperance. In general, your dreams have been providing you with a creative outlet that you may be denied in your waking life. Your sleep is not only invigorating but entertaining, and you have been using the otherwise "unproductive" hours of sleep to spin some fascinating yarns.

XIII Death. In general, your dreams have been giving you the opportunity to confront your innermost fears and insecurities. And in this respect, your hours of sleep have a cathartic quality that helps you better cope with life.

XII The Hanged Man. In general, your dreams have been playing a healing role in your life. Your hours of suspended animation have been helping you get over something, or helping you restore your soul. You awaken with a renewed sense of purpose.

XI Strength. In general, your dreams have been revealing something that you have been careful to suppress in your waking hours. In your sleep you have been wrestling with your feelings and rationalizing your behaviors. In time, you will overcome these things.

Position 5–This is behind you.
Position 6–This is before you.

This same table will give you the Readings for cards in either position 5 or position 6.

In position 5 the cards should be read as **Just recently . . .**

In position 6 the cards should be read as **Just coming up . . .**

XX	Judgement	you experience a spiritual rebirth.
XIX	The Sun	you experience a new lease on life.
XVIII	The Moon	you experience a mood swing.
XVII	The Star	you experience internal conflict.
XVI	The Tower	you experience some emotional upheaval.
XV	The Devil	you experience some repressed feelings.
XIV	Temperance	you experience an emotional outburst.
XIII	Death	you experience an emotional showdown.
XII	The Hanged Man	you experience a time of emotional recovery.
XI	Strength	you experience a time of emotional equilibrium.

Position 7–This is who you are.
Position 8–This is who they want you to be.

This same table will give you the Readings for cards in either position 7 or position 8.

In position 7 the cards should be read as **In this dream, you are . . .**

In position 8 the cards should be read as **In this dream, others want you to be . . .**

I	The Magician	the one who is cool.
II	The High Priestess	the one who is calm.
III	The Empress	the one who is collected.
IV	The Emperor	the one who is in absolute control.

Positions 7 and 8 *(cont.)*

V	The Hierophant	the one who is on solid ground.
VI	The Lovers	the one who is compulsive.
VII	The Chariot	the one who is destructive.
VIII	Justice	the one who is well balanced.
IX	The Hermit	the one who is eccentric.
X	Wheel of Fortune	the one who is on top of things.
XX	Judgement	the one who is oblivious.
XIX	The Sun	the one who is carefree.
XVIII	The Moon	the one who is hyper.
XVII	The Star	the one who is relatively stable.
XVI	The Tower	the one who is upset.
XV	The Devil	the one who is obsessed.
XIV	Temperance	the one who is creative.
XIII	Death	the one who is overwhelmed.
XII	The Hanged Man	the one who is trying to fit in.
XI	Strength	the one who is restrained.

Position 9—This is what you want.

I The Magician. You want to prove yourself.

II The High Priestess. You want to know yourself.

III The Empress. You want to fulfill yourself completely.

IV The Emperor. You want to feel superior to others.

V The Hierophant. You want to browbeat yourself.

VI The Lovers. You want somebody to love.

VII The Chariot. You want to escape the person you believe is out to get you.

VIII Justice. You want to procrastinate.

IX The Hermit. You want to feel inspired.

X Wheel of Fortune. You want to control the uncontrollable.

Position 9 (*cont.*)

XX Judgement. You want to conquer your fear of the hereafter.

XIX The Sun. You want to conquer your fear of growing old.

XVIII The Moon. You want to conquer your fear of things that go bump in the night.

XVII The Star. You want to conquer your fear of running out of the things you need.

XVI The Tower. You want to conquer your fear of falling out of favor.

XV The Devil. You want to conquer your fear of being taken captive

XIV Temperance. You want to conquer your fear of change.

XIII Death. You want to conquer your fear of the inevitable.

XII The Hanged Man. You want to conquer your fear of punishment.

XI Strength. You want to conquer your fear of predators.

Position 10–This is what you get.

I The Magician. You can figure it out for yourself—and in the end you must. For the answer lies within you, and you alone are capable of taking charge of your own life.

II The High Priestess. You must get over your own past first, if you ever expect to go on with your life. The future is neither open nor closed to you. The possibility of what will be exists in the seeds of your own vision, but you alone determine the outcome.

III The Empress. You need to finish what you've started, even if you have taken on more than you can chew. If the conditions remain favorable, you will be able to pull it off for sure. But even if the weather fails you, you must not give up. Patience counts in this world, too.

IV The Emperor. You need to take responsibility for your own actions (and reactions). Things may not always turn out the way you hoped

Position 10 (*cont.*)

or promised. But nothing remains the same forever. If you want to stay at the helm, you will have to adjust to changing times.

V The Hierophant. You feel the need to make a confession to yourself or deliver an apology to someone else in order to get out from under the nagging guilt that haunts you lately. And a few prayers probably wouldn't hurt either.

VI The Lovers. You need to take things to their natural conclusion, for better or worse. This may involve either the cementing or the severing of a relationship, but only you can decide which is the right choice. The time has come to make up your mind.

VII The Chariot. You need to take decisive action, for this is no time for either modesty or hesitation. Something is pulling you in opposite directions—your emotions perhaps. Think fast! before you tear yourself apart.

VIII Justice. You need to resolve something once and for all, so that you can forgive and forget some past wrong done to you (or that you have perpetrated upon another). Get over it and get on with your life.

IX The Hermit. There is something that you feel you need to do at this moment in your life. Though only you can decide for sure, it would probably be best for you to pursue the thing that calls you, if only for a while—or else be willing to live with your regrets.

X Wheel of Fortune. You need to ride out the phase that you are in—take this stage to its ultimate conclusion—so that you can make the transition to the next phase of your life. Though it may seem to you to be a major crisis, perhaps it is only a rite of passage.

XX Judgement. You need to reestablish contact with reality. Your head has been in the clouds a bit lately, you've been out of touch with the real world, and you have been holding out too much hope in miracles. You must take charge of your own life if you want to determine your destiny.

XIX The Sun. You have been out chasing rainbows again, but enough is enough already. You might want to settle down a bit before you tire the patience of those who are in charge of the reins and the purse strings.

XVIII The Moon. You have been out baying at the moon again, burning the midnight oil, and prowling around at all hours of the night. Maybe it's time to quit while you're still ahead.

Position 10 *(cont.)*

XVII The Star. You have been trying to perform double duty, but there is only a limited number of hours in the day, and your supply of energy is not entirely unlimited. Be careful that you don't burn out.

XVI The Tower. You are trying to recover from some catastrophic (at least it seems that way now) experience. And though what has happened is unfortunate, the time has come to pick up the pieces. What happened cannot be prevented now, but there is still an opportunity to go on with your life.

XV The Devil. You have been feeling trapped by your current circumstances. But what you have to realize is that—though it may not be easy, and you may have to make some hard choices—you still have the chance to dig your way out of the dilemma you find yourself in.

XIV Temperance. You have been feeling as if something is about to break loose in your life, bringing with it monumental changes for the better. And perhaps you are right! Keep doing what you're doing, and keep your fingers crossed.

XIII Death. You have been feeling as if you can't possibly deal with the fate that has befallen you, for the changes that have occurred recently are of the irrevocable kind. You have no choice but to make the transition now, for despite the loss we feel sometimes, we must keep on keeping on.

XII The Hanged Man. You have been feeling as if you are playing the role of a martyr lately. But before you completely sacrifice yourself, wake up to the fact that you cannot do it all on your own and that, to some extent, you bring your burdens upon yourself. Lighten up.

XI Strength. You have been feeling lately as if you need to get in better control of the forces that rage within you. Perhaps you actually do need to tame your beast a bit; but in the process be careful not to discard that thing that makes you the very person you are.

EXTRA CREDIT

For a quick Reading about what's been bugging you lately, shuffle all the Trumps (I–XX) together and ask: **What am I trying to work out?** When the cards are done, deal out the top Trump. Then read the answer as if the card were in position 10.

Scratch Pad
Jot down your card here.

EXTRA EXTRA CREDIT!

What the heck, put a pad of paper by your bed and write down your dreams first thing every morning. Then conduct this Reading for each dream to see if a pattern develops.

Go on to the next Reading whenever you are ready to continue.

Reading #26

WHAT IS MY LIFE'S PURPOSE?

In Reading #26 you will be working with all the cards to consider the purpose various stages of your life have served and to project from these your overall life's purpose.

TAROT TOOLS

You will need all the cards.

HOW TO

In order to investigate such a serious question, we will be using a special layout called the Pyramid.

Shuffle all the cards together while you ask your question: **What is my life's purpose?** or **What is the purpose of _____?**

When the cards are done, deal up the top three and place them in a row in front of you, from left to right. Deal up two more cards and place them above the three you dealt before. Deal up one final card and place it above the two you just dealt.

If a card comes up upside down in your Reading, leave it that way, and focus on the *italic* portion of the answers.

Look up your cards by their position in the layout (1 through 6) in the Answer section.

Scratch Pad

Note your cards and answers here.

Card 1
Card 2
Card 3
Card 4
Card 5
Card 6

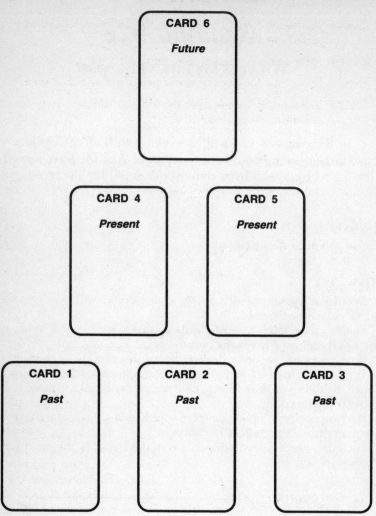

HINT: In this Reading, you will need to interpret the answers a bit for each card. The following chart gives you the context of the cards in each of the various positions:

Card 1 represents the purpose your early childhood served, or it indicates the initial period of any situation.

Card 2 represents the purpose your adolescence served, or it indicates how the situation developed.

Card 3 represents the purpose your early adulthood served, or it indicates how the situation came to a head.

Card 4 represents the purpose your current situation is serving.

Card 5 represents the purpose of the period just ahead of you.

Card 6 represents your life's purpose, or your ultimate purpose in the situation you have asked about.

If you are conducting a Reading to find out the purpose of a specific event in the past, read the Pyramid as if it were all in the past, except for Card 6, which remains the future. The sequence will often be in chronological order.

For additional information on any card, consult the Quick Reference Guide.

THE ANSWERS

The Trumps–I

0	The Fool	To spread your wings. To go where no one has gone before. To be an explorer. To be an adventurer. To be a dreamer. *To take the road less traveled.*
I	The Magician	To come into your own. To develop your body, mind, and soul. To determine your own destiny. To gain experience. *To give it your best shot.*
II	The High Priestess	To be a part of the whole. To develop your feelings. To understand how you fit in. To find your niche. *To help others envision the future.*
III	The Empress	To give birth to new things. To plant, nurture, and cultivate ideas. To bear offspring. To be a creative force. *To care for those who depend on you.*

The Trumps–I (*cont.*)

IV	The Emperor	To assert your own identity. To define who, what, and where you are. To create order out of chaos. To provide leadership. *To act in the interest of others.*
V	The Hierophant	To assume your proper place. To find your niche. To develop a good relationship. To be spiritual. To work for the common good. *To fight for the rights of others.*
VI	The Lovers	To love and be loved. To seek a mate. To be fruitful and multiply. To carry on the family line. To make a commitment. *To join forces with another.*
VII	The Chariot	To fight for a good cause. To overcome the things that threaten your existence, identity, position, or ideas. To protect others. *To stick your neck out for others.*
VIII	Justice	To achieve equilibrium. To strike a balance between opposing forces, ideas, and individuals. To seek peaceful solutions. *To help others resolve their differences.*
IX	The Hermit	To learn from the experience. To seek and discover your own truth. To hold up a light for others to follow. *To set a good example.*
X	Wheel of Fortune	To take a chance. To risk something on the roll of the dice. To ride out a winning streak. *To make the most of whatever happens.*

The Trumps—II

XX	Judgement	To overcome your human limitations. To rise above the common and ordinary. To do something that has a lasting impact. *To trust that all things work for good.*
XIX	The Sun	To be a free spirit. To play. To laugh. To sing. To not have a care in the world. To ride high in the saddle. *To delight in each new day.*
XVIII	The Moon	To evolve over time. To grow and change. To complete a full cycle. To start a new phase. To let your instincts guide you. *To howl the night away.*
XVII	The Star	To let your light shine. To achieve your full potential. To take your place in the scheme of things. To be dependable. *To remain constant.*
XVI	The Tower	To generate new ideas. To open yourself to innovation. To be inspired. To see the light. To tear down what is old and outworn. *To get knocked to your senses.*
XV	The Devil	To escape persecution. To break loose of the bonds that bind you. To rise above your current situation. *To overcome difficulty.*
XIV	Temperance	To bring new things into being. To create new substance. To invent things. To realize things for yourself. To improve yourself. *To generate new ideas.*
XIII	Death	To clear the way for a new era. To remove the old, outworn, obsolete. To put an end to the past and create a new era of growth. *To finish something for good.*

XII	The Hanged Man	To make a clean break from the past. To pay your debt to society. To make a transition. To make a personal sacrifice. *To turn over a new leaf.*
XI	Strength	To come to terms with yourself. To get in touch with yourself. To be a force for good. To overcome great odds. *To overcome the violence of this world.*
XXI	The World	To drink up the experience. To take it all in. To celebrate the act of existence. To experience it all for what it is. *To have fun doing what life asks of you.*

The Wands

Ace of Wands	To play a productive part in things. To get things started. To produce offshoots. To plant seeds. *To pursue a new line of work.*
2 of Wands	To be stretched to your limits. To extend the normal boundaries. To go to the ends of the earth. *To go about improving the world.*
3 of Wands	To go the distance. To try out new things. To be an observer of human nature. To set things in motion. *To launch new ventures.*
4 of Wands	To cultivate good relationships. To extend your own reach. To work with and through others. *To cement relations.*
5 of Wands	To develop your own skills. To better yourself by competing against your peers. To struggle. To measure up. *To achieve the highest standards.*
6 of Wands	To achieve a victory. To brave the cold, cruel world and come out a winner. To attempt to make the world a safer place. *To perform your duty.*

The Wands (*cont.*)

7 of Wands

To find a place to call your own. To take care of your corner of the planet. To stand your ground.
To stand up for the rights of others.

8 of Wands

To be a straight arrow. To be determined and diligent in following your chosen course. To keep your sights focused.
To hit the mark.

9 of Wands

To be dependable and conscientious. To protect community interests. To perform your duties with diligence.
To hold down the fort.

10 of Wands

To carry your weight. To complete much work. To struggle toward your goal. To accomplish your mission.
To be prolific in your work.

Page of Wands

To be vocal. To deliver an important message. To spread the word. To speak from the heart.
To get the message.

Knight of Wands

To be proactive. To be prepared for trouble. To aid those in distress. To come to the rescue of others.
To get ready.

Queen of Wands

To care for others. To nurture things. To help things achieve their full potential.
To achieve your own potential.

King of Wands

To be a role model. To provide direction. To foster confidence. To make progress. To taste success. To take responsibility.
To achieve results.

The Cups

Ace of Cups

To pour out your love. To overflow with compassion. To be a source of joy. To add to the quality of life.
To touch the hearts of others.

2 of Cups

To meet the love of your life. To love and support another person completely. To support and comfort another.
To share your love openly.

3 of Cups

To be a good friend. To provide a shoulder to lean on. To care for others. To confide in others.
To be a participant in life.

The Cups *(cont.)*

4 of Cups

To sort things out for yourself. To long for what you don't have. To seek the thing that will complete you.
To search for your soul mate.

5 of Cups

To make up for mistakes. To undo past wrongs. To atone for a past life. To pick up the pieces. To suffer rejection.
To get something out of your system.

6 of Cups

To have a romantic experience. To benefit from a good environment. To make a lifelong friend.
To express your true feelings.

7 of Cups

To dream dreams. To have visions. To strive for the good things in life. To determine what it is you really want.
To live out a fantasy.

8 of Cups

To be progressive. To leave the past behind. To journey abroad. To see what color the grass is on the other side.
To appreciate what you've got.

9 of Cups

To be satisfied. To be comfortable. To be free of care. To enjoy a period of abundance and happiness.
To learn how to be satisfied.

10 of Cups

To share the experience. To appreciate natural wonders. To marvel. To share a tender moment with someone special.
To enjoy the simple life.

Page of Cups

To express your emotions. To deliver a message of love, comfort, or consolation. To brighten the spirits of others.
To deliver a speech.

Knight of Cups

To be at the right place at the right time. To meet your true love. To rescue your love. To discover what it is you love.
To deliver a proposal.

Queen of Cups

To be caring and comforting. To be a force for good in the lives of the people who depend on you.
To develop a lasting relationship.

King of Cups

To be understanding and kind. To be a role model for those closest to you. To rule the roost with compassion.
To remain true to your word.

The Coins

Ace of Coins	To be a person of high values. To contribute to the material and spiritual well-being of your people. To add value to the world. *To bring new wealth into being.*
2 of Coins	To add more than you subtract. To give more than you take. To come to terms with your material desires. *To learn the value of money.*
3 of Coins	To create things of lasting value and enduring worth. To appreciate the work of others. To grow in self-esteem. *To learn how to invest money.*
4 of Coins	To amass net worth. To protect your assets. To hang on to the things that you value. To preserve the past. *To sock a little money away.*
5 of Coins	To brave the elements. To value the things that are essential. To transcend the situation and seek a light in the darkness. *To make it on your own.*
6 of Coins	To be generous. To contribute to the general welfare. To help those who need a hand. To look out for others. *To share what you have.*
7 of Coins	To cultivate things that have a market value. To invest your time in efforts that bear fruit later. To be enterprising. *To tend to your investments.*
8 of Coins	To produce a useful product. To finish something. To build something. To keep your hands busy. To learn a skill. *To do your best work.*
9 of Coins	To improve the environment. To enhance your personal appearance. To put your spare time into something that shows. *To prove what you can do.*
10 of Coins	To build something that will stand the test of time. To live the good life. To experience a period of prosperity. *To enjoy your good fortune.*

The Coins (cont.)

Page of Coins	To give your two cents worth. To handle money. To deliver services or friendly advice to others. *To put your money where your mouth is.*
Knight of Coins	To come to the aid of those who lack means. To provide assistance. To perform extra duty to earn extra pay. *To put your money to good use.*
Queen of Coins	To appreciate beautiful things. To acquire the things that money buys. To admire your possessions. To plan for the future. *To accomplish something.*
King of Coins	To establish your command. To assert your control. To manage your resources. To do something productive, constructive. *To reap the financial rewards of life.*

The Swords

Ace of Swords	To fight for the right. To conquer. To triumph. To feel the thrill of victory. To taste power. *To be successful.*
2 of Swords	To temper yourself. To sharpen your skills. To come to grips with reality. To make peace with yourself and others. *To experience a period of calm.*
3 of Swords	To be sensitive to the feelings of others. To mend a broken heart. To dry a few tears. *To learn to appreciate how others feel.*
4 of Swords	To be patient. To allow the forces outside you to work through you. To lie in wait for the voice to call. To prepare yourself. *To gather your strength.*
5 of Swords	To be brave and courageous. To fight for a cause. To make a name for yourself. To make an important rite of passage. *To learn how to defend yourself.*
6 of Swords	To flee from a troubled place. To journey to a safe haven. To pick up your roots. To make a drastic move. *To journey to a new place.*

The Swords (cont.)

7 of Swords	To escape. To do what you must in order to survive. To get away with something. To pull off a strategic move. *To make your big move.*
8 of Swords	To make a personal sacrifice. To get free from the things that bind you. To wrap up loose ends. To make a plan to escape. *To restrain yourself.*
9 of Swords	To overcome a bad experience or an emotional upset. To face up to the facts. To resolve a burning issue. *To face your fears.*
10 of Swords	To get the message. To experience the agony of defeat. To learn an important lesson. *To sacrifice your ego.*
Page of Swords	To fight for the truth. To be intolerant of injustice. To experience conflict. To boldly state your position. *To prepare for the inevitable.*
Knight of Swords	To be strong of body and resolute of will. To commit heroic acts. To rush in where others are afraid to go. *To come to the defense of others.*
Queen of Swords	To organize others in a common effort. To use constructive criticism. To develop a support system. To build a network. *To work toward something crucial.*
King of Swords	To be a force to be reckoned with. To establish a firm position. To play a dominant role. *To learn not to abuse power.*

EXTRA CREDIT

For a quick Reading of the purpose for a particular situation or event, just shuffle the cards as you ask your question (for example: **What is the purpose of my relationship with** _____? or **What is the purpose of my job with** _____?). When the cards are done, deal up the top three cards, consult the answers, and read them as one continuous thought.

Scratch Pad

Jot down your cards and answers here.

Card 1
Card 2
Card 3

Card 1
Card 2
Card 3

EXTRA EXTRA CREDIT!

What the heck, conduct this Reading as a Celtic Cross spread. (Consult the Quick Reference Guide for an illustration of the layout.) Interpret the cards as if they describe: Card 1—the purpose of your current situation; Card 2—the purpose of the challenge you face; Card 3—the purpose that will be served by addressing this challenge; Card 4—the purpose of something that happened to you in the past; Card 5—the purpose of a recent event; Card 6—the purpose of an upcoming event; Card 7—the purpose you have in the current situation; Card 8—the purpose others want you to have; Card 9—the purpose you want to have; and Card 10—the purpose you ultimately achieve.

Go on to the next Reading whenever you are ready to continue.

Reading #27

WHAT IS MY MISSION?

In this Reading you will use all of the cards to help you
decide which way you want to go with your life. This
Reading also works for making everyday decisions about
things that involve a couple of different options.

TAROT TOOLS

You will need all the cards.

HOW TO

For the purpose of helping you make a critical choice in life, this Reading
will use a special layout that lets you choose between two options. It's called
the Horseshoe. Here's how it works.

Shuffle all the cards together as you ask your question: **What is my
mission?** or **What is my mission with regard to _____?**

When the cards are done, deal up the top six and place them in a U, in
the order indicated below. If a card comes up upside down in your Reading,
leave it that way, and focus on the *italic* portion of the answers.

> ### Scratch Pad
> *Note your cards and answers here.*
>
> Card 1
> Card 2
> Card 3
> Card 4
> Card 5
> Card 6

HINT: In this Reading you will need to interpret the answers a bit for
each card. For your answer, the cards are going to give you two alternative

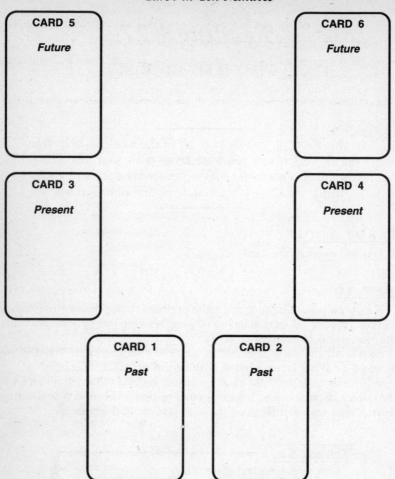

| CARD 5 | | CARD 6 |
| Future | | Future |

| CARD 3 | | CARD 4 |
| Present | | Present |

| CARD 1 | CARD 2 |
| Past | Past |

answers for you to choose between. Read your cards in the context of their position in the layout.

The left-hand branch of the Horseshoe shows you one option:

Card 1 represents a mission you have already completed.

Card 3 represents an option open to you now.

Card 5 represents the outcome you can expect if you choose this course.

The right-hand branch of the Horseshoe shows an alternative path you can take:

Card 2 represents another mission you have accomplished in the past.

Card 4 represents an option open to you now.

Card 6 represents the outcome you can expect as a result of this course of action.

For additional information on any card, consult the Quick Reference Guide.

THE ANSWERS

The Trumps—I

0	The Fool	To know who you are. *To go as the spirit moves you.*
I	The Magician	To work wonders. *To channel your energy.*
II	The High Priestess	To read minds. *To be connected to the eternal stream.*
III	The Empress	To tend to your duties. *To follow the path of the stars.*
IV	The Emperor	To exercise your authority. *To carve out a niche for yourself.*
V	The Hierophant	To occupy a responsible position. *To create order out of chaos.*
VI	The Lovers	To pursue a romantic interest. *To strive for perfect union.*
VII	The Chariot	To conquer the enemy. *To conquer the opposing forces within you.*
VIII	Justice	To decide for yourself. *To achieve inner balance.*
IX	The Hermit	To come to terms with yourself. *To offer something of yourself to the world.*
X	Wheel of Fortune	To change with the times. *To change yourself.*

The Trumps—II

XX	Judgement	To hear the call and rise up to it. *To rise again.*
XIX	The Sun	To heed the call and ride off toward it. *To rise and shine.*

XVIII	The Moon	To answer the call and pursue it. *To rise and go.*
XVII	The Star	To follow the call and stick to it. *To ebb and flow in your own rhythm.*
XVI	The Tower	To respond to the call and leap at it. *To come to your own rescue.*
XV	The Devil	To recognize the call and submit to it. *To get out from under your limitations.*
XIV	Temperance	To work with the call and fulfill it. *To open yourself up to the possibilities.*
XIII	Death	To react to the call and dismiss the past. *To kick off a new beginning.*
XII	The Hanged Man	To make your own calls. *To get your act together.*
XI	Strength	To get with your call. To understand it. *To balance internal and external forces.*
XXI	The World	To be who you are. *To go with the flow.*

The Wands

Ace of Wands	To receive your calling. *To feel the spark of passion.*
2 of Wands	To pursue your own interests. *To go where the spirit moves you.*
3 of Wands	To pursue other interests. *To go where the journey takes you.*
4 of Wands	To pursue common interests. *To grow with your soul mate.*
5 of Wands	To fend for yourself. *To establish your position.*
6 of Wands	To rise above the rest. *To make a name for yourself.*

The Wands (*cont.*)

7 of Wands	To organize things.
	To develop strength in numbers.
8 of Wands	To set things in motion.
	To help things on their way.
9 of Wands	To define things.
	To put things in their proper context.
10 of Wands	To put it all together.
	To add it all up at the end of the day.
Page of Wands	To spread the word.
	To share what you have learned.
Knight of Wands	To champion a cause.
	To fight the good fight.
Queen of Wands	To dedicate your life.
	To serve a good purpose.
King of Wands	To follow your calling.
	To achieve your purpose.

The Cups

Ace of Cups	To receive the spirit.
	To feel the forces at work in your life.
2 of Cups	To know another.
	To discover your soul mate.
3 of Cups	To know your friends.
	To discover your kindred spirits.
4 of Cups	To know yourself.
	To complete your vision quest.
5 of Cups	To right wrongs.
	To let your conscience be your guide.
6 of Cups	To cheer hearts.
	To speak from the heart.
7 of Cups	To dream dreams.
	To look forward to the future.
8 of Cups	To journey places.
	To add to your experience.
9 of Cups	To live life.
	To enjoy the experience.
10 of Cups	To experience life.
	To take something out of the experience.
Page of Cups	To relate your story.
	To share your experience.
Knight of Cups	To offer your assistance.
	To give something of yourself.

The Cups *(cont.)*

Queen of Cups	To be spirit.
	To establish your spiritual side.
King of Cups	To express your feelings.
	To get in touch with your emotions.

The Coins

Ace of Coins	To acquire the wherewithal.
	To put your possessions to work for you.
2 of Coins	To develop the discipline.
	To handle your own affairs.
3 of Coins	To earn a living.
	To apply your art to commercial use.
4 of Coins	To acquire possessions.
	To gather your strength from material objects.
5 of Coins	To overcome poverty.
	To avoid becoming homeless.
6 of Coins	To redistribute the wealth.
	To help those who are less fortunate.
7 of Coins	To prepare for the future.
	To invest your efforts in something that will pay off later.
8 of Coins	To pay your own way.
	To keep the cash flowing.
9 of Coins	To enjoy your leisure time.
	To appreciate when you have accomplished enough for the day.
10 of Coins	To live well.
	To enjoy the things that come your way.
Page of Coins	To respect your treasures.
	To realize your native abilities.
Knight of Coins	To use your treasures.
	To offer your services.
Queen of Coins	To grow your treasures.
	To put your free time to good use.
King of Coins	To acquire the means.
	To put your possessions to work for others.

The Swords

Ace of Swords	To achieve honor.
	To fight for the right.

The Swords (cont.)

2 of Swords	To save face.
	To negotiate a win/win situation.
3 of Swords	To honor your commitments.
	To be true to your word.
4 of Swords	To honor your duty.
	To live up to your obligations.
5 of Swords	To do honor to your name.
	To establish your own reputation.
6 of Swords	To do the honorable thing.
	To know when it is time to retreat.
7 of Swords	To avoid dishonor.
	To remain discreet.
8 of Swords	To honor your debts.
	To pay your debt to society.
9 of Swords	To honor your victims.
	To show signs of remorse.
10 of Swords	To restore yourself to honor.
	To get back on your feet again.
Page of Swords	To honor your native abilities.
	To stand and be counted.
Knight of Swords	To honor your commitments.
	To take up the just cause.
Queen of Swords	To honor your superiors.
	To carry out orders.
King of Swords	To achieve glory.
	To fight for the truth.

EXTRA CREDIT

For a quick Reading on what you are supposed to accomplish with a particular project or person, just shuffle the cards, deal up three, and look up your answers. Read the answers as if they were a continuous thought. For cards in reversal, consult the portion of the answers printed in *italics*.

Scratch Pad

Jot down your cards and answers here.

Card 1
Card 2
Card 3

Card 1
Card 2
Card 3

EXTRA EXTRA CREDIT!

What the heck, mix your cards up really well and conduct a Celtic Cross reading for your mission in life. The Quick Reference Guide will show you how to lay out the cards. To interpret your answers, follow these guidelines: Card 1—describes your current mission; Card 2—describes a conflicting mission; Card 3—describes the adjusted mission you can expect as a result; Card 4—describes a past mission that relates to this one; Card 5—describes a recent milestone in meeting your mission; Card 6—describes an upcoming achievement; Card 7—describes the mission you think you are pursuing; Card 8—describes the mission others want you to pursue; Card 9—describes the mission you want to pursue; and Card 10—describes the mission you fulfill in the end.

Go on to the next Reading whenever you are ready to continue.

Reading #28

WHAT DO I NEED TO LEARN?

In Reading #28 you will be working with all the cards to discover the moral of your story. In this Reading you will learn what you need to learn. You can also use this Reading to find out what lesson you should get out of a particular event or series of events in your life.

TAROT TOOLS

You will need all the cards.

HOW TO

For the purpose of asking such an important question, we will be using a very special layout called the Crescent Moon.

Shuffle all the cards together, as you ask your question: **What do I need to learn in this life?** or **What should I learn from _____?**

When the cards are done, deal up the top six and place them in the shape of a Crescent Moon in the sequence shown in the illustration.

If a card comes up upside down in your Reading, leave it that way, and focus on the *italic* portion of the answers.

Look up your cards by their position in the layout (1 through 6) in the Answer section.

Scratch Pad

Note your cards and answers here.

Card 1
Card 2
Card 3
Card 4
Card 5
Card 6

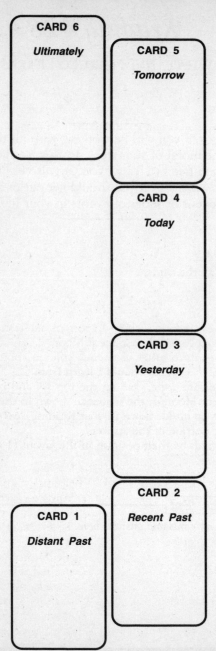

CARD 6

Ultimately

CARD 5

Tomorrow

CARD 4

Today

CARD 3

Yesterday

CARD 2

Recent Past

CARD 1

Distant Past

HINT: In this Reading you will need to interpret the answers a bit for each card. Read your cards in the context of their position in the layout.

Card 1 represents something you learned in the distant past (anything over a year ago).

Card 2 represents something you learned recently (within the last six months or so).

Card 3 represents something you learned yesterday.

Card 4 represents something you learn today.

Card 5 represents something you will learn tomorrow.

Card 6 represents the lesson you will ultimately learn as a result of all of this.

For additional information on any card, consult the Quick Reference Guide.

THE ANSWERS

The Trumps–I

0	The Fool	What innocence teaches. *How to experience.*
I	The Magician	What a young man knows. *The physical experience.*
II	The High Priestess	What a young woman knows. *The emotional experience.*
III	The Empress	What a woman knows. *The growth experience.*
IV	The Emperor	What a man knows. *The learning experience.*
V	The Hierophant	What a priest knows. *The religious experience.*
VI	The Lovers	What a lover knows. *The earth-shaking experience.*
VII	The Chariot	What a hero knows. *The life-threatening experience.*
VIII	Justice	What a judge knows. *The precedent-setting experience.*
IX	The Hermit	What a sage knows. *The spiritual experience.*
X	Wheel of Fortune	What experience teaches. *To take from the experience.*

The Trumps–II

XX	Judgement	What the end brings.
		The beginning.
XIX	The Sun	What the sun brings.
		Life.
XVIII	The Moon	What the moon brings.
		Rebirth.
XVII	The Star	What the stars bring.
		Destiny.
XVI	The Tower	What the sudden light brings.
		Inspiration.
XV	The Devil	What the darkest hour brings.
		Passion.
XIV	Temperance	What the stream brings.
		Creation.
XIII	Death	What the stream carries away.
		Completion.
XII	The Hanged Man	What the plants know.
		To everything there is a season.
XI	Strength	What the animals know.
		Only the strong survive.
XXI	The World	What it's all about.
		Ain't it good to be alive.

The Wands

Ace of Wands	What opportunity is.
	A self-fulfilling prophecy.
2 of Wands	What ambition accomplishes.
	The way to self-esteem.
3 of Wands	What appearance accomplishes.
	The way to self-image.
4 of Wands	What cooperation accomplishes.
	The way to self-fulfillment.
5 of Wands	What competition accomplishes.
	The way to self-improvement.
6 of Wands	What success accomplishes.
	The way to self-realization.
7 of Wands	What determination accomplishes.
	The way to self-assertion.

The Wands (cont.)

8 of Wands	What effort accomplishes. *The way to self-direction.*
9 of Wands	What diligence accomplishes. *The way to self-sacrifice.*
10 of Wands	What hard labor accomplishes. *The way to self-determination.*
Page of Wands	What words accomplish. *The way to self-expression.*
Knight of Wands	What good deeds accomplish. *The way to self-satisfaction.*
Queen of Wands	What going with the flow accomplishes. *The way to self-actualization.*
King of Wands	What right actions accomplish. *The way to self-enlightenment.*

The Cups

Ace of Cups	What love is. *"Feelings, nothing more than feelings."*
2 of Cups	What commitment is. *A solemn feeling.*
3 of Cups	What friendship is. *A kind feeling.*
4 of Cups	What longing is. *A restless feeling.*
5 of Cups	What rejection is. *A cold feeling.*
6 of Cups	What romance is. *A warm feeling.*
7 of Cups	What desire is. *A hot feeling.*
8 of Cups	What distance is. *An empty feeling.*
9 of Cups	What closeness is. *A full feeling.*
10 of Cups	What love feels like. *Nothing else.*
Page of Cups	What puppy love feels like. *The waters rising.*
Knight of Cups	What first love feels like. *The waters rushing.*

The Cups (cont.)

Queen of Cups	What true love feels like. *The tide coming in.*
King of Cups	What undying love feels like. *The endless sea.*

The Coins

Ace of Coins	What money is. *"All that glitters . . ."*
2 of Coins	What cash flow means. *The odds fluctuate.*
3 of Coins	What credit means. *The odds can be counted on.*
4 of Coins	What savings means. *You can bank on the odds.*
5 of Coins	What poverty means. *The odds can work for or against you.*
6 of Coins	What charity means. *You can even out the odds.*
7 of Coins	What risk means. *You can chance the odds.*
8 of Coins	What investment means. *You can stack the odds.*
9 of Coins	What success means. *You can get the odds on your side.*
10 of Coins	What luck means. *You can beat the odds.*
Page of Coins	What money says. *Put your money where your mouth is.*
Knight of Coins	What money buys. *Whatever it can afford.*
Queen of Coins	What money does. *Go through your hands.*
King of Coins	What money gets you. *Exactly what you pay for.*

The Swords

Ace of Swords	What power is. *"Let the force be with you."*
2 of Swords	What conflict proves. *There are opposing forces at work.*
3 of Swords	What love proves. *There are forces beyond your control.*
4 of Swords	What dreams prove. *There are forces below the surface.*
5 of Swords	What winning proves. *One force can overpower another.*
6 of Swords	What retreat proves. *One force can repel another.*
7 of Swords	What escape proves. *The forces can be redirected.*
8 of Swords	What surrender proves. *The forces can be harnessed.*
9 of Swords	What defeat proves. *The forces can be reversed.*
10 of Swords	What betrayal proves. *The forces can be unpredictable.*
Page of Swords	What a good defense proves. *One force can hold off another.*
Knight of Swords	What a good offense proves. *One force can break through another.*
Queen of Swords	That the word is mightier than the sword. *One force can silence another.*
King of Swords	That the sword cuts both ways. *Nothing lasts forever.*

EXTRA CREDIT

For a quicker Reading, ask, **What are the three things I need to learn about _____?** Simply shuffle, and turn up the top three cards. Focus on the *italic* portion of the answers for cards in reversal.

Scratch Pad

Jot down your cards and answers here.

Card 1
Card 2
Card 3

Card 1
Card 2
Card 3

EXTRA EXTRA CREDIT!

What the heck, ask what you need to learn in your life right now, shuffle the cards, and deal them up into a Celtic Cross layout. Consult the Quick Reference Guide for an illustration of the layout and for instructions about interpreting your answers. Look up your answers in the Quick Reference Guide's Master Answer Section.

Go on to the next Reading whenever you are ready to continue.

Reading #29

WHERE DO I GO FROM HERE?

In Reading #29 you get to fly solo. You can ask any question, use any combination of cards, and deal your cards out into any layout. For answers, just consult the Quick Reference Guide at the back of the book. In this Reading the Tarot Tools and How To sections review the techniques you've already learned.

TAROT TOOLS

Select the cards that are "best at" answering the type of question that's on your mind:

For questions about **work** . . .   **Wands** (Ace through King) and **Trumps** (0–XXI)

For questions about **love** . . .   **Cups** (Ace through King) and **Trumps** (0–XXI)

For questions about **money** . . .   **Coins** (Ace through King) and **Trumps** (0–XXI)

For questions about **strategy** . . .   **Swords** (Ace through King) and **Trumps** (0–XXI)

For **all other purposes** . . .   **Trumps** (0–XXI)

Or just use *all* the cards for a complete reading on any subject.

At this point you can also select a "significator." A significator is a card that helps you focus on the subject of your Reading. If you are reading for yourself, use your Key Card from Reading #1. Or if you are using a deck (such as Rider-Waite) that includes a blank card, you can make this card your permanent significator by signing your name to it. For Readings conducted for others, first select their Key Card by completing Reading #1 for them. Just place this significator faceup on the table as you prepare and conduct your Reading.

This is also a good time to light a candle or burn some incense to put you in the mood for a Reading. Some people like to begin each session with a prayer for guidance.

HOW TO

After selecting the cards you want to use in your Reading, you need to decide on a layout.

Which layout (or spread) you choose to use is largely a matter of personal preference, but each is good at certain things. The book teaches eight ways:

One-Card Readings are good at giving you something to think about. Just deal up a single card to get some guidance for the day ahead.

Three-Card Readings are good at quickly sizing up a situation—past, present, and future—or at suggesting a course of action.

Two-card Cover and Cross Readings are good at getting quickly to the point. Just deal up two cards, placing the second crosswise over the first, in order to go directly to the bottom line on any question.

Three-pair Cover and Cross Readings are good at hitting the highlights. Deal up the three cards and cross them with three more to look at your questions past, present, and future.

Celtic Cross Readings are good at considering all the angles. Eight cards are dealt up and placed around a central Cover and Cross formation for a complete assessment of you and your situation.

Pyramid Readings are good at helping you focus in on a complex relationship. Six cards are placed in the shape of a triangle to help you organize your own thoughts about the subject at hand.

Horseshoe Readings are good at helping you determine your own destiny. Six cards are arranged in the shape of a U to identify two actions you can take to influence the future outcome of anything.

Crescent Moon Readings are good at establishing timeframes. Six cards are arranged in the shape of a moon, with each card representing a given point in time, to help you pinpoint key developments over time.

Next, formulate your question.

With Tarot you can ask virtually any question that is on your mind, but Tarot is best at handling **how, what, where,** and **what if** questions:

HOW	How should I proceed with _____ ?
	How's it going with _____ ?
	How will _____ turn out?
	How will I do at _____ ?
	How does _____ feel about me?
	How is _____ coming along?
WHAT	What will the outcome of _____ be?
	What does _____ expect from me?
	What should I do about _____ ?
	What's the story with _____ ?
	What's up at _____ ?
	What should I know about _____ ?
	What's the status of _____ ?
	What are the prospects for _____ ?
	What does the future hold for me?
WHERE	Where is my relationship with _____ going?
	Where is my job with _____ headed?
	Where will I be in _____ years?
	Where will I wind up?
WHAT IF	What if I _____ ?
	What if I don't _____ ?

Tarot also works quite well with **should I, will I, can I,** and **am I** questions:

WORK:	Should I apply for this job?
LOVE:	Will I go out with so-and-so?
MONEY:	Can I afford to buy this house?
STRATEGY:	Should I be more aggressive?
GENERAL:	Am I going to make it big?
SPIRITUAL:	Am I on the right path?

You can also ask **who, when,** and **why** questions:

WORK:	When will I find out about my raise?
LOVE:	Who is my secret admirer?
MONEY:	When will my ship come in?
STRATEGY:	Who can be of help to me?
GENERAL:	When will the letter arrive?
SPIRITUAL:	Why am I dreaming of water?

Once you have formulated your question, you are ready to proceed with your Reading. Shuffle the cards as you ask your question.

There is no right way to do this, and there is no way you can do it wrong—honestly! All you really have to do is take the cards in your hands and mix them up while you ask your question. Shuffle them hand over hand, riffle them together, or swirl them around on the table in front of you. Keep shuffling until your cards are "done."

There are two good ways of knowing when the cards are done: (1) when the cards get sluggish and don't want to go into one another anymore, or (2) when one leaps out of the deck. Sometimes it takes a long time for one of these things to happen, and sometimes it takes no time at all. Another surefire way of knowing when the cards are done is when you simply get tired of shuffling them. Whenever you quit, it will be the right time.

At this point you can cut the cards one, two, or three times and gather them up again before you deal, or you can just stop shuffling and deal from the top of the shuffled deck. Cards that leap should be used as the first cards in the spread.

Consult the Quick Reference Guide for the sequence and arrangement of cards in your layout, for instructions on interpreting the meaning of cards in the various positions of each spread, and for complete answers. But first, a couple of general tips:

Cards in reversal. At the beginning of the book, I said you could worry about reading the cards in reversal later. Now is your opportunity, since the Quick Reference Guide includes answers for cards that appear upside down in your layout. But if the first card you deal up is reversed, turn it upright and flip the deck around in your hands. (You have probably inadvertently picked up the entire deck upside down.) Otherwise, cards should be left in the upright or reversed position as they have fallen. Cards that "cross you" in a Cover and Cross formation are always read as if they are upright.

Interpreting the cards. The Quick Reference Guide includes a brief description and a general reading for every card in the deck, with special sections devoted to work, love, money, and strategy questions. Just look up each card in your layout and read as much of the answer as you think applies to the matter at hand. These answers will give you a feeling for what each card might mean in various instances, but you will need to apply the meaning to your own situation. A solo Reading involves reading between the lines and looking at the pictures on your cards to see what message pops out at you today. Don't ever be afraid to draw your own conclusion about what a card means. Don't ever hesitate to influence your own destiny.

Godspeed, my friend.

Quick Reference Guide
to
Reading the Cards and Their Messages

For Use with Any Question
For Help with Any Reading

CARD LAYOUTS

Before using this section, you might want to complete Reading #29, which gives you some tips for selecting which cards to use, choosing a layout, formulating your question, and shuffling the cards. The instructions here assume you know these steps and are now ready to deal out your cards and conduct a reading.

In conducting your own readings, use the answers provided in the second part of this Quick Reference Guide. There is a complete answer for each card, followed by separate sections relating specifically to questions about work, love, money, and strategy. Upright and reversed answers are included for each card. Use these answers as a starting point for developing your own interpretations and drawing your own conclusions.

One-Card Readings

Sometimes just drawing a single card from the deck will give you the information you need. For people on the go, this is a good way to benefit from Tarot every day, without having to devote the time to a full-scale Reading.

HOW TO

Simply shuffle the cards while you ask your question. When the cards are done, deal up one. Place it faceup in front of you.

Look up your card in the Answer section of the Quick Reference Guide.

TIPS

A one-card Reading works best if you simply ask, "What's the thought for the day?" or "What guidance do you have to give me today?" To get your thought for the day, read the Strategy section of the answer for your card. This type of Reading works fine with the whole deck or with just the Trumps (0–XXI).

VARIATIONS

Tarot in Ten Minutes uses one-card Readings to conduct character analyses. If you want to construct a complete Tarot profile for yourself or a friend, just complete Readings #1 (personality), #5 (occupation), #9 (relationships and popularity), #12 (appearance), #14 (money), #17 (success), #20 (foibles), and #23 (true self). Reading #2 also uses a one-card Reading, to tell you what "Tarot Year" you are in and what you can expect from it. Conducting these Readings all together makes for a fun evening.

Three-Card Readings

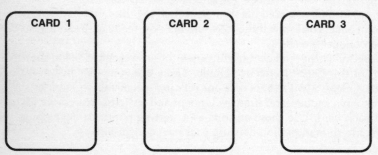

Three-card layouts provide a simple, effective assessment of any given situation. The method employed is similar to that used with Celtic runes, in which three stones engraved with symbols are drawn from a pouch, placed in a row, and then interpreted.

HOW TO

Shuffle your cards while you ask your question. When the cards are done, deal up the top three and place them in a row in front of you, from left to right. Look up your cards in the Master Answer section.

TIPS

To interpret your answers, read the cards like Runes:

Card 1 represents the current situation.
Card 2 represents the action you should consider taking.
Card 3 represents the outcome you can expect.

Consult the entire answer for your cards, but focus on the sections that relate directly to the question you asked.

Reading #4 demonstrates this kind of three-card spread.

VARIATIONS

The three-card Reading can also be interpreted like the I Ching—a method of Chinese fortune-telling that uses three coins to cast a fortune. If you would like to try this method, make up your mind before you shuffle. The cards that come up are read as if they are a continuous thought. The first represents the main subject, with each subsequent card adding detail. You don't have to stop at three cards—you can continue dealing up cards until you are satisfied that the cards are done. Reading #13 demonstrates this approach.

Three-card spreads also make a nice past, present, and future Reading, if you decide before you shuffle the cards that you want to read the layout as such. See Reading #7 for an example of this kind of reading. You can also conduct a three-card Reading by shuffling and cutting the cards into three stacks, then reading the top card in each stack.

Cover and Cross Readings

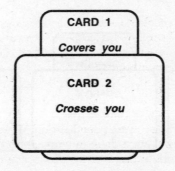

This simple two-card Cover and Cross Reading is a fundamental Tarot tool. As the central element of the long-standing, tried-and-true Celtic Cross method of reading the cards, the Cover and Cross is used to size up what's going on in your life right now.

HOW TO

Shuffle your cards while you ask your question. When the cards are done, deal up the top card (or use the leaper) and lay it in front of you. *This card covers you.* Across this first card, place the second card. *This card crosses you.* Look up your cards in the Answer section.

TIPS

To interpret your answers, read your cards in the context of their position in the layout:

Card 1 describes your current situation.

Card 2 describes the challenge you face.

Together, the two cards sum up a situation and tell you what you need to do next. Focus on the Strategy section of the answers.

Such basic Cover and Cross layouts are used in Readings #3, #6, and #10.

VARIATIONS

Since the Cover and Cross Reading quickly gets to the bottom line, it is ideally suited for asking straight yes/no questions (see Reading #22).

Three-Pair Cover and Cross Readings

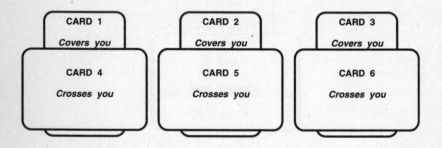

This layout is particularly well suited for tracing the development of a relationship, the progress of a career, the stages of a financial situation, or the course of a given strategy.

HOW TO

Shuffle your cards while you ask your question. When the cards are done, deal up the top three and place them in a row in front of you, from left to right. *These cards cover you.* Deal up three more, and place them crosswise over the three cards you dealt before. *These cards cross you.* Look up your cards in the Answer section.

TIPS

To interpret your answers, read your cards in the context of their positions in the layout:

Card 1 represents the early days of a relationship.

Card 2 represents a significant event that occurred along the way.

Card 3 represents how the relationship changed as a result.

Card 4 represents the situation as it now stands.

Card 5 represents the challenge you face.

Card 6 indicates the action you should take.

VARIATIONS

Pyramid Readings are good at sorting out matters of long standing. For this reason, the Pyramid is also an excellent Reading for tracing your soul's progress over this or many lifetimes, as demonstrated in Reading #26, where the question concerns your life's purpose.

Horseshoe Readings

This is a good Reading to do whenever you are not sure which way to turn in a situation. A Horseshoe Reading provides you with two different options and projects the outcome of each so that you can decide which way you want to proceed.

HOW TO

Shuffle your cards while you ask your question. When the cards are done, deal up the top six, moving from left to right, from the bottom up the curve of the horseshoe, as indicated in the illustration. Look up your cards in the Answer section.

TIPS

Be sure to arrange your cards with the horseshoe open end up, or else—as the superstition goes—your luck may run out.

To interpret your answers, read each card based on its position in the layout. Read each branch of the horseshoe separately.

The left-hand branch shows you one option:

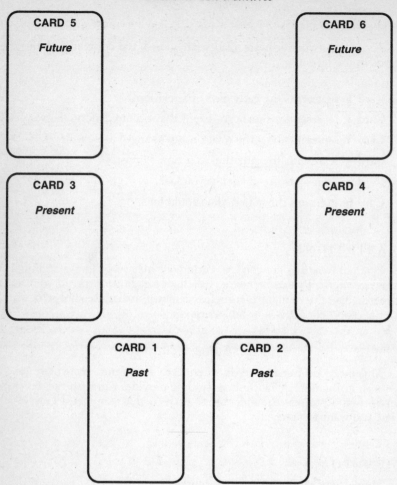

Card 1 represents a past experience that you can build on.

Card 3 represents an option open to you now.

Card 5 represents the outcome you can expect as a result.

The right-hand branch shows an alternative path you can take:

Card 2 represents a past experience that you can build on.

Card 4 represents an option open to you now.

Card 6 represents the outcome you can expect as a result.

Card Layouts

For cards in positions 1 and 5, and 2 and 6, consult the Answer section in the Quick Reference Guide for each card, focusing on the portions that relate directly to the subject of your question (work, love, money, or strategy). Focus on the Strategy section for cards in positions 3 and 4.

VARIATIONS

For spiritual matters, the Horseshoe is a particularly useful layout, because at various points in our soul's journey, we must choose between taking one road or another. In this book, the Horseshoe is demonstrated in Reading #27, a Reading that involves choosing your mission in life.

Crescent Moon Readings

The Crescent Moon layout is good whenever you want to understand your answer in the context of time. Use it to identify the developments in a relationship or to forecast the sequence of events in any unfolding situation.

HOW TO

Shuffle your cards while you ask your question. When the cards are done, deal up the top six and place them in the shape of a Crescent Moon, as illustrated in the diagram. Look up your cards in the Answer section.

TIPS

To interpret your answers, read your cards in the context of their positions in the layout.

Card 1 represents events or situations from the distant past.

Card 2 represents developments in the recent past.

Card 3 represents something that happened yesterday.

Card 4 represents something that happens today.

Card 5 represents something that will happen tomorrow.

Card 6 represents the eventual outcome of this matter.

Read the Quick Reference Guide's entire answer for each card, but focus on the portions that relate directly to your question.

VARIATIONS

Instead of using the default timeframes listed above, prior to shuffling you can set the timeframe yourself. For example, Card 1 could be designated

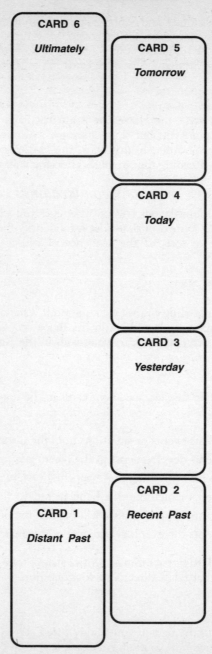

CARD 6

Ultimately

CARD 5

Tomorrow

CARD 4

Today

CARD 3

Yesterday

CARD 2

Recent Past

CARD 1

Distant Past

as one year ago; Card 2 as six months ago; Card 3 as last month; Card 4 as this month; Card 5 as next month; and Card 6 as "by the end of the year." For long-range planning, each card can be designated as a year. In this case, Card 1 would be three years ago; Card 2 would be two years ago; Card 3 would be last year; Card 4 would be this year; Card 5 would be next year; and Card 6 would be two years from now.

The Crescent Moon layout is demonstrated in Reading #28, where it is used to trace the lessons you have learned in life.

MASTER ANSWER SECTION

0 THE FOOL

This is a card about fresh starts. *Look at your card.* It is the dawn of a new day. The Fool is setting out to seek his fortune. This card describes a person with a good sense of adventure, someone who is not afraid to take a risk, someone who is about to take a big leap, or someone who is going through a rite of passage. Major transitions or radical departures are involved. Perhaps you've felt like running away lately. *Reversed.* There is a possibility that you are headed in the wrong direction. An uninformed choice has been made. Someone is off on a wild-goose chase.

For WORK questions. It's time for a change! A new job, new position, or whole new line of work is indicated. You may be tempted to seek employment in a different part of the country, to switch careers, or to start all over again. *Reversed.* The grass is no greener on the other side. False starts, vain hopes, or misrepresented opportunities are the outcome.

For LOVE questions. That old urge calls! Someone is looking high and low for a companion. A new partner is being sought, a change in friends is desired, or an affair is contemplated. You want to form new relationships. *Reversed.* You may be tempted to seek love in all the wrong places or to turn your back on a good thing.

For MONEY questions. Money is withdrawn! New investment opportunities open up, the urge to travel calls, or a new way to put your money to work is explored. Possessions are redirected, given away, or sold. You may be tempted to splurge. *Reversed.* Don't spend all your money in one place. Investment schemes turn sour.

For STRATEGY questions. A leap of faith is required! Strong views, firm conviction, and relentless desire are involved. It takes a true believer to pull this one off. *Reversed.* Your hopes may be unfounded. Or you may have to make a supreme sacrifice in order to achieve your goals.

I THE MAGICIAN

This is a card about energy. *Look at your card.* There is something that needs to be accomplished. The Magician taps into the energy and directs it to the task at hand. This card describes an energetic, dedicated, and focused person—a person who practices hard at a craft or who concentrates on achieving personal goals, aspirations, or ambitions. Perhaps you have been feeling a little charged up recently. *Reversed.* There is the possibility that the person drawing this card is spinning wheels. Personal energies are being misdirected, wasted, or dissipated.

For WORK questions. Apply yourself! This is a time for taking the bull by the horns. You should throw yourself into your work. Brush up on your skills. Practice what you've learned in the past. Give it your very best shot. Something wonderful happens on the job. *Reversed.* You are being underutilized or you are not achieving your full potential. Promising projects meet with snags.

For LOVE questions. Assert yourself! This is a time for making the first move. Someone is sending out signals, picking up on what someone else is thinking, or being admired from afar. A surge of sexual energy pulses through you like lightning, and you need to do something about it. There is a little magic in your life. *Reversed.* There are mixed messages and crossed signals. You may feel unsatisfied or pent-up and frustrated to the point of distraction. A relationship goes nowhere.

For MONEY questions. Apply your resources! This is a time for employing your assets or channeling your financial resources. Make the most of the cash you have on hand. Direct it toward realizing your financial goals and objectives. You can work magic with money. *Reversed.* Money slips through your fingers, is misapplied, or spent without proper consideration of financial aims. This is not the time to invest.

For STRATEGY questions. Focus your energy! This is a time when you need to direct your energies and resources to the job that needs to be done, to a goal or desired outcome. Performance counts. Output is measured. Strong results are realized. You score. *Reversed.* Lay off for a while. Nothing can be accomplished right now, no matter how hard you try.

II THE HIGH PRIESTESS

This is a card about intuition. *Look at your card.* Cycles and continuity are involved. Everything passes by in an endless stream, a continuous cycle, like the moon and the tides, and there is a natural rhythm to everything. This card describes a person who is in touch with reality, who goes with the flow, or who simply "knows without knowing." Perhaps you've had a psychic experience recently. *Reversed.* The tide of events has suddenly changed and something unexpected occurs. A natural cycle is disrupted. You feel a bit out of sorts.

For WORK questions.
Go with your gut! There are choices to make, promises to keep, or goals to realize. The past is studied. The future is envisioned. New plans are laid. A hunch of yours is likely to pay off big. *Reversed.* For every two steps you go forward, there will be a step back. Promises made in the past may not materialize as expected.

For LOVE questions.
Go with your heart! There are coincidences. There are premonitions. There is love at first sight, and love that endures. There is a calm feeling inside you when you know it's right. Somebody is coming into your life. *Reversed.* It will be, if it is meant to be; and otherwise it wasn't right anyway. Be careful not to let your hormones do the talking.

For MONEY questions.
Anticipate! There is an unexpected change in income, or a decrease in expenses, which improves the bottom line. Interest rates are fluctuating to your benefit, the market is going in the right direction, or your financial situation in general is coming around. You are operating in the black. *Reversed.* The books don't quite balance. There is an unexpected reversal in the financial situation.

For STRATEGY questions.
Psych up! This is a situation that calls for more of the mental than the physical. You need to be "up" for the game or "on" for the event. Prepare well in advance. But before the contest, clear your mind, take deep breaths, and listen to the silence within you. Everything will be okay. *Reversed.* Seek some kind of emotional or cathartic release. Screaming helps, or a good cry might suffice.

III THE EMPRESS

This is a card about productivity. Creativity or procreation may be involved. *Look at your card.* The Empress is waiting to harvest what she has planted in a prior season. To everything there is a season, and everything occurs in its own time. This card describes a person who is productive, maybe even prolific—especially in the creative arts or sciences. It could also stand for someone who is very close to nature, in touch with the physical world, or an excellent parent. A bright idea may have occurred to you recently. Something from the past pays off. *Reversed.* The things you started have not developed as rapidly or abundantly as you had hoped. Don't count your chickens before they're hatched. Bad weather is brewing.

For WORK questions. Keep up the good work! Things may take a while longer to pay off on the work scene, but good progress is being made. All the bases are covered, and the plans are unfolding as expected. Knock on wood. Someone is rooting for you. *Reversed.* Growth is sluggish and there may need to be cutbacks in order to pull through some difficult times. Hang in there and hope for the best.

For LOVE questions. Expect the best! This is a serious relationship that involves marriage (or at least a firm degree of commitment), wives, mothers, the birds and bees, and doing what comes naturally. Children or childbirth may be involved. Everything looks good on the home front. *Reversed.* Infertility, trouble with a pregnancy, or menopause are possibilities. A wedding may be postponed.

For MONEY questions. Watch over your assets! Savings, investments, money market funds, insurance policies, and retirement plans are all favored. You might want to start following the commodities exchange. An account you opened in the past is about to produce a yield. *Reversed.* The market bottoms out. Funds do not grow as expected. There is a substantial penalty for early withdrawal.

For STRATEGY questions. Sit tight! The best thing to do right now is nothing. Watch and wait for any new developments that demand your attention or immediate response. But for the most part, everything is done that you can control. The rest is out of your hands. Keep your fingers crossed. *Reversed.* The fates do not always cooperate with even best-laid plans. The apple cart is upset. Be ready to salvage what you can.

IV THE EMPEROR

This is a card about the powers that be. *Look at your card.* The sun is rising on the empire—or is it setting? The Emperor has staked out his claim over these lands for another day. But there is no telling for how long. This card describes a person who has a strong physical—maybe even charismatic—presence; a sure person; a certain person—someone who does well in a highly structured environment, or someone who rises to the top. The sale of real estate may be involved. This card also suggests an audience with a higher-up. *Reversed.* There is a sudden reversal of the rules. Boundaries are disputed. You may stand to benefit from a change in the power structure.

For WORK questions. Ask the boss! Rules, policies and procedures, or standard operating practices are involved. Good performance is expected. When in doubt, ask. Service beyond the call of duty earns a reward or special recognition. *Reversed.* You may need to present an accounting, report on your activities, or make adjustments to please the powers that be. A reorganization may be in the works. Watch for opportunities.

For LOVE questions. Who's the boss? Somebody wants to have the upper hand in this relationship, lay down the law, or control the moves. A parent/child relationship may be involved. You need to discuss something with your husband or father. *Reversed.* Someone you thought was your friend turns into a stone wall. There is a change for the better in a one-sided relationship.

For MONEY questions. Aim for the top! The financial situation you are in requires foresight and planning. Prepare a budget or financial plan and stick to it. Have funds deducted automatically from your pay in order to achieve your goals. *Reversed.* Federal, state, and local taxes are coming due. Your returns are subject to audit.

For STRATEGY questions. Hold the line! The best offense is a good defense. Keep an eye on the competition, but let the other guy make the first move. Before you react, make sure popular opinion is on your side. Someone in authority wants to speak with you. *Reversed.* Your guard is down. Things are plotted in silence. Look out behind you!

V THE HIEROPHANT

This is a card about beliefs. *Look at your card.* The benediction has just been said. The Hierophant confers the final blessing on the worshipers. This card describes someone who believes in right and wrong, good and bad, or in abiding by the rules. It also describes someone who has achieved a good station in life based on high personal standards, moral character, or ethical behavior. The present situation may require a vow or commitment. A grace period is involved. For now at least, you can do no wrong. *Reversed.* You may find yourself feeling guilty or confused. Your beliefs about something are holding you back. Someone falls from grace.

For WORK questions. Have faith! Though all the things in your environment are not in your control, do the best you can with what you've got and let the rest take care of itself. Believe! Someone is looking out for you. When in doubt, pray. *Reversed.* Things are not what they seem. A secret comes out of the rumor mill, but don't believe everything you hear.

For LOVE questions. Make a commitment! This is a relationship that is all or nothing. There is no halfway. Pledges, promises, or formal vows are involved. You may even hear wedding bells. True love remains true to its word. If you roam, try not to go too far. A period of celibacy is good for the soul. *Reversed.* A difficult confession is made. Ask to be forgiven. Learn to forget.

For MONEY questions. Tithe! Try to set aside one-tenth of your net income. Take 10 percent off. Or try to get a 10 percent increase. You are asked to contribute to a worthy cause. Help out with a fund-raiser. *Reversed.* Operating funds come up a bit short this month. You may need to ask for an extension on a note or put off a discretionary expense.

For STRATEGY questions. Go for the "Hail Mary" play. You can't plan everything down to the wire. Remain confident and convicted. An opportunity comes in the final seconds. Give it your best shot. *Reversed.* Things may not turn out exactly as you expected. Disappointments are possible. You may have to hold out until the bitter end in order to get what you want.

VI THE LOVERS

This is a card about physical union. *Look at your card.* The Lovers run toward each other in slow motion as the camera pans, their arms open for the coming embrace. This card signifies the true love in your life. It can also describe a would-be suitor, a lover, or someone who must make a difficult choice. An affair of the heart is involved. Look forward to a romantic encounter, perhaps over the weekend. *Reversed.* Someone seems distant. This may be a time of physical separation, emotional drift, or loneliness.

For WORK questions. Consolidate! Staff realignments, mergers, or reorganizations occur. Proposals are made. An offer of employment is extended or renewed. There is a love interest in the workplace. *Reversed.* Coworkers are reluctantly split up. A resignation is handed in. Business and pleasure do not mix.

For LOVE questions. Merge! This relationship adds up, comes together, or simply clicks. Things are said with the eyes. Things are whispered in the dark. A question is popped, and the obvious answer is given. A monumental decision becomes easy in the end. *Reversed.* This is love on the rebound, infatuation, or wishful thinking. It could be a one-night stand. You could be stood up. Or a long relationship could end.

For MONEY questions. Combine resources! Your finances can be leveraged now by consolidation. Joint accounts, joint tax returns, or jointly held property may be involved. Make sure you read the fine print of a legal agreement. *Reversed.* Joint assets are split up. Partners do not agree on the profit split. A handshake deal disintegrates.

For STRATEGY questions. Extend feelers! The situation calls for giving things the once-over or sizing things up. Tact, charm, and diplomacy are involved. But in the process it's best to make your true intentions known. *Reversed.* Someone is not being entirely up-front with you. Be suspicious of sweet nothings.

VII THE CHARIOT

This is a card about opposing forces. Conflict and its resolution are involved. *Look at your card.* The hero of the hour rides at the front of the parade. For the moment peace reigns triumphant, and the balance of power is restored. The Chariot describes a person who comes to the rescue—an athlete, perhaps, or a soldier—or someone who prepares thoroughly, reacts quickly, or performs well under pressure. You deserve some recognition. A new car may be in your future. *Reversed.* Tensions are strained. The stakes are too high. A truce is only temporary.

For WORK questions. Victory! Bonuses, raises, perks, or plaques are handed out. Loyalty and endurance are appreciated, but in the end performance counts. You may be asked to make a speech. A conflict is resolved to your mutual benefit, a common goal is reached with celebration, or a leader emerges from the ranks. *Reversed.* A turf battle brews. Staff grumble. A promotion or raise is delayed. Employees jockey for position.

For LOVE questions. Conquest! In a battle for the heart, yours is won over. Someone in a uniform or dressed fit to kill attracts your attention. Eyes lock across a crowded room. It all seems too good to be true. Enjoy the moment. *Reversed.* The object of your affection may seem bigger than life. Someone is keeping score, and you are one of the touchdowns.

For MONEY questions. Triumph! To achieve your financial goals, divide and conquer. Control over money comes from working through the numbers and creating a plan of attack. An important milestone will soon be reached. *Reversed.* Others stand to gain from your loss. For some reason, you can't seem to get ahead. Accounts are overdrawn. You may have car trouble.

For STRATEGY questions. Dress for success! Your chances are good right now, but you must continue to put your best foot forward. Dress the part. Keep your shoes shined. Throw your hat in the arena. Enlist. The victory promises to be a landslide. *Reversed.* Fame is fleeting. It's important to maintain a semblance of order while the balance of power is restored or a defeat is overcome.

VIII JUSTICE *(In some decks, Card XI)*

This is a card about reaching decisions. *Look at your card.* The judge weighs all the evidence in the scales. Legal precedent is considered, and then the sword of decision comes down. This card describes a person who is a logical or analytical thinker, or someone who upholds or enforces the law. Lawyers, judges, police officers, or critics may be involved. Evidence is collected. Facts and feelings are expressed. A case is presented. A verdict is reached. *Reversed.* There are extenuating circumstances. A decision is postponed or reversed. The jury is still out.

For WORK questions. Play by the rules! Employee agreements are signed, procedures and job descriptions are updated, or long-standing policies are enforced. Performance is reviewed and documented. A test must be passed. Perhaps you will receive your just reward. *Reversed.* A blunder is discovered. A request for time off is denied. Or the rules are bent for somebody else. There is no justice now.

For LOVE questions. Tell the truth, the whole truth! Nothing but the truth will save this relationship. Openness and honesty are called for now. Don't jump to a conclusion until you hear the whole story. Consider your decision carefully and deliver it calmly. *Reversed.* An indiscretion is revealed. The facts don't jibe. There is the shadow of a doubt, and no one benefits from it.

For MONEY questions. Weigh the alternatives! Pros and cons are involved. Consider the pluses and minuses of various investment options or spending plans. Review past financial performance. Identify discretionary expenses to cut. Itemize deductions. Balance your checkbook. *Reversed.* Bills are paid late or monies due you are not received on time. Legal action is contemplated.

For STRATEGY questions. Consider the consequences! You are accountable for your own actions. Make sure that binding agreements are duly executed in writing. Don't cut corners when it comes to getting required permissions in advance. *Reversed.* The ends do not justify the means.

A price may have to be paid later for the decision you reach today. A person's integrity is questioned, or his or her intentions. Be careful whom you trust.

IX THE HERMIT

This is a card about seeking the truth. Time and distance are often involved. *Look at your card.* The Hermit returns from the wilderness to give you his two cents worth. Or The Hermit waits to guide you on your vision quest. This card represents people who are old and wizened or wise beyond their years—visionaries, counselors, advisors, teachers, and others who tend to give good advice. This card could also stand for someone at a distance, a loner or recluse, a monastic, or someone who is good at finding his or her own way around. You can soon expect to see a little light at the end of the tunnel. Perhaps a journey is in store. *Reversed.* The message is not what you wanted to hear. Someone expected at a certain time arrives late or doesn't come at all. It is a dark and stormy night outside. You are stranded somewhere.

For WORK questions. Consult! Advisors are brought in from the outside, specialists are employed, or experts are asked their opinion. An old hand shows you the ropes. You burn the midnight oil in order to meet a deadline or impress the higher-ups. If offered, take a friendly word of advice. *Reversed.* Uncertainty about the future—or a fondness for the past—prevents progress. Good advice is ignored. Bright ideas are thrown out.

For LOVE questions. Abide! The one you await with a candle burning in the window returns. Or the long road leads back to the place where it all began. A pilgrimage to an old haunt may be involved. A time of abstinence begins or ends. You seek expert advice. *Reversed.* A marriage counselor, religious leader, or a Reader and Advisor tells you nothing new. Weather conditions prevent the timely return of a loved one.

For MONEY questions. Divest! Make use of the material assets you have assembled, or else dispose of them. Sacrifice short-term profits for long-term gains. Invest in education, take a self-improvement course, or seek financial advice. *Reversed.* You are in a financial rut. Assets are frozen. Utilities may be shut off for nonpayment.

For STRATEGY questions. Retreat! You will gain new perspective by getting away from it all, having a change of scenery, or getting off by yourself. Take refuge in a secluded place. Or hide out and lie low for a while until things blow over. *Reversed.* There is a risk of solitary confinement. A clandestine meeting enters into the plans. After hours, a secret life is being led. Or someone comes out of the closet.

X WHEEL OF FORTUNE

This is a card about risk. Luck, fate, and change are involved. *Look at your card.* The lucky wheel goes round and round on its axle, and "where she stops . . ." When you spin the wheel, you take your chances. This card describes people who are risk takers or who appear to be lucky by nature—the rich, the successful, the happy. There is a good chance you will soon be feeling on top of the world. The odds turn in your favor. Conditions improve with a change in the seasons. *Reversed.* Your lucky streak ends. The odds oppose a wish of yours. The house wins. Storm clouds blow in. You feel a bit under the weather.

For WORK questions. Anticipate change! Management turnover is likely now. You have a chance to rise up the corporate ladder. New ventures and strategic plans are completed. Investors are sought and found. Cash flow improves. Loans come through. Someone is betting on you. *Reversed.* Boom is followed by bust. There are layoffs or demotions. Revenues or profits take a nosedive. Recession rears its ugly head.

For LOVE questions. Risk getting hurt! This relationship may not be forever, but it will be good to you and for you . . . for as long as it lasts. There is a good possibility you will "get lucky" this weekend. Your love life spices up when the seasons change. You may be lucky with love. *Reversed.* A fling ends suddenly. A romance heads downhill quickly. You fall head over heels for someone who treats you like @#$%.

For MONEY questions. Speculate! The market is guaranteed only to fluctuate. Sometimes it's a bull and sometimes it's a bear. You get by on a wing and a prayer. Deposit accounts, savings bonds, and government securities round out your portfolio and create a reserve. *Reversed.* Hunches fail to pay off. The market crashes. You lose your shirt. You may be tempted to buy a lottery ticket.

For STRATEGY questions. Play the odds! Depend as much on your skill in keeping track of the cards as on the luck of the draw. Minimize your risk by preparing well and considering the "what if's." When going into an uncertain situation, leave room for escape. *Reversed.* Risk aversion stands in the way of your progress. The possibilities pass you by. No gain comes from nothing ventured.

XI STRENGTH (In some decks, Card VIII)

This is a card about mental telepathy. Animal instincts and unspoken feelings are involved. *Look at your card.* The lion tamer calms the beast by looking straight into its eyes. Somehow an understanding passes between them. The raging beast turns into a pussycat. This card represents people who act instinctively, who think intuitively, or who relate well to animals. It describes someone who communicates without speaking, someone who practices gentle persuasion, or someone who has a calm voice. You may be picking up on something a friend is thinking. Something that has been gnawing at your insides suddenly relents. Try to remain calm. *Reversed.* Signals get crossed. There are mixed messages. The mind goes blank. Your stomach growls at an inopportune moment.

For WORK questions. Pat on the back! You deserve, get, or hand out a little stroking for good behavior. You read the boss' mind, the customer walks away satisfied, or a challenging assignment is pulled off. You pass the test. *Reversed.* A mouse roars. More is bitten off than can be chewed. The workplace is a zoo. You walk away with your tail between your legs.

For LOVE questions. Be gentle! You are about to have a close encounter with someone who runs on the wild side. A look passes between you, not a word is spoken, and yet . . . you get the message. Be careful. A friend of yours would like to see you settle down. *Reversed.* Someone's got you by the hair of your chinny-chin-chin. Or, try not to let this one get away.

For MONEY questions. Creature comforts! Funds are automatically withdrawn, deposited, or electronically transferred from one account to another to cover expenses for food, clothing, and shelter. Someone picks up the check for your next meal or helps you out with the rent. *Reversed.* You may need to cut back on luxuries and expensive habits, or in other ways modify your spending behavior. There is no such thing as a free lunch. Never bite the hand that feeds you.

For STRATEGY questions. Give a little, get a little! You may sometimes need to mark your territory, bare your teeth, or puff out your chest to get your point across. But in general, a spirit of cooperation will see you through the day. Sometimes you win by rolling over and playing dead. Sometimes you have to be the mouse that roars. You have to feel your own way. *Reversed.* A voice is raised. Try not to stick your foot in your mouth. You may have to eat your own words.

XII THE HANGED MAN

This is a card about transitions and turning points. *Look at your card.* The Hanged Man is undergoing a rite of passage. He has come to a crossroads. And he must now decide whether to continue following the same path, or to branch off in a different direction. This card describes people who think about their past actions, who try to improve themselves, or who seriously consider their next move. A test of bravery or courage may be required. Preparation, prayer, and meditation come into play. The answer emerges from within. *Reversed.* Someone passes the test. Sacrifice or martyrdom pays off. Public ridicule, self-punishment, or personal humiliation go by the wayside.

For WORK questions. Hang it up! Or hang in there—only you can decide whether it is better to stay where you are. Perhaps the time has come to look for greener pastures or try something entirely different. You mull over a dilemma. Your own stamina is your saving grace. A difficult test is passed. *Reversed.* You have come through a personal sacrifice. Past errors have been surmounted. A light has gone off in your head.

For LOVE questions. Personal preference! A big decision weighs on your mind. You have a choice to make between two people, two different relationships, or two alternate life-styles. You must decide something about and for yourself. The right choice is made. *Reversed.* What have you gotten yourself out of this time? Think twice before you get entangled again. Someone jumps to conclusions.

For MONEY questions. Austerity! Money falls out of your pocket. Funds are tied up. Or you must pay now for something you bought in the past. The time has come to get back on your feet. Changes in spending, investment, or savings patterns are required. Cutbacks are in order. You must remain firm in your newfound resolve. *Reversed.* A sudden realization alters you forever. Your financial situation turns around. You restore your balance.

For STRATEGY questions. Sleep on it! A new idea, proposal, or plan promises to turn things around. Try not to make the same mistakes twice. Get out of a current jam by applying your experience. Close a chapter on the past. Turn over a new leaf. Let a thought incubate 24 hours before acting upon it. *Reversed.* A little white lie prevents others from being hurt. Keep your fingers crossed.

XIII DEATH

This is a card about permanent change. *Look at your card*. Death rides in on a white stallion to claim the life of a fellow who has lived out his days. The sun sets. A eulogy is said. The past is buried. The slate is clean. This card describes someone who is undergoing a dramatic, profound, or radical change; someone who is good at adjusting to change; or someone who is attempting to resist change. The inevitable occurs. A new chapter begins. Someone wants to shield you from reality, but you must go on with your life. *Reversed*. You are grieving over the past; or someone grieves over your loss. The sun rises on a new day. A season of difficulty passes in its proper time.

For WORK questions. Resign yourself! Massive changes shake up the workplace. Terminations occur. People are unexpectedly shuffled. A few heads roll. Or a leader falls. A product line goes into decline or a business is killed off. Arrangements are made in a hurry. Things change for good. *Reversed*. Severance programs go into effect. Transitional arrangements are made. An era ends, and a door is closed forever.

For LOVE questions. Say your good-byes! Someone goes on ahead, leaving you behind, for something comes between you, or sparks that once flew simply no longer ignite. A juncture has been reached in this relationship. You stand to suffer a permanent loss. A friendship runs its course. *Reversed*. Avoid a scene. Shed a few tears in private. Hold what is left silently to yourself.

For MONEY questions. Cash in your chips! It's time to call in your IOUs, convert bonds and securities into hard currency, or make draws against equity stakes or cash values. Residual benefits are distributed in lump sums. You stand the chance of receiving an inheritance. Add up your current assets before you launch new plans. *Reversed*. Plan for the long-term welfare of your heirs and successors. Review insurance policies and monitor retirement funds. Organize your papers. You may be audited.

For STRATEGY questions. Start over from scratch! Clear away the past, clean up after a project is finished, or prepare a fresh surface to build up from. Pay your respects to those who have influenced you. Keep something of sentimental value with you at all times. Someone wants to see you succeed on your own. *Reversed*. There is a skeleton in your closet. In case it gets out, be ready with a quick response. Put your mistakes behind you.

XIV TEMPERANCE

This is a card about dynamics. *Look at your card.* The angel mixes two substances together. A chemical reaction occurs, and presto chango! Something else appears. This card describes someone who is good at working with the things that are just lying around, or someone who seems to know instinctively how to make something out of nothing. Inventors, cooks, and craft enthusiasts come to mind. You can look forward to a period of high creativity and personal growth. An attempt is made to transform the environment. A miracle may soon occur in your life. Wonders never cease to amaze you. *Reversed.* Chemical spills are experienced, or raw materials are depleted. The ecological balance is screwed up. A magic formula produces inconsistent results.

For WORK questions. Walk on water! Someone attempts to create order out of chaos. New strategies are employed. Fresh ideas are sought. A dynamite suggestion is made. You are expected to perform the impossible overnight. A breakthrough occurs suddenly. *Reversed.* The full potential of a fresh, new idea is not realized. A competitor reaches the market first. Or a chemistry experiment blows up.

For LOVE questions. Body chemistry! You find yourself attracted to someone who exudes a special scent. A whiff of cologne turns your head. Someone wants to get close to you. What starts as a physical attraction expands into long-lasting rapport. Body fluids are exchanged. The chemistry works. *Reversed.* Someone is experimenting with your heart, and the experiment doesn't pan out. The earth fails to move as expected. The relationship lacks magic.

For MONEY questions. Leverage your assets! Put your financial resources to work in a way that allows them to grow. Compute your net worth. Channel funds into accounts that produce higher yields. Refinance debt loads at more favorable interest rates. Turn a hobby of yours into a money-maker. *Reversed.* Quit pouring money down the drain. Convert liquid assets into cash reserves. Don't wade into debt any deeper.

For STRATEGY questions. Synergy! This is a situation that requires you to mix and match existing components into something new, bigger, or better. More than one variable is involved in coming up with the winning solution. The problem requires you to go out on a limb or take a dynamic approach. Scientific principles may be involved. Test your hypothesis in a controlled way. Someone expects you to demonstrate results. *Reserved.* Vent steam. Make full use of the by-products resulting from your work. Recycle your best ideas. Clean up your own messes.

XV THE DEVIL

This is a card about entrapment. *Look at your card.* The Devil keeps a naked man and woman as his slaves. They remain tethered to him because they are afraid to make a break for freedom. This card describes someone who feels helpless, someone who is oppressed, or someone who can't see a way out of a bad situation. Binding legal agreements, promises made a long time ago, or a masochistic sense of duty may be involved. The current situation has you kowtowing to someone else, yet no viable option presents itself. Someone has you right where he or she wants you. Your own beliefs are limiting you. *Reversed.* Get out while you still can. Existing relationships are redefined for the better. A bad situation is escaped just in the nick of time. You walk a fine line.

For WORK questions. Trapped! You have sold your time to a company that now thinks it owns you. If you think there is a real possibility for getting ahead with these people, think again. You might as well be working for the devil himself. Apply for other work just as soon as you can. This job is going nowhere fast. *Reversed.* Allegations go back and forth. Legal action is threatened. Anything you gain comes at a huge price.

For LOVE questions. Mental cruelty! You are being used. Someone wants to control you, body and soul. Verbal or sexual abuse, physical threats, or games of dominance and submission are all distinct possibilities. Perhaps your friend is sick, but that's beside the point. Get out while you still can. Fend for yourself. *Reversed.* You walk a fine line. A relationship gets out of hand.

For MONEY questions. A slave to money! You are living way beyond your means, gambling too much, or spending too much on bad habits. Perhaps your house or car is a money pit. At any rate, you are caught in a downward spiral. Materialism has sucked you in. Bankruptcy may look like the only answer now, but it would be better to learn how to dig your way out. Seek professional help. *Reversed.* You are so enamored of having money in the bank that you live a life of poverty. It's your money, but be careful of the dark allure of the almighty dollar.

For STRATEGY questions. Get it in writing! Document informal agreements, but before signing, take time to read the fine print. Enact the escape clauses on deals that have gone bad. Stand up for your rights. *Reversed.* Plot your escape from the things that hold you back. Work on your self-image. Discard the beliefs that hold you back or keep you "in your place."

XVI THE TOWER

This is a card about electrical impulses. *Look at your card.* A bolt of lightning strikes the lid off The Tower. Two people—knocked off by the shock—are now falling headlong into the abyss. This card describes someone who is subject to fits of inspiration, mental lapses, or visions. Perhaps you work with computers or electronic equipment. Electricians, deejays, or paramedics may be involved. In the near future you can expect to pick up some static, to be shocked into your senses, or to witness a shocking event. An idea suddenly comes to you in the shower. One heck of a storm blows through your part of the world. *Reversed.* Someone attempts to light a fire under you. The "acts of God" clause in your insurance policy is invoked. You are shocked by what you hear on the radio or TV.

For WORK questions. People in high places! The high and mighty have spoken. The confidence of staff is eroded by a scandal that gets around via electronic mail. Or a sudden change in management leaves you temporarily without a boss. Someone wants to make sure you get the message. The phone rings off the hook. *Reversed.* The computer network goes down unexpectedly, leaving everyone helpless. Work or school is called off on account of the storm. Or, lucky day, you get to participate in a fire drill.

For LOVE questions. Was it good for you, too? Earthquakes, thunderstorms, waves crashing on the beach in the wake of Hurricane Bob, tornadoes swirling on the open plains . . . You get the idea. This is a relationship that makes you feel pretty good. *Reversed.* Not quite, but almost. Perhaps you've had a falling out. You're pretty much left to your own devices. The phone rings unexpectedly.

For MONEY questions. Red alert! Money is burning a hole through your pocket again. Wait for the next going-out-of-business sale to get the best deal. Save enough to insure everything against fire, theft, or loss. Or charge it on something that assures you buyer protection. *Reversed.* The computer denies your credit card. Funds are misapplied during an ATM transaction. Hang on to your receipts.

For STRATEGY questions. Kiss it good-bye! Loss and destruction are real possibilities unless you think fast. The ground is coming up quicker than you think—you could fall flat on your face. This situation is about to explode or collapse into itself. Seek cover at the first sign of imminent danger. *Reversed.* Back up all important documents on the computer. Prepare disaster plans just in case.

XVII THE STAR

This is a card about cosmic consciousness. *Look at your card.* A prolific Universe pours out the "waters of life." Above her head, in a dramatic grand finale, a supernova in a cluster of companion stars glows with the combined light of the entire Universe before it finally sputters out. This card describes people who live up to their highest potential, people who have great hopes, or people who are particularly well suited to their environment. You may be regarded as a rising star or a big fish. Somebody thinks you can walk on water. A lot of things are going on at once. *Reversed.* There is the distinct possibility of burnout. You are wasting too much of your limited energy supply.

For WORK questions. Priorities! Many things are competing for your interest or attention. Focus on the things that matter most, and dispense with the rest with one hand tied behind your back. Even efforts that come to nothing have their purpose. Success tends to come to those who plant the most seeds. *Reversed.* You are spreading yourself too thin. It is difficult to juggle both a career and a family.

For LOVE questions. Companionship! Most stars make their way through the heavens accompanied by a companion. It is time you sought out yours. Or perhaps you need to take this opportunity to renew the commitment you have made to your soul mate. Someone looks at you with starry eyes. *Reversed.* You may have a little something going on the side, but your heart belongs to the one you chose forever.

For MONEY questions. Cash flow! Money enters your life in a steady stream, but flows away just as quickly. Most of it goes for current living expenses, but a little bit is squandered or set aside for later. The situation requires you to manage both sides of the equation. Protect your sources of income. Watch your expenses. Manage to the bottom line. *Reversed.* The money dries up. Savings are dipped into, if not already depleted. Your income is fixed.

For STRATEGY questions. Consult the stars! Make full use of the limited energy available to you by deciding about how best to spend your time. Apply yourself. Focus on the goals that matter most to you. Put other interests and distractions out of mind. Let your energy flow. Track performance over time. *Reversed.* You burn your candle at both ends. You cannot go on like this. Consult your horoscope today.

XVIII THE MOON

This is a card about endless cycles. *Look at your card*. It is a Full Moon that rises here, bringing the dogs out to bay and driving the sea creatures into mating frenzy. This card describes people who follow their instincts, people who like a strong beat to dance to, and people who adore the sea. Poets, painters, and performing artists are involved. Magic, music, and interesting people flow through your life. Schedules, calendars, and clocks are critical to you. You are inclined to act on impulse and to think intuitively. A psychic experience has recently occurred. Perhaps your cards are really hot tonight. *Reversed*. A lunar eclipse occurs. An era, epic, or period in your life comes to its end. Your routine is interrupted. Your schedule is off.

For WORK questions. Time management! Break up your day into its component parts and pace yourself according to your own daily rhythm. Keep track of how you spend your time. Note the things you have written on your calendar. Someone wants you to go out prowling with him or her after work. Mix business with pleasure. *Reversed*. Stop watching the clock.

For LOVE questions. Wild thing, you make my ... ! Howling, prowling, maybe even dancing in the streets—you name it. Anything goes when the moon is full. It's a night for driving around in your car. Nobody gets much sleep. Someone comes on to you. *Reversed*. By Quarter Moon you will be interested in someone or something entirely different. Take a glance in the mirror.

For MONEY questions. Interest rates, spot points, and stock quotes go up and down with the tides. Your own funds shrink away at the same rate as they grow. Lucky for you, there's another payday coming in another couple of weeks. Your financial situation diminishes and improves as often as the phases of the moon. And yet you always seem to have enough to get by. *Reversed*. Mostly it's the cost of living that soaks up all your dough. What's money for, anyhow?

For STRATEGY questions. Consult the cards! In dealing with your current situation, you need to feel your own way, go with your instincts, or follow your hunches and gut feelings. The answer that you seek will come in the morning, if not in the cards tonight. Sleep on it. *Reversed*. Shed your skin. Crawl out of your shell. Dream your troubles away. Follow your natural rhythm.

XIX THE SUN

This is a card about personal freedom. *Look at your card.* It is summer. The naked child rides bareback through the garden on a gray mare as the sun rises up over the garden wall. This card represents people who are only as old as they feel, innocent children, and free spirits. Close relationships with nature are involved. Perhaps you relate well to plants or are a "sun worshiper." Things measured in seasons and years are involved . . . and a strong sense of independence. You have been given a free rein lately, you are testing your wings, or you are feeling footloose and fancy-free. A ride through the country would do your soul a world of good. Work in the soil. Stretch out in the sun. *Reversed.* Draw back on the reins. Settle down. Get out of the sun before you burn.

For WORK questions. Rise and shine! Get an early start on the day, try having something different for breakfast, wear something new, or take a different route to work. Take time to look at the scenery on the way. On the job, try out fresh ideas or new approaches to old problems. Someone wants to see you strut your stuff. Show what you can do. *Reversed.* Leave early or stay late to avoid the rush-hour traffic. Tone down your appearance, or work on the way you present yourself.

For LOVE questions. Ride it out! This relationship happens spontaneously and burns with a bright flame. Everything is out in the open. What you see is what you get. Let it run its course. Someone invites you for a day out of doors, perhaps to an amusement park or playground. Don't be afraid to let your hair down. *Reversed.* Something goes on "behind the barn" or in a parked car. Hold your horses.

For MONEY questions. The sky's the limit! Pull out your wallet, checkbook, or credit cards for a shopping spree or major purchase. Something with plenty of horsepower or a canvas top tempts you. Or perhaps it's time to spruce up the house, landscape the yard, outfit the kids, or furnish a nursery. A big feed is put on for the entire family or all your friends. Buy a little something on impulse. *Reversed.* Cut back on out-of-pocket expenses, especially for clothes.

For STRATEGY questions. Fly by the seat . . . ! Go as the spirit moves you. Approach the world with the innocence and the enthusiasm of a child at play. Whistle, laugh, or sing your way through the day. And don't worry about tomorrow—it will take care of itself. *Reversed.* It is easier to ask for forgiveness than for permission. Live and learn from your slipups.

XX JUDGEMENT

This is a card about destiny. *Look at your card.* The sky opens, the trumpet sounds, and the dead rise from their graves to answer the question: What have you learned? This card describes people who are facing a final decision about something very critical in their lives. Students awaiting grade cards, employees waiting to hear about a raise, or patients awaiting the results of tests are possibilities. Prayers may come into play. Perhaps you feel as if something is a matter of life and death. A letter or telephone call seals your fate one way or the other, but how you respond to the news is what gives you control over your own destiny. A surprise is in store for you. *Reversed.* The awaited news does not come, is delayed for a considerable time, or is different than you had hoped. Something gets lost in the shuffle. You remember the dead.

For WORK questions. The last stand! This is it—the final attempt, the final decision, or the final resolution. The business booms or busts. All rise or fall, depending on how they've performed in the past and what they're made of now. A mixed message suddenly becomes blindingly clear. The bottom line is revealed. You see now what it was all leading to or how it all ends. A decision is made for you. *Reversed.* "Is that all there is?" You wish you could go back and do it all over again. You wish you had known then what you know now.

For LOVE questions. Voice from the past! A long-lost love reenters your life. Soon you will share a very special experience with a dear friend. Good news is heard. An engraved invitation is received. *Reversed.* A long-standing relationship ends. Things blurted out are actually meant. The news cuts you to the marrow. You want to curl up and die.

For MONEY questions. Manna from heaven! Money suddenly comes to you from out of the blue . . . and it's just enough. The check arrives just in the nick of time. Your material troubles end. Your tab is covered. Your accounts are cleared. Congratulations. *Reversed.* An inheritance is received—or is it a legacy of debt and excess? You come out of it with not even the shirt on your back. It could all go down the tubes.

For STRATEGY questions. The bitter end! Your struggle is about to be over. You have done everything you can, and it's too late to go back and do anything else or do anything differently. All you can do now is wait for the verdict. At last it will be decided once and for all. All in all, the news is good. *Reversed.* You cannot prepare for everything. Neither can you live up to every expectation or second-guess the critics.

XXI THE WORLD

This is a card about rebirth and reincarnation. *Look at your card.* The soul dances within an egg—the symbol of fertility. The Universe is constantly recycling itself. This card describes people who have lived many lives before, people who have done many things in their current lives, or people who have lived for many years. This card signals the start of a new life. You are going through an emotional or spiritual rebirth. It is the new you that will emerge from this metamorphosis. Happy birthday. Happy Bar Mitzvah. *Reversed.* You are thinking of breaking camp, of going somewhere else in order to get a fresh start. A karmic debt or two may remain to be settled before you make your final exit. You are invited to a farewell party. Happy New Year. Happy New You.

For WORK questions. Give it a year! An entire season, cycle, or sequence needs to be completed before you can get a true reading of this employment situation or a better feeling for your chosen line of work. You have great potential, but it takes the right conditions for anything to grow. Use the next 12 months—use the next 13 moons—to see how it goes. *Reversed.* This particular line of work or employer may not suit you in the long run, but—what the heck—you can use the experience. Build up your kit of personal survival skills.

For LOVE questions. April love! Everything in your life seems fresh and new again. There has never been a spring like this before—or a summer, fall, or winter for that matter. And it is all because of the new love in your life. This is the real thing. *Reversed.* September love! You never thought you'd feel this way again, certainly not at this stage in your life. Love is always better the second time around. This, too, is the real thing.

For MONEY questions. The financial year! It's time to start a new ledger, set up a new budget, or open a new set of books. A calendar year starts or a new fiscal year begins. You are optimistic about the potential of the next 12 months (or 13 moons). You have a year to prove the outcome for yourself. *Reversed.* The monthly or year-to-date figures are less favorable than you originally projected. Adjustments are needed now if you are going to catch up to your goals by the end of the year.

For STRATEGY questions. Things take time! You can't judge a book by its title. And you can't foresee the outcome of your life's work. What you can do is this: Plant seeds. Water. Wait. Give ideas a chance to incubate. Give efforts a chance to take hold. Give seeds a chance to grow.

Some attempts will flourish and some attempts will not. Give it your best shot. That's all that's required of you. That's all you can ever do. *Reversed.* If at first you don't succeed . . .

ACE OF WANDS

This is a card about opportunities that knock at your door. *Look at your card.* A hand bursts forth from the clouds bearing a budding club. Since the Wands are about the things we do for a living, this fertility symbol is a good sign that your career prospects are looking up. You will be very productive in your chosen line of work. You can't believe your luck. *Reversed.* Thumbs down on a particular career prospect. If you proceed with an idea, you will have to pull it all off on your own.

For WORK questions. Offers! You can expect to receive an offer of employment. A promotion may be handed out or a special assignment given. Students are accepted to the schools where they have applied. Athletes and soldiers are drafted. Jobbers and free-lancers receive contracts or orders. *Reversed.* Applications are turned down. Work is hard to find. Or you hold out for a better offer.

For LOVE questions. Favors! A close friend offers you a job in exchange for something else or in repayment for the past. You may be asked to perform a favor. Someone is hitting on you at work. Or, someone from your arts and crafts class asks you out. *Reversed.* An innocent-sounding invitation from the boss may turn out to be something else. Business and pleasure do not mix.

For MONEY questions. Pay hikes! Cost-of-living raises go into effect, bonuses are handed out, or merit increases take effect. Even after taxes and deductions, the net improves. A retroactive adjustment by Payroll puts a little extra in your pocket. Allowances are raised for improving grades or doing chores around the house. *Reversed.* You may be asked to take a cut in order to remain on the payroll. Or your net pay goes down as a result of onetime retroactive adjustments or new deductions. Tuition rates soar.

For STRATEGY questions. Opportunity knocks! Offers like these don't come along every day. When the door of opportunity opens up a crack, at least peek in. Apply for openings. Go to interviews. You never know unless you try. *Reversed.* Possibilities are ruled out in advance. Due to the limitations you place on yourself, a door is closed to you before it even had the chance to open up.

2 OF WANDS

This is a card about strategic alliances. *Look at your card.* The prince in this picture looks out upon his piece of the world with thoughts of expanding his influence or the size of his territory. He has the choice of attempting to do it all himself, but he will probably call others in to help. You, too, will be successful in pursuing your own ambitions with the support and cooperation of others. People in high or faraway places are involved. *Reversed.* Your own ambitions come head to head against another's. Needed support does not come in time.

For WORK questions. Partnership! Achieving your own goals requires you to play well with others. Teams are formed. Group assignments are made. Alliances are negotiated. Joint ventures are outlined. Cooperative bargains are struck. Or partnerships are formed. You have an important ally at a distance. *Reversed.* Others do not always share your vision or appreciate what things need to be done. Stick to your own agenda. Go it alone.

For LOVE questions. Marriage of convenience! This relationship is based on something other than love. It may be a union that helps advance someone's status, career, or social ambitions. To be successful for any length of time, such a deal needs to benefit both partners equally. You pass by each other in the hall. You hear from someone at a distance. *Reversed.* Someone is attempting to use you. Perhaps it's time to go your separate ways.

For MONEY questions. Backing! Expansion plans are financed by loans, donations, or promises to share the proceeds later. Fund-raising activities are undertaken. Somebody at a distance puts up the capital, bankrolls the deal, or underwrites the production. Someone else's property (or cosignature) may be needed as collateral to finance a joint undertaking. *Reversed.* Financing falls through at the last moment. Backers withdraw their support. The time comes to pay up.

For STRATEGY questions. Alliance! Most people do not have the personal resources, the range of skills, or the wherewithal to make it big on their own. If you want to climb the ladder, you will most likely need to do it by networking, striking bargains with others, playing politics, or making use of all your connections. Seek out those who share your vision and whose desires overlap with yours. *Reversed.* In accepting the support of others, you open yourself up to meddling. There are too many cooks in the kitchen.

3 OF WANDS

This is a card about products and productivity. *Look at your card*. The merchant stands on a hillside watching his fleet go out to sea loaded with exports. They will return some time later with imported goods. You find yourself involved in work that deals with the manufacture, distribution, or sale of products on the open market. Soon you will travel across state lines or international borders in order to pursue career or academic interests. *Reversed*. There is an upset in the balance of trade. Your industry is suffering from temporary overproduction or recession. Travel plans are put on hold.

For WORK questions. Quotas! Input and output are measured on the job. Inventories are taken. Orders are delivered and filled. And, in general, merchandise is moved. But someone is always watching over your shoulder. Strive for excellence. *Reversed*. Quality takes second place to volume. The goods delivered are shoddy and overpriced. The customer complains. Inventory is marked down for quick sale.

For LOVE questions. Packaging! Appearance counts. You may need to dress the part in order to attract the sort of date you're looking for or to hang on to your current mate. Clothes, cosmetics, and personal hygiene products come into play. You may have to travel to the mall to find exactly what you're looking for. Something special you sent for in the mail is winging its way. *Reversed*. The current styles don't suit you. Return items that don't fit. Mix and match products to develop your own look.

For MONEY questions. Let's make a deal! Shop around until you find what you're looking for on sale, deal with a contact who can get things at wholesale, or barter with the clerk for a discount. Join consumer clubs and co-ops in order to stretch your consumer buying power. Save credit for things that last longer than their installments. *Reversed*. Get a rain check for advertised sale items that are out of stock. Something you've sent for is back-ordered until the supplier delivers.

For STRATEGY questions. Productivity! The game is to get as much as you can for as little as possible. This is how business works in producing and delivering goods. This is how consumers must behave in order to live on their income. Price is the critical factor in economics of this type. In business, deliver value for the money. At consumer levels, insist on quality for the price. You strike a hard bargain, but it is accepted. *Reversed*. You can't even give away a bad product. Let the buyer beware.

4 OF WANDS

This is a card about celebrations. *Look at your card.* A party is being held or a ceremony has just been conducted under the bower. Restaurant workers, hotel staff, repair people, clergy, and grounds keepers may be involved. You would like a job with lots of people contact or that requires public relations skills. Perhaps you will soon be asked to participate in organizing or attending some kind of social event. *Reversed.* The level of service provided does not measure up to expectations. The arrangements for an event get all screwed up.

For WORK questions. Opening night! The work you have chosen brings you in contact with all sorts of people with widely varying personalities and expectations. You are evaluated on your performance and on the number of complaints or compliments received about you. You will soon need to attend to something on the spot and on the double. Showing up on time counts, but you also need to play your part well. As they say in the theater, break a leg. *Reversed.* It's impossible to satisfy all of the people all of the time. A performance receives bad reviews.

For LOVE questions. Wedding bells! If you're in the market for a date, there's no better place to shop than at a wedding . . . unless, of course, it's yours. Get a haircut and have your shoes shined or your nails done. When a special occasion is celebrated, be sure to dress the part. The look you want to go for is the look that appeals to those you want to impress or attract. *Reversed.* Attending a special occasion gives you nothing to write home about. Perhaps you are overdressed.

For MONEY questions. Personalized attention! Attend grand openings, open houses, or business anniversary bashes in order to meet people you want to do business with. Select a bank that does more than take your money. Choose a realtor, tax service, doctor, lawyer, or travel agent who understands that you are the customer. *Reversed.* Check your next order carefully before you leave the drive-through window. If you pay for full service, make sure you get full service.

For STRATEGY questions. Common courtesy! A big smile makes a difference even when answering the phone. Pleases and thank yous go a long way. Be sure to thank your host or hostess for their hospitality. *Reversed.* Sometimes you may have to pretend that you're in a good mood or that you are having a better time than you actually are.

5 OF WANDS

This is a card about competition. *Look at your card.* Two boys pit their strength against three others in this joust. In terms of numbers, they are not fairly matched, but such is life. Still, there's no telling who the winner will be. You are up against some stiff competition yourself. A sporting event or contest may be involved. Someone wants to see you slug it out. You may need to prove yourself. *Reversed.* The best "man" does not always win. An internal conflict threatens to get the better of you.

For WORK questions. Strife! Labor does not see eye to eye with management, bickering and feuding divide the ranks, or fights break out on the playground. An aggressive competitor arises. You face a test of physical strength or a battle of the wits. Your team prepares for the play-offs. Your company fights for survival in the marketplace. *Reversed.* Unfair competition. Someone is bending the rules. The playing field is less than level. You suffer a blow below the belt.

For LOVE questions. Rivalry! Multiple suitors fight over you or show off to get your attention. A good friend helps you defend your honor or restore your good name. You play the field or run with a group of close friends. A physical relationship may be involved. You get together in the gym or at a sporting event. You may be asked on a double date. *Reversed.* Internal conflict divides you. An important choice or decision is complicated by mixed emotions. A love interest estranges former friends.

For MONEY questions. High stakes! You're asked to put your money where your mouth is. Keeping up with the Joneses (or playing with the big boys) may involve getting in over your head. Competing wants and needs vie for your limited financial resources. You may have to struggle to make ends meet. *Reversed.* Bills mount up. Creditors are beating a path to your door. You are tempted to wager on a sporting event or risk your entire purse on a single outcome. The deck is stacked against you.

For STRATEGY questions. Strength in numbers! When going up against a strong rival, it's a good idea to have help beside you or reinforcements waiting in the wings. Preparing offensive maneuvers and defensive strategies in advance can't hurt. A good mental attitude comes into play. Psych up for the big game. *Reversed.* If attacked, hold your ground, think fast, and do some fancy footwork. Sometimes bluffing works.

6 OF WANDS

This is a card about campaigns. *Look at your card.* A captain leads his troops back from a successful mission. The victory parade in full regalia passes by, and everyone is cheering. You can expect to triumph in a current business, athletic, or scholastic undertaking. A victory celebration is involved. *Reversed.* The mission proves impossible, or fails by a narrow margin. A celebration is tainted by some bad news. The price of the victory was too high.

For WORK questions.
Sales promotion! Discounts, giveaways, premiums, incentives, and limited-time offers are involved in an effort to boost sales. The workplace is decorated for a real or mock celebration. You may be required to wear the team colors or a special uniform. You can expect to triumph in an upcoming competition. *Reversed.* Things calm down following a flurry of activity. Promotional campaigns bomb. A special event turns out to be a dud.

For LOVE questions.
Public relations! Public displays of affection are involved in this relationship. You are enamored of a public figure, someone who occupies a high position, or someone who wears a uniform. A rock star, movie great, or professional athlete may serve as your idol or hero. You are invited to see someone you care about compete, perform, or receive an award. In turn, you are rewarded for your loyalty. You triumph in a relationship. *Reversed.* Something unsavory is exposed about your hero. An affair becomes public knowledge. You may be subjected to ridicule.

For MONEY questions.
Advertising! Watch the newspaper for announcements of sales events, special offers, or giveaways. Changes in the stock market are signaled by the news of political events. Strong performance on the job improves your bank balance if you blow your own horn a bit. Efforts to raise cash are successful now. You triumph over money. *Reversed.* Financial programs fall short of their mark. Plans to raise funds are aborted.

For STRATEGY questions.
Plan of attack! In order to achieve your goals, you first of all need to define what they are. Once you understand the purpose of your mission, you will be in a good position to assess the situation and come up with a plan of attack. Success comes mostly to those who prepare. If you make the extra effort, you will triumph in your current undertakings. *Reversed.* Unforeseen circumstances stymie your efforts. It is time to retrench. Put contingency plans into effect.

7 OF WANDS

This is a card about positioning. *Look at your card.* A man who appears larger than life holds his ground against invasion. By his words, his actions, and his body language, he communicates exactly where he stands. You may need to protect your turf, defend your views, or rally people to your battle cry. Someone envies your courage. *Reversed.* You are outnumbered. Your views are unpopular. Your territory is too weakly defined. Your soft spots are uncovered.

For WORK questions. Turf battles! Divisional barriers, departmental lines, or job descriptions are subject to challenge. Things are a little shaky right now at work or school. You may need to speak your piece before a matter can be resolved. The boss wants you to get behind the program. Always take the high ground. Fight to keep your position. *Reversed.* It's a different day, but the same old !@#$. Some things never change.

For LOVE questions. Standoffs! A line of suitors forms at your door. You have to beat them off with a stick or put up a good line of defense against unwanted advances. A big daddy or big brother reads the riot act. Explain your position. Remain firm in your resolve. If it's no you want to say, just say no. *Reversed.* Mace may be involved, or a flying kick to the groin. Your privacy may be invaded.

For MONEY questions. Property lines! Deeded land and real estate are playing a big role in your life right now. Others want to buy your land, take your property away for a song, or bully you into selling. Keep up your monthly payments. Property surveys are worth the price of harmony with your neighbors. Someone may approach you about donating money to a civic crusade. *Reversed.* Protect your investment with added insulation, additional landscaping, or natural barriers. Hedge against inflation.

For STRATEGY questions. Rally! To establish your position, territory, or moral purpose, you must define *and* defend it. You must champion your rights or your cause with a vengeance. To make sure you win, rally the support of others—get your ducks lined up. Detractors and attackers will surely come. Be ready and waiting for them with your best ammunition. *Reversed.* Your reputation is at stake. Just how far are you willing to go to hang on to what you've got? Gird your loins for an upcoming battle.

8 OF WANDS

This is a card about projects. Goals and targets are involved. *Look at your card.* Eight arrows sail toward an unseen target. Whether these projectiles hit or miss the mark has already been determined by the throw, for sometimes it is all in the wrist. You have launched a lot of projects of your own recently. There are a lot of things up in the air. You are waiting to see how something turns out. *Reversed.* You are aiming for something that is out of sight. You simply have too many irons in the fire. Or something may boomerang or backfire on you.

For WORK questions.
Goals! Many things vie for your attention. The mailbox overflows. The fax machine rings off the hook. There are many conflicting goals and competing interests at play. And there is always enough busywork to go around. Keep sight of your corporate purpose. Dispense your duties with efficiency. Launch long-term projects. Aim for realistic targets. *Reversed.* Details you overlooked come back to haunt you. The workplace lacks a common sense of purpose. Projects miss their mark.

For LOVE questions.
Ongoing interests! This relationship involves something of an Olympic nature. It just goes on and on. It hits the nail right on the head. It's on the money. The two of you share a common wavelength, a similar past experience, or various interests. In general, your separate lives take you in parallel directions. You may be invited to a track-and-field event or to a marathon. *Reversed.* The two of you have been through a lot together or have shared a lot of things, but perhaps the time has come for you to go your separate ways. Or it's possible you bump into someone with whom you share a past.

For MONEY questions.
Installments! Things like car loans, revolving accounts, mortgage payments, and other accounts that must be paid on time are involved. It may seem like everything is due at once this month. Perhaps money due you is coming in the mail. You may launch new money-making projects in your spare time. *Reversed.* You may have been shortchanged. IOUs are called in. Your supplemental income dips.

For STRATEGY questions.
Give them all you've got! One way to get someone's attention is to fire off a barrage. Deluge the market with resumes. Submit lots of ideas or proposals, and volunteer for extra assignments. The more projects you have in the works, the greater the odds that something will hit. A winning idea comes to you. *Reversed.* The recipient of your own barrage fires back at you. Your efforts add up to overkill. You've got more things going than you can handle.

9 OF WANDS

This is a card about duties. *Look at your card.* The wounded sentry stands watch over a besieged fort. Nothing gets in the way of him fulfilling his duty. No doubt you have obligations to perform, too. Someone on active reserve may be involved. Perhaps you are on call in case there's an emergency. You are expected to take your responsibilities seriously. *Reversed.*

You have let down your defenses. Someone has been sleeping on the job or shirking his or her duty. If you are not careful, someone will trick you.

For WORK questions. Mind your post! You have a job where you have to ask permission to go to the potty. Work involving a shift, a tour of duty, or a fixed starting and ending time may be involved. You are expected to be on time, every time. And no excuses. You need to keep up your guard at work or school. Your degree of loyalty or dedication to the job is being tested, but passing a test is not so important as not failing it. *Reversed.* You may have to put in overtime or perform double duty for a while. You feel like your job is demanding too much of you.

For LOVE questions. Mind your p's & q's! There may be jealousy involved in this guarded relationship. Someone wants to make sure you remain loyal, that you do not cross over an imaginary line, or that you do not get too close until it's certain you can be trusted. Personal secrets, military intelligence, or trade secrets may be involved. Perhaps you have been asking too many questions . . . or telling too much. *Reversed.* The cat gets out of the bag, and you are suspected of letting it loose. Or you get in trouble because of something your friend did or did not do. Someone is telling tales on you.

For MONEY questions. Meet your obligations! Protect your sources of income, guard your savings, or maintain your credit rating. These may well be times of austerity, but, more or less, all's quiet on the financial front. While you're ahead, stash a little money around the house, just in case of an emergency. Keep a stiff upper lip. *Reversed.* Be suspicious of strangers who approach you for help over the next few days; they may have ulterior motives. Carry a little mad money in your shoe. Get back on your budget.

For STRATEGY questions. Keep your eyes open! In this situation you really can't trust anyone—or be too careful. Exert discretion, follow instructions to a T, stay alert, and be careful. Guard the secrets that are entrusted to you. Use a secret password or speak in code. Don't be fooled by diversionary tactics. *Reversed.* You may need to go underground for a while, or sneak behind enemy lines to find out what you need to know. If you need to get around someone, create a diversion.

10 OF WANDS

This is a card about burdens to bear. *Look at your card.* At the end of the day, the worker carries home the results of his labor. It looks like it's been a good day for gathering firewood—almost too good, in fact. Weary from his effort, the worker trudges along. Perhaps you've been putting in a lot of hours lately or have been allowing your work to get to you. Make sure that one last straw doesn't break you back. *Reversed.* Seek work that makes you want to sing or whistle. If you're going to put in so much effort, you might as well enjoy what you're doing.

For WORK questions.
Work loads! Your employer's expectations of you are too high, or your teacher has loaded you down with homework. Just as likely, you have taken on an additional burden yourself, turned a molehill into a mountain, or become committed to too many extracurriculars. Overachievers or workaholics may be involved. Your responsibilities are stretching you to the limit. *Reversed.* Lighten up before your job consumes you and you lose everything else. Take a weight off your shoulders or a load off your feet. Always lift from your knees.

For LOVE questions.
Mouths to feed! This relationship requires a lot of effort to keep it going. Perhaps there are children involved or older people to attend to. At any rate, family obligations seem to tie you down. Perhaps someone is heaping a lot of blame on you—or you may be heaping guilt on yourself. You need to get away from it for a while to gain some perspective. *Reversed.* You are having a hard time seeing your way clear. You ask yourself, What's it all about? You may be tempted to chuck it all. Careful not to get a hernia.

For MONEY questions.
Roof over your head! Your primary residence, beach house, or RV is making you a slave to the monthly payments, the repair bills, and the insurance costs. Or you find yourself working at a dead-end job just to keep up the standard of living you have grown accustomed to. It's time to step back and reassess whether all this stuff is everything it's cracked up to be. Are your possessions making you happy? *Reversed.* You work for the day when you will retire. Invest in a physical before you perform hard labor.

For STRATEGY questions.
Pedal to the metal! You're in a situation that requires plenty of muscle, elbow grease, or strenuous mental activity. Impossible deadlines may be involved. The amount of effort that is required and the output that is desired may stretch the human potential to its limits. This is a job that calls for reinforcements. See if you can get some help. *Reversed.* Put one foot in front of the other—just a little while longer. You're almost there. You can do it. You can make it.

PAGE OF WANDS

This is a card about official communications. *Look at your card.* The blond messenger stands waiting for the crowd to gather so he can deliver the news that has been dispatched with him. Someone may have something to tell you. More likely, you are about to receive some important news that relates to your studies, your job, or your career. Keep your ears cocked. *Reversed.* An awaited message about work or school is delayed, not sent at all, not entirely clear, or different from what you expected to hear.

For WORK questions.
Take a memo! Official correspondence, memoranda, or notices are prepared, sent, and received. A job in communications may be involved. You may have luck finding employment by reading the want ads this week or chasing down leads on the grapevine. You hear a piece of important news via official channels. *Reversed.* Someone gets the story backward. The news is not what it appears to be or not what you wanted to hear. Don't kill the blue-eyed messenger.

For LOVE questions.
An unsolicited testimonial! You have been telling others about the love of your life. Or the love of your life has been telling others about you. All in all, a favorable review is given, maybe right down to the intimate details. Others are a little envious of you . . . and a little jealous. Who's the blonde in your life? *Reversed.* A bit of gossip reaches your ear, but don't believe it. Someone just wants to see your reaction. In your response, be careful not to reveal what's really going on.

For MONEY questions.
Take notice! Amid that avalanche of direct-mail catalogs, free circulars, and perennial bills that fills your mailbox, an important notice lies buried. At work you are reimbursed for a business-related expense, or news about your salary or benefits is announced. Perhaps you have applied for a loan. If so, you will hear about it shortly—the news looks good. *Reversed.* The bill collectors just won't quit hounding you with past-due notices. Notify your bank in writing—as required—of billing errors or discrepancies in your account, but don't expect to get a written response.

For STRATEGY questions.
Word of mouth! The situation you are in requires you to get your point of view—or your side of the story—across quickly. Use the telephone, fax machine, or electronic mail to get the word out to as many people as possible. For even faster results, call a reporter or tell a couple of people who are well connected on the grapevine. *Reversed.* The rumors circulating on the network are a red herring. Someone has planted them to distract your attention from what's really going on.

KNIGHT OF WANDS

This is a card about aggressive behavior. Impulsive actions may be involved. *Look at your card.* A knight in shining armor dashes in on his charging steed. This card may signal the need for you to be more aggressive in pursuing your own career, financial, or love interests. You may have the sudden opportunity to travel. Dress for the occasion. Someone sweeps you off your feet. *Reversed.* Your hero turns out to be more talk than action. Get both feet planted firmly on the ground. Watch out for flat tires.

For WORK questions. Rarin' to go! You hit the ground running; you zoom to work as fast as the car in front of you will allow; or you charge into the office bright-eyed, bushy-tailed, and ready for whatever challenge awaits you. Answer the want ad that seeks an "aggressive self-starter." Look for work that involves travel. Snap up an opportunity that comes out of left field. *Reversed.* You are spinning your wheels. Check the tread on your tires. Beware the blond wonder.

For LOVE questions. Hot to trot! This is a relationship that's in a hurry or in which you are aggressively pursued by your suitor. The two of you find yourselves swept up in it—one of you, at least, gets carried away. A quick trip down a dusty country lane may be involved or a car that comes to a sudden halt in a remote place. A platinum blonde knocks your socks off. *Reversed.* You are tempted to pick up a stranded motorist. A good Samaritan comes to your rescue when your car breaks down.

For MONEY questions. Born to charge! Visa, MasterCard, American Express, Diners Club, Discover—you name it—this is where the plastic meets the road. There's this sudden, pressing need that just can't wait for a rainy day. A set of threads or something capable of handling rough terrain calls your name. Leather, metal, and fringe may be involved—hats, gloves, boots, or something in athletic gear. *Reversed.* Credit limits are reached. It's time to get back on the austerity bandwagon. Watch out for pushy sales clerks.

For STRATEGY questions. Gung ho! An alarm sounds or a bell goes off in your head. The situation calls for an immediate response. You must dress hurriedly—perhaps for battle, to go on a rescue mission, or to make a sudden conquest. There is really no time to think it over—and it's probably better that way. You must spring into action with enthusiasm. It is now or never, you see. You must respond to this fateful moment by following your impulses. *Reversed.* A sudden call to action turns out to be a false alarm. There are neither fires to start nor flames to put out.

QUEEN OF WANDS

This is a card about survival. *Look at your card.* The Earth Mother sits on her garden bench to admire her prizewinning sunflower and everything else she has grown this summer. She waits, perhaps, for the Harvest Moon to rise, marking the conclusion of her seasonal work. You, too, have to work hard for your living, even if your hands never touch the soil or plead for rain. But all in all, it's been a good year. You will have something to show for your efforts by fall. *Reversed.* Things are coming up a little short this year. Salvage what you can. A freeze comes early.

For WORK questions. Survival of the fittest! The workplace is just like the rest of the world—a cross between jungle and zoo. You may be driving a truck or pushing paper for a living, but it all comes down to the primitive instincts. There will always be wolves and there will always be sheep. There will be good years and bad, storms and calms. Some will flourish and grow in the work climate—you'll probably be one of them. *Reversed.* Consider transplanting yourself to a more hospitable place, perhaps the Midwest.

For LOVE questions. Survival of the species! The facts of life come home to roost: Of all the callings on this Earth, the urge to be fruitful is the strongest and most ancient. We are here to plant seeds, and plant seeds we must. But seedlings that are too crowded cannot grow. Beware the Full Moon! Use birth control. *Reversed.* You are outnumbered or outvoted. There is a permanent change in the climate. There is one more mouth to feed.

For MONEY questions. Survival of the shrewdest! Money does not grow on trees, yet it is planted, picked, and plundered just the same. It is like everything else in the Universe. Each buck is a seed. Some grow where they land, some blow away. Idle money rots, and pretty soon there are vultures circling around it. *Reversed.* There is the possibility of an inheritance. A casualty insurance policy pays off.

For STRATEGY questions. Survival of the sharpest! It would help if you had eyes in the back of your head or the night vision of the Queen's black cat, but in this incarnation you are required to live off your wits, even if not off the land. Make use of your noggin. It is an old-fashioned idea, but in all things, you stand a chance of reaping only what you plant. *Reversed.* Not everything that's planted grows. Keep sowing seeds.

KING OF WANDS

This is a card about being in charge. *Look at your card.* An accomplished businessman sits at the helm. This captain of industry, having climbed to the highest rung of his occupation, now appears to be in full command of everything he sees. Chairpersons, CEOs, presidents, or other executives may be involved. Perhaps you have accomplished quite a lot in your own right lately. At any rate, the boss would like a word with you. A request is granted. *Reversed.* The top brass got up on the wrong side of the bed, and someone gets chewed out. You are out of line.

For WORK questions. Request authorization! A full signature or three key initials are involved at the bottom of a form. A line backs up outside the boss's door. The fax machine rings. A special meeting is called to discuss plans. Someone holds a quick briefing in the wings. You are free to proceed. *Reversed.* Someone comes up against a brick wall. Your request is denied. . . . End of discussion.

For LOVE questions. Schedule a meeting! Synchronize your watches and get out your pocket organizers. Calendars, time slots, and agendas are involved in this relationship. There are hurried lunches and late dinners. Calls are placed from a car phone or a booth along the way. And once in a while you have the opportunity to be alone together. You are summoned to a place. *Reversed.* Someone dozes off during an otherwise passionate moment.

For MONEY questions. Watch the bottom line! There are expenses and revenues, assets and liabilities, and changes in cash flow to review and manage. The boss has it calculated several ways before reaching a final decision. Do your part to keep expenses down and revenues up. *Reversed.* This is not a good time to ask for a raise. In fact, some people may have to be let go.

For STRATEGY questions. Judge character! When you work for somebody else, you do not always get to do things your own way. When you are the boss, it is no different. Management can be fickle and unpredictable, and staff can be resistant in undocumentable ways. Consultants and advisors will tell you what they think you want to hear. You must learn to read people. *Reversed.* Paper trails will be left and quick talkers will cover their own behinds, perhaps with your hide. Be careful.

ACE OF CUPS

This is a card about blessings that come from out of the blue. *Look at your card.* A hand extends from the clouds with a cup that "runneth over."

You can look forward to an overwhelming experience. Your heart is about to be moved. Your eyes are about to well up with tears of joy. This is a perfect moment. This is a happy time. Someone cares about you. Somebody does something nice for you. You can't believe your luck. *Reversed.* A fair-weather friend may be involved. A relationship needs further development. Catharsis may help. Have a good cry.

For WORK questions. Deep friendship!

You have warm feelings, mutual respect, or compassion for the people you work with. Friendly greetings are exchanged, special days are shared together, and when the going gets tough, someone comes to your rescue. A favor is repaid many times over. *Reversed.* Someone you care about needs to be cheered up. There is a farewell party for a good friend. Your emotions about the people you work with go back and forth.

For LOVE questions. Overwhelming love!

There is a special someone in your life, or someone special is coming into your life. Your heart leaps. Your eyes drink in the sight. Warmth spreads through your veins. The sound of a voice is music to your ears. And at a touch, your knees go weak. I see a Hollywood kiss coming on. The music swells in the background. The waves crash. *Reversed.* The experience leaves you drained, but these things have a way of renewing themselves. Your love is a bottomless cup.

For MONEY questions. Cash flowing in!

Money pours in from various sources. Your accounts are replenished, even as they are drained. Fortune rains on you. A raise, inheritance, rebate, or gift comes just when you need it. Your accounts earn interest. At times like these, you can't believe your luck. *Reversed.* Money slips through your fingers. The more you have, the more you seem to need.

For STRATEGY questions. Drink in the moment!

This is a rewarding time that brings with it a feeling of great happiness. There is nothing you need to do, except enjoy it. Count your blessings. Give thanks. Yes, you do deserve it. *Reversed.* An emotional high is followed by doubts, fears, or equally great emotional lows. Take the downs with the ups. All in all, it's worth the price.

2 OF CUPS

This is a card about cementing relationships. *Look at your card.* A man and a woman seal their agreement with a ceremonial toast. A pledge is made. Vows are exchanged. You find yourself in a situation that requires you to make a commitment. You enter into a permanent living arrangement. A license, prenuptial agreement, or blood test may be involved. Someone looks you in the eye and tells you how he or she feels about you. *Reversed.* A relationship is not as permanent as it first appeared. You do not see eye to eye with someone. The results of a physical exam are a determining factor.

For WORK questions.
Partnerships! Someone wants to "get in bed" with you. A joint undertaking is proposed, an offer of employment is extended, or a merger proposal is submitted. A big deal is sealed. Contracts, letters of intent, or binding agreements are signed. You receive an offer you can live with. *Reversed.* Someone resigns or uses the escape clause of an agreement to back out on a commitment. A requirement of employment is violated.

For LOVE questions.
Pairings! A proposal is made. It could be a proposal to "go steady," to live together, or to tie the knot. It could also be a proposal to renew vows taken long ago. Whatever the exact situation, the intentions are serious. There is commitment on both sides. Congratulations. Best wishes. *Reversed.* A commitment is less serious than it appeared at first. A trial period turns out to have been a good idea.

For MONEY questions.
Joint ventures! Assets are consolidated, funds are merged, or financial risks are shared. A friend or acquaintance approaches you about a money-making deal or investment opportunity. Put your money where your mouth is. Get in on the ground floor. *Reversed.* Shared assets are split up. An unequal distribution of funds may occur.

For STRATEGY questions.
Two heads are better than one! There's nothing wrong with going it alone and there's no guarantee that working with others will be any easier, but a good relationship with a trusted friend can help both of you achieve your common goals. Make sure you agree to the terms up front. Put things in writing. *Reversed.* Misunderstandings result from differences in opinion or differing expectations about the arrangements. Be honest with each other. Discuss the facts. Express your feelings.

3 OF CUPS

This is a card about shared experience. *Look at your card.* Three women dance in a circle—perhaps under a Harvest Moon—with their glasses upraised. They are celebrating the conclusion of something or the mere fact that they are friends. Your own friends are playing an important part in your life. Caring and sharing are involved. You will be invited to a get-together. *Reversed.* Someone is moving on, moving away, or leaving the group for reasons beyond your control. A pact remains in force but is no longer what it once was. You are growing apart from your friends.

For WORK questions.
Sharing! A team effort is concluded in victory, a group project ends on a high note, or the group just enjoys working together. The job provides you with a social outlet as well as a work experience. You are invited out to lunch or to an after-hours party. *Reversed.* A lot of socializing isn't allowed at work. You get in trouble for talking when you're supposed to be on the job. Your so-called friends can't be trusted.

For LOVE questions.
Caring! Friends provide you with a shoulder to lean on, a hand to hold, or a smile to greet you. You are in good company. Your support system sustains you. Someone invites you over for the evening. A wedding reception may be involved. *Reversed.* Someone you thought you could count on through thick and thin disappoints you. Marriage takes a friend of yours out of circulation.

For MONEY questions.
Giving! A friend foots the bill for a party, picks up the tab for dinner, or buys you a cup of coffee. You return the favor in kind. A sentimental gift is given. Tokens of affection are exchanged. Without asking, your glass is refilled. After all, this is what money is for. *Reversed.* You get stuck with the check. A social event costs more than you can afford. Oh well, everybody had a good time.

For STRATEGY questions.
Socialize! You can never tell when a personal contact will prove useful. Wining and dining is an important part of life. Get to know others on a human level. Mix at mixers. Hobnob at receptions. Fraternize with peers and higher-ups. A little small talk goes a long way to reinforce your image. *Reversed.* People are kissing up to you. Your "friends" are using you.

4 OF CUPS

This is a card about relationships that are tested. *Look at your card.* A young man considers his current situation. Three out of four of his criteria are being met. The one thing that is lacking is being offered, but he remains troubled. Perhaps you, too, are a bit confused. You need to sort things out in your own head. An affair, fling, or flirtation tempts you, or a recurring fantasy distracts you. A brooding individual may be involved. Someone else appeals to you. *Reversed.* The alternatives are dismissed. Or it's possible that in chasing after some whim, you end up sacrificing everything that once mattered to you.

For WORK questions. Moonlighting! A different employer, line of work, or profession seems to offer you a little more than your current situation. A career change is contemplated. A proposition is dangled in front of your nose. *Reversed.* Your priorities shift away from your primary responsibilities to a temporary diversion. In going after a promise, you sacrifice a sure thing.

For LOVE questions. Extracurricular activities! Though a current relationship is desired and satisfying, there is a temptation to stray. Someone has been flirting with the possibility of having an affair. These desires may be purely physical, but even so, they cloud an existing relationship. Doubts begin to surface. *Reversed.* The temptation proves to be too great. An affair backfires.

For MONEY questions. Risky business! Though not all that bad to begin with, a financial situation promises to be improved by an investment opportunity. A careful decision is involved, since a promised return on investment is never certain, and you will be risking capital in this endeavor. *Reversed.* An investment scheme soaks up your dough. You get ripped off by idle promises.

For STRATEGY questions. Enough is never enough! Think carefully about whether something you want to go after is worth the effort and the potential consequences. You may not have everything you want right now, but no matter how much you get, there will always be something more you desire. Learn where to draw the line. Proceed with caution. *Reversed.* A pipe dream turns into a bitter reality. This is not what you wanted either. Snap out of it before it's too late.

5 OF CUPS

This is a card about deep regrets. *Look at your card.* A cloaked figure mourns over the loss of something that cannot be recovered. The better part of a relationship has been destroyed, yet important pieces remain. Perhaps you, too, are crying over spilt milk. An apology is certainly in order. Someone has a confession to make. *Reversed.* Things appear pretty bleak at this moment, but perhaps they are not as bad as they seem. Someone is hiding something from you, but it is fairly insignificant.

For WORK questions. Minimize your losses! Plans have not turned out as well as envisioned, a situation deteriorates in the workplace, or success comes at too great a price. Someone is wearing a long face. Or someone is giving you grief. *Reversed.* There is a slight upturn following a disappointing season. You hear a bit of gossip that distresses you, but whatever was insinuated turns out to have been untrue.

For LOVE questions. The truth comes out! Trials, tribulations, and blunders upset this relationship. Someone has betrayed a confidence, broken a silent pledge, or committed some other near-fatal error. This relationship is damaged—perhaps beyond repair. If an apology is offered, accept it. If an apology is due, give it. But this is a case where just saying, "I'm sorry" is probably not enough. *Reversed.* Idle gossip does damage unjustly to someone's reputation. There is a tendency to get even. Feelings are hurt on purpose.

For MONEY questions. Cash in your chips! The market has crashed or gone down dramatically. Money that was there—at least on paper—is suddenly reduced. Investments fail. Real estate values drop unexpectedly. Or some other money calamity befalls you. However, there is still a chance to recover. Focus on what to do with what you have held in reserve. *Reversed.* There is a minor downward adjustment in your accounts. A period of mild recovery comes following a temporary recession.

For STRATEGY questions. Don't look back! When things bottom out in your life and you feel as if you've had the screws put to you, take a deep breath, inspect the damage, and then get down to work again. Recover what you can and pitch the rest. It is not the end of the world. *Reversed.* Avoid making the same mistake twice, but don't be gun-shy either. By the time it's all said and done, this may turn out to be the best thing that ever happened to you.

6 OF CUPS

This is a card about sentimental value. *Look at your card.* A boy—who is just about grown-up—stops to give his childhood sweetheart a bouquet before crossing the bridge into his new life. Perhaps you have been thinking about someone from the past. Romantic and nostalgic feelings are involved. Someone remembers you as you once were. *Reversed.* You can't go home again. Let old acquaintance be forgot. . . . Let bygones be bygones.

For WORK questions. Trade anecdotes! Get to know the people you work with. Exchange favors. Swap stories. Read each other's resumes. In dealing with people, it helps to know a little something about their past. You can see now where someone is coming from. *Reversed.* The good old days are missed. You want to live in the past.

For LOVE questions. Exchange greetings! Letters, cards, or unexpected presents from an old or secret admirer show up on your doorstep. A voice from out of the past is heard on the phone. An old relationship is rekindled, but on a new basis. You remember old friends and times that are no more. *Reversed.* Something that happened a long time ago is not necessarily enough to sustain a relationship now. You can't live in the past.

For MONEY questions. Send the gift that counts! You don't have to spend much to make a good impression when family and old friends are involved. A little goes a long way. It's the thought that counts. *Reversed.* An old friend drops in from out of the blue to sell you insurance or ask for a loan. You hear disturbing news about someone you used to know.

For STRATEGY questions. Learn from the past! History has a way of repeating itself, even if the circumstances are never exactly the same. To understand the present, study and learn from the past in general and from your own past. The times have changed, but people remain the same. *Reversed.* The past comes back to haunt you. You slip into an old pattern of behavior. Think twice before you open old wounds.

7 OF CUPS

This is a card about pipe dreams. *Look at your card.* A dark figure stands gazing into the clouds where his fantasies unfold. He is building castles in the air. You yourself have been daydreaming recently. Wishes about big houses, jewels, power, lovers, or glory may be involved—or any incredible scheme. A relationship promises to improve your financial position. Your head is full of hopes and desires. Dream a little. *Reversed.* Disillusionment takes the place of dreams, which now lie scattered on the ground. A longstanding fantasy is realized, but the reality falls short of the ideal.

For WORK questions. False prophecies! Future plans are drawn on the board, the computer projects a rosy picture, or the analysts have nothing but good news. Someone promises you the world. Career paths are sketched out. Potential earnings are estimated, but there may be strings attached. *Reversed.* A promised raise or promotion turns out to be unsubstantial. Work interrupts your sleep.

For LOVE questions. False promises! This relationship promises to keep you in the style to which you would like to grow accustomed. Or it provides you with the connections to advance your status or career. A marriage of convenience is not out of the question. *Reversed.* This relationship evaporates as quickly as it formed. You'd better check to see if that diamond is really a cubic zirconium.

For MONEY questions. False sense of confidence! The future may look bright, but don't spend all your potential earnings just yet. The lure of luxurious living is great. Realtors and bankers would like to see you borrow as much as you possibly can, but stretching to the point of no return will not make you any happier than you are right now. *Reversed.* Your material acquisitions bog you down. You are trapped in a money pit.

For STRATEGY questions. Paint a pretty picture! The situation you are in calls for you to dream a bit, believe implicitly in yourself or your grand plan, and provide a convincing argument to anyone willing to listen to you. In the process, you may have to substantiate your claims as well as demonstrate your sincerity. You stand a chance of dazzling someone. *Reversed.* Someone wants to pull the wool over your eyes. You lack the wherewithal to pull off your schemes.

8 OF CUPS

This is a card about retreating. *Look at your card.* A man turns his back on everything he has built, crosses the chasm, and goes off in an entirely different direction. His moon is waning now. Perhaps you, too, are having a midlife crisis. Or maybe it's just been one of those days. At any rate, the past doesn't seem to add up to what you wanted—or, having achieved what you set out to accomplish, it suddenly no longer matters to you anymore. Someone wants to chuck it all, go away, and start all over again. It's never too late to go . . . it's never too late to stay. *Reversed.* Someone who has gone, returns. A month needs to pass before this matter can be completely resolved—give it a moon to work itself out.

For WORK questions. Diversification! An old line of business or an employment relationship isn't satisfying anymore, isn't making it anymore, or has gone about as far as it can go. Maybe it's time to get into something new or change directions in midstream. Take a couple of weeks off yourself to think about your own past and the prospects for your future. *Reversed.* Within four weeks things will become clearer. Old, familiar faces around the coffeepot go on to bigger and better things.

For LOVE questions. Separation! This is a long-standing relationship, but it requires a little breathing space right now. Give the one you love a little slack. Separate vacations or dedicated time alone may be required. The relationship itself is not necessarily in danger, but if you want to save it, the best thing to do is to let go. Someone needs to work something out alone. *Reversed.* A trial separation results in a new opportunity for growth and personal development. Someone who has gone away, returns—possibly around the New Moon.

For MONEY questions. Traveler's checks! Take a little money out of the bank for a retreat or a vacation. Getting away right now is worth it. In fact, it may be some of the best money you ever spent. You might even want to spring for a trip to another continent. *Reversed.* You return from a trip with empty pockets and a fresh perspective. Everything old looks new again.

For STRATEGY questions. Expand your horizons! You can't always appreciate something right under your nose. Or, because you're just too close to things, you can't always see what you should do next. The secret is to get away from it for a while, even if just to take a drive in the country or go on a moonlit stroll. *Reversed.* A pause refreshes. Look up from your work. Go out to lunch. Take the evening off.

9 OF CUPS

This is a card about contentment. *Look at your card.* A well-fed man sits among his trophies. He has accomplished much, and it makes him happy. There are many reasons that you should be happy, too. This is the time for taking an inventory of the good things that have happened in your life and in your relationships with others. All in all, things look pretty good. Someone jovial may be involved in your life. *Reversed.* Things could be better, but at least you have your health. You remain in good spirits.

For WORK questions. Personal fulfillment! Your career is working out for you, you like the people you work with, or the effort you are putting into work is paying off. An awards ceremony is possibly in the offing. You may even be honored in some way. These things are nice, but your sense of accomplishment is most likely coming from doing the work itself. *Reversed.* Your job's okay, and it has its moments, but it's not really fulfilling you.

For LOVE questions. Mutual satisfaction! This relationship makes you feel warm and cuddly. It answers your needs. It satisfies your caprices. And it puts a big smile on your face from time to time. You feel good about it. Hang on to it. *Reversed.* One person is happier in this relationship than the other—or should I say all the others? A person who goes through a lot of relationships—perhaps simultaneously—is involved.

For MONEY questions. Ample returns! Money matters are rewarding at this time. Everything in the bank is adding up nicely. You are well fed and well clothed, and there's a roof over your head. Sit back. Enjoy. *Reversed.* It looks like your money's all tied up right now and busy working for you. Money on paper gives you a false sense of confidence in the future.

For STRATEGY questions. Hang on to a good thing! This situation doesn't require you to change anything or do anything differently than you have in the past. You have a winning formula under your belt. Why mess around with a winning streak? *Reversed.* In your confidence, be careful not to be blindsided. A sudden reversal could put everything you've worked so hard for at risk. Get off your duff and react. Think fast.

10 OF CUPS

This is a card about happy endings. *Look at your card.* A man and woman make a wish on a rainbow as their two children dance gleefully at their feet. This is the ideal picture of a happy family riding off into the sunset together. This is as good as it gets. This is the relationship you want to have, or perhaps it is the relationship you have already. At any rate, you are happy with your life right now. Someone shares a special moment with you. *Reversed.* There is a pot of gold at the end of your rainbow. Quick! Make a wish!

For WORK questions. First things first! As good as your career prospects are and as much as you love your work, you need to keep your priorities in order. Your family really ought to come first. Work can wait, children cannot. They will be with you long after the gold watch is given; they will never fire you; and they will not lay you off. *Reversed.* Your work takes you away from your family. Hurry back.

For LOVE questions. A storybook romance! The hero sweeps the maiden off her feet . . . they ride off into the sunset together . . . to a little cottage in the woods . . . where they raise perfect little children . . . and live happily ever after. . . . This relationship lives up to your highest expectations—and gives all the rest of us hope. Good luck to you. *Reversed.* It probably won't turn out quite as good as you hoped, but you're going to be very happy together. Best wishes.

For MONEY questions. Living expenses! The mortgage, the utility bills, the grocery tab, the clothes, the medical expenses, and the car payments will eat you alive—not to mention the birthday presents, parties, and outings you'll have to underwrite in your lifetime. But what the heck, what's money for? *Reversed.* If it's not one thing, it's something else. But the people you care about are so darn cute, how can you resist? Pull out your wallet. Write checks.

For STRATEGY questions. Get out a little! The best way to spend quality time is to go someplace where you can all be together without any distractions or ordinary concerns to command your attention. Get out there and commune with nature a bit—a walk in the park or a camping trip will do everyone a world of good. *Reversed.* Pack slickers or carry an umbrella just in case. Don't let a little downpour dampen your spirits.

PAGE OF CUPS

This is a card about greetings and salutations. *Look at your card.* The messenger bears a sloppy or mushy message in his cup. He brings good tidings of glad joy to all who gather to listen. There may be a dark-eyed lad in your life. More than likely someone sends you a love letter, a greeting card, or a thank-you note. A good deed is written up in the area newspaper. A wedding or an engagement is announced. *Reversed.* An expected message of appreciation, admiration, or sweet nothings is not forthcoming. A note or letter that is received bears a half-truth.

For WORK questions. Company news! News about new appointments, accomplishments, or marriages among staff comes out in the official company newsletter—but most know about it in advance. Word of mouth travels faster than light these days. You hear something from someone close to someone who heard it from the horse's mouth. *Reversed.* There is no truth to some of the rumors on the grapevine, but you'll never know which ones. Be suspicious of a note you receive from someone with hazel eyes.

For LOVE questions. Love letters! Scented letters are smelling up the mailbox these days—or perhaps the letters are a bit salty. Passions spill from the page, even if the words are spelled wrong. These are messages that are kept in a shoe box forever. These are the letters you would never dream of throwing away. They send a thrill from your head through your socks. They mush. They gush. *Reversed.* You hear from an anonymous or secret admirer. The news may not be welcomed.

For MONEY questions. Unsolicited offers! Someone offers you a preapproved credit card through the mail or you get a once-in-a-lifetime opportunity to save big if you respond quick. An invitation arrives for preferred customers only. Your bank raises your credit limit, and it makes you feel good about your credit rating—but then again, there are the payments, interest rates, and shipping and handling charges. Oh well, tomorrow is another day. *Reversed.* You receive a friendly reminder that your monthly payment is past due. Have you forgotten???

For STRATEGY questions. Only believe half of what you hear! Someone's hormones are working overtime, or someone really doesn't have your best interests in mind. Filter out the messages you receive. Discard most of them. Read between the lines of the rest. *Reversed*. No news is good news.

KNIGHT OF CUPS

This is a card about deliberate behavior. *Look at your card*. A dark-eyed knight wearing wings comes into the picture on a prancing steed. At this moment, someone is winging his or her way to you. It could be a lover or it could be a newborn. The progress may be a little slower than you would like, but the entrance that is made is memorable, maybe even spectacular. *Reversed*. You may find yourself traveling via a roundabout route or a quaint means. You will be invited to attend a military ceremony or a parade.

For WORK questions. Incremental progress! Take one step at a time, work at your own pace, and keep plodding. Eventually you will finish the assignment or mission you have taken on. An ultimate goal or final destination is reached. You come through with flying colors. *Reversed*. Someone with light brown hair appears in the workplace . . . before dashing off again.

For LOVE questions. Propositions! Someone attempts to sweep you off your feet with a little sweet talk, outright flirtation, or a series of suggestive remarks. Though nonchalant and slow in its way, the action is fast—perhaps too fast for you. Someone is delivering a few well-rehearsed lines. *Reversed*. An offer is turned down flat. An invitation is refused.

For MONEY questions. The check is in the mail! Money is sent or automatically transferred into your account on a routine basis. In a pinch money is wired or a certified check comes via express mail. Or a promotional offer in a time-dated envelope is printed on paper that resembles a check. Something you sent for comes via direct mail or courier service. You could also receive a fax. *Reversed*. Funds get lost during transfer or never were actually put in the mail. An electronic message arrives scrambled or illegible.

For STRATEGY questions. Deliver on your promises! The situation calls for swift action, but there are many details to attend to in fulfilling a request or executing an instruction. Buy yourself some breathing room by relying on a delivery service or an electronic means of communication. Focus on preparing and packaging a message first, then on delivering it. *Reversed*. Things done to a T that arrive late might as well not have been sent at all, at least not in these circumstances. Deliver the best quality you can in the time you've got. Settle for a field goal if you can't make the touchdown.

QUEEN OF CUPS

This is a card about foresight. *Look at your card.* A wise woman gazes into her chalice as the sea washes about her feet. She is attempting to anticipate the future. Since the tides are quite high, it is probably a New or Full Moon. You, too, will find it easiest to predict the things that happen in recurring cycles, such as your own biorhythms. There is a particular time of the month when you will do your best work, feel your sexiest, and have your best luck in general. Pay attention to the phases of the moon. *Reversed.* Watch for changes in the wind, waves, or currents. Someone reads your fortune in the bottom of a teacup or by casting stones.

For WORK questions. Anticipate the next moves! The winds of change are blowing through the workplace. Individuals rise and fall in the wake of a reorganization. Sales cycle with the seasons. Product life cycles are charted on a growth curve that rises, peaks, and sinks again in a crashing wave. Watch for the signs that tell you it is time to make your move. *Reversed.* Things settle down again after a major upheaval.

For LOVE questions. Foresee where it is all leading! Romance follows its own cycle. A relationship rises, peaks, and declines. There are ups and downs and in-betweens. The trick is to ride the crest of the wave for as long as you can. Take the lows with the highs. Take the ups with the downs. Things will even out in the end. Try to get in sync with your partner. Swim in parallel. *Reversed.* This relationship is like swimming against a strong current. A brown-haired stranger delivers a timely warning.

For MONEY questions. Prepare forecasts! There are times when money is in short supply and times when it is flowing freely. Check your spending patterns against income to see where the peaks and troughs exist and if there is any pattern. You may feel rich right now, but you still need to make what you have stretch until the next influx of cash is due. *Reversed.* Your money washes away. Savings are eroded.

For STRATEGY questions. See which way the wind blows! This situation demands that you consult the weather forecast, test the waters before you dive in, or stick your head outdoors before you decide what you're going to wear. The point is, make plans that consider your environment. There is no use attempting to do things when conditions do not support them. Wait for the time to be right. *Reversed.* Conditions change suddenly only for those who have not been paying attention to the signs.

KING OF CUPS

This is a card about keeping afloat. *Look at your card.* A would-be seaman attempts to go boating on a concrete slab. Somehow he manages to keep his rocky craft on top of the water. You, too, despite your solid exterior, ride on an undercurrent of emotional tides. Don't let the little things upset you. Don't dive off the deep end either. Perhaps you will travel across water shortly to get where you are going. *Reversed.* Wear a life vest or use your seat cushion as a flotation device. Keep your head above water. Sink or swim.

For WORK questions. Ride out the waves! Work styles come and go, along with the business gurus who purport them. Hang in there; these fads change with the moon and the tides. Common sense pays off in the long run. Someone asks you to do the impossible. Try not to spout off. Remain calm on the outside even though your emotions are churning on the inside. *Reversed.* The latest management rage swamps the workplace and threatens to undo the business. You are up to your ears in alligators. Swim for the nearest shore.

For LOVE questions. Bail! Emotional currents swirl below the surface of this relationship. If they get out of control, the boat will not only list, it will fill up with water and sink under the added weight. Keep irrelevant things secret, but get the churning issues out in the open. Bail out the troubled waters. Someone confesses his or her true feelings. *Reversed.* Bail out of this relationship . . . and quick. You are in over your head.

For MONEY questions. Use the float! What with electronic fund transfer and automatic payments, there isn't much float left these days, but take advantage of any delay in the receipt of a bill and the payment due date. Use your credit cards to postpone payments by 30 days—but be sure to pay them off each month. Time things so that you hang on to your cash as long as you can, and make sure you earn interest on it in the interim. *Reversed.* Float a loan to get yourself out of hot water.

For STRATEGY questions. Stay on top of things! The situation you are in is ludicrous, it defies all common sense, or it is contrary to anything you have known in the past. Perhaps if you have enough faith and believe enough, it can work—but the odds would seem to be against it. Ride out the current tide as best you can, and pray for a miracle. Meanwhile monitor everything going on and react at the first sign of danger. Trust your gut feelings. *Reversed.* Tread water until you can be rescued.

ACE OF COINS

This is a card about money out of thin air. *Look at your card.* A hand comes forth from the clouds bearing a giant gold coin. On the ground, things blossom under an infusion of capital. A little money drops suddenly into your lap. A gift is received or given. Funding comes from unexpected sources. Material assets may be involved. Maybe you win a contest. You can't believe your luck. *Reversed.* Money is taken from you, taken back, or rescinded. Debts are paid back. Credit limits are raised to higher ceilings.

For WORK questions. Working capital! Financial backing comes in the form of a gift. Someone underwrites a project, gives you a grant, or puts up the money you need. You may get a little advance against future earnings to tide you over until the big money comes in. That raise you were hoping for comes through, a bonus is bestowed, or benefit programs are improved. *Reversed.* Funding is withheld, wages are cut, or benefits are eroded gradually.

For LOVE questions. Diamonds are forever! A proposal comes with a rock attached, gold rings are exchanged, or a dowry is put up. The material trappings of love are involved. For some reason gifts with big price tags are said to measure the extent to which the heart believes. In your case, it is true. *Reversed.* Money matters more to you than love. An expensive gift is given, but you cannot accept it. A gift is returned.

For MONEY questions. Cold, hard cash! Money jangles in your pockets, swells in your wallet, and drips from your bank accounts. Money falls out of the sky. You are showered with money. Money fills your hands. Or somebody offers you a gold card with one heck of a limit. Maybe you win the lottery. *Reversed.* Something is being withheld. Someone is holding out on you. Maybe you get a tax refund, a check for back wages, or a rebate for having bought something.

For STRATEGY questions. Hold out your hands! When that old slot machine lines up on triple sevens, get your plastic cup ready to scoop up the jackpot. Feel the weight of all those casino chips being counted out by the cashier. Count along with the teller as those big bills are stacked up on one another. There's really nothing much to do—when it's your lucky day, just sit back and rake it up. Your ship comes in. *Reversed.* Count your change. Tip the dealer.

2 OF COINS

This is a card about balanced accounts. *Look at your card.* A performer on the boardwalk entertains the holiday crowds by juggling two gold coins.

Out to sea, two big boats are tossed in the same motion. They go up and down, like a checkbook bouncing. Have you balanced your own lately? Debits and credits are involved. Assets and liabilities come into play. Some things go up, while some come down. You are attempting to keep your expenses in line with your income. You may need to spend less. *Reversed.* You are attempting to keep your income in line with your expenses. You need to earn more.

For WORK questions. Income and expenses! Whether this month turns out in the red or in the black is anybody's guess until the figures are tallied. You may need to juggle the columns a bit to get things to line up straight. But the numbers are the numbers, and you'll have to live with them. The income situation is not all that bad, really. If you can just keep a lid on the expenses, this picture will be improved. *Reversed.* Sales need to come up in order to cover ongoing operational costs. A little belt tightening is in order. Do your part to cut back.

For LOVE questions. Assets and liabilities! This relationship has its pros and cons, its pluses and minuses, and its strengths and weaknesses. Quite possibly there are conflicting views over money and money matters. The financial picture tends to change from time to time, but more for the good than for the bad. *Reversed.* This is a financially troubled relationship, and things are unlikely to get any better. Someone's spending is out of control.

For MONEY questions. Cash flow! Nothing says you have to come out ahead every month, as long as things even out over time. There is a time to charge and a time to pay in cash. Study payment schedules, interest rates, and monthly budgets before deciding which way to go. Balance your checkbook. *Reversed.* At present, you are cash-poor. Pay back what you owe just as fast as you can.

For STRATEGY questions. A balancing act! The situation requires you to weigh two things, compare two things, keep two things going at once, or establish a balance between two different things. It would be even better to establish a favorable *im*balance in which the positive outweighs the negative. Focus on what you want to accomplish. Manage to the bottom line. *Reversed.* Someone drops the ball. You will need to follow up on loose ends. There may be some unexpected expenses.

3 OF COINS

This is a card about intellectual property. *Look at your card.* A sculptor works on his masterpiece while two patrons look over his shoulder. In order to receive their continued financial support, his work must please them. Perhaps you, too, are a starving artist. If you expect to make a living at your craft, you will need to give your public what they want without sacrificing your artistic integrity. You are offered some support in an undertaking, or you are given creative license. *Reversed.* The backers back off suddenly. Your artistic creation does not stand up under critical review. No one understands you.

For WORK questions. The go-ahead! A pet project, innovative effort, or experimental approach is approved. However, you will have to show progress and demonstrate that your ideas do indeed have commercial or academic merit or that they are novel enough to receive intellectual protection. Apply your highest skills to the task at hand. *Reversed.* Your work gets a little carried away with itself—or you, with yourself. Come back down to Earth. Accept constructive criticism.

For LOVE questions. Chaperoned! Someone tags along on a date or accompanies the two of you on an outing. It's not that you can't be trusted—it's that somebody doesn't trust you. There is a fear that you will do something socially questionable if left to your own devices. Be on your best behavior and maybe it will buy you a little slack in the future. Try to make a good impression when meeting somebody's parents. *Reversed.* You are given the benefit of the doubt. Somebody backs off from you.

For MONEY questions. Support the arts! Donations, charitable contributions, and endowments for the humanities are implied by this card. Participate in fund-raisers or buy something from a struggling artist or craftsman. Pay royalties on the music you listen to, the videos you watch, the books you photocopy, and the software you load. Protect your own creations with trademark, patent, or copyright. *Reversed.* Someone pirates your ideas or steals your work. Intellectual property is ripped off or intentionally meddled with.

For STRATEGY questions. Novelty! In this situation you will have to prove or demonstrate that your work is your own and that it represents something new or unique. You may have to be the first one to voice an idea if you are to get credit for it. If you take money from those who offer to sponsor you, establish in advance what the conditions are. *Reversed.* In order to have your work seen at all, you may need to consider signing over the rights or sharing the royalties with your financial backers.

4 OF COINS

This is a card about ownership. *Look at your card.* A man holds on to four coins by clutching them to his body. These four things clearly belong to him, or he's at least staking claim to them. You may be feeling a little possessive, too. You are clinging to something. You are holding on for dear life. What belongs to you may not add up to all that much, but it's all you've got. Possession is nine-tenths of the law. *Reversed.* Someone is attempting to pry something out of you. You are unwittingly parted from your money or swindled out of something you treasure.

For WORK questions.

Span of control! Requirements, duties, and responsibilities are listed in a way that helps management determine what they are willing to pay you. To get ahead, you will have to gather as much territory and authority under you as you can manage. Or you will have to make a contribution that exceeds a normal person's weight in gold. Money for additional compensation is tight at this time. Inventories may be excessive. *Reversed.* Your authority is being eroded. Somebody wants a piece of your territory. At best you can expect a cost-of-living increase.

For LOVE questions.

Jealousy! Someone is clinging pretty tightly in this relationship, perhaps out of fear that the other person will somehow get away. Someone watches closely for any sign of possible encroachment. Someone watches every little move. Casual hellos and fleeting glances are no-nos. Someone is jealous of you. *Reversed.* You can't keep another person entirely to yourself, especially if you love him or her. Neither can you be kept very long in a relationship like this.

For MONEY questions.

Hoarding! Cans of food are stocked up in the pantry for the winter, emergency money is stuffed in the mattress, or mad money is slipped into the lining of a hat or money belt. It's good to be prepared for a rainy day, but this card indicates excessive or compulsive behavior with regard to storing things up. You are thought of as being cheap . . . which pleases you. *Reversed.* You can't take it with you. Don't pinch pennies when it comes to the ones you profess to love.

For STRATEGY questions.

Finders keepers! Cash, assets, or secrets are entrusted to you for safekeeping. Stash things of worth in safe places. Keep a lid on plans for a financial deal under consideration. Lock important papers up in your briefcase and carry them with you. *Reversed.* Secrets leak or something entrusted to your care gets lost or stolen. Be careful whom you trust. Don't leave your luggage unattended at the airport.

5 OF COINS

This is a card about lacking the means. *Look at your card.* A poor woman and her crippled child have nowhere to go on a bitter night. Not even the church provides them with sanctuary. You may be feeling as if you have been left out in the cold yourself. Needed support has not come through. Special assistance is denied. You simply do not have the means at your disposal to get out of the jam you find yourself in. Your strength is drained. And you may not know which way to turn. *Reversed.* In times of trouble your system of beliefs helps you get by. Though material or physical comforts may be lacking, spiritual empowerment gives you the strength to go on.

For WORK questions.
Layoffs! Ends are no longer meeting in the workplace, and drastic measures result. People are let go on short notice. Pet projects are abandoned. There are cutbacks in discretionary budgets. Charitable donations are cut out. The employment situation looks bleak. *Reversed.* Assistance comes from unlikely sources. Another person of equally limited means shares what little he or she has with you—if only companionship.

For LOVE questions.
Toughing it out together! This relationship is built on coming through some tragedy or crisis together. The experience draws you closer, for you have no one to lean on but each other at this time. You comfort and console each other, prop each other up, or give each other the strength to go on. Despite difficult conditions, this proves to be an enriching personal experience. *Reversed.* A weather emergency brings strangers together for the night.

For MONEY questions.
Empty pockets! You are left with the change in your pockets and a couple of pieces of lint. The prospects for getting through these difficult times are more a factor of personal resourcefulness than of financial leverage. You have few options but to depend upon the kindness of strangers and upon your own wits . . . mostly the latter. *Reversed.* Things may not be materially better in the morning, but your spirits will have improved.

For STRATEGY questions.
Get through the night! You are in a pretty desolate situation right now. You are feeling downright desperate. Seek some kind of shelter even if you have to invent it. Seek warmth, even if you have to build a fire. And seek food even if you have to forage for it. Bolster your courage. *Reversed.* You may be hungry, cold, or miserable right now, but relief is just around the corner. Rely on someone with experience in living off the land.

6 OF COINS

This is a card about charity. *Look at your card.* A rich man finds he has a little spare change for the needy who kneel around him begging for handouts. You may be asked to contribute to a worthy cause shortly. Perhaps you will find yourself canvassing door to door, soliciting for contributions. If asked, give what you can. If asking, forgive those who slam the door in your face. *Reversed.* You may find yourself waiting in line for public assistance. Take only what you need and try not to resent the reluctant giver.

For WORK questions.

Collections and distributions! You may be asked to chip in on a gift for a coworker or to bring in canned goods for a company-wide food drive. In order to raise capital, stocks may go public, agency funding may be sought, or the government may be called in to bail you all out. Unemployment benefits, workers' comp., or disability insurance plans go into effect. *Reversed.* Dividends, though small, may be distributed. Or an advance against future wages couldn't come at a better time.

For LOVE questions.

Allowances! A spouse, a child, or a relative living with you requires a little spending money of his or her own. A few bucks are doled out or the car keys are lent. The handout may not be enormous, but it is given lovingly and without any strings attached. This is a healthy relationship in which people unbegrudgingly help each other out from time to time. *Reversed.* Whatever is given is peanuts . . . just enough to get by; yet the recipient may be required to beg for it just the same. This relationship is less than generous.

For MONEY questions.

Spare some change! In balance you have more than enough to cover your own needs and meet your current obligations. Or if not, there is something you could really live without in order to help somebody who has a lot less than you. It doesn't have to be much to make a big difference. Besides, it's bad luck not to give a beggar a hand out, no matter how unlikely the person's story is. *Reversed.* It shouldn't hurt you so much to ask for help when you need it. Besides, it's bad luck to turn away a free lunch.

For STRATEGY questions.

Take care! In this situation people are looking up to you for help and encouragement. In some ways you are rich, while they are impoverished. If you have more money than they do, help them out when they ask. If they come to you for advice, give them your two cents worth. If they are down in the dumps, share your optimism and courage. You may get nothing but a thank you or a warm feeling inside in return. It is more than enough. *Reversed.* The tables are reversed, and you have something to learn from people who are less fortunate than yourself.

7 OF COINS

This is a card about returns on investment. *Look at your card.* A farmer stands looking at a bush bearing fruit. His crop is not quite ready to harvest yet, except for one thing that has ripened early. There is nothing you need to do right now but be patient and wait for the things you have cultivated to come along. Some things happen in their own time. You get a sudden craving for something that grows on a vine. An early dividend is reported. *Reversed.* You can't force a situation that simply requires more time. Don't count your chickens before they're hatched. What you hunger for is not in season.

For WORK questions. Early returns! The first results of a money-making effort dribble in. A project that has occupied you full-time promises to be nearing its end. All that remains are a few loose ends to clean up. It looks as if all your hard work and dedicated effort are about to pay off. Enjoy the fruits of your labor. *Reversed.* Money is advanced against future sales. A watched kettle never boils.

For LOVE questions. The start of something big! You're off to a good beginning in this relationship. You've hit it off together. And so far, so good. There's still room for growth. More time needs to pass until you see what it amounts to. But at this very moment, someone is thinking about you. You may be distracted by someone yourself. Someone brings you an apple. *Reversed.* You are trying too hard to make this relationship happen. Give it some space and the time it takes. Stop at a roadside stand for a glass of cider.

For MONEY questions. Proceeds! There is money to be distributed following the sale of a property or after a product is delivered to the market. Earnings from an investment or stock option plan may be spent now or reinvested—it's your call. You may see a little cash now from something you've been doing around the house or growing in your garden. There may soon be a few bargains in the produce section. *Reversed.* The returns are a little less than you projected, but you get your money back out of an investment deal or business plan.

For STRATEGY questions. Rake it in! There's not much you can do at this time to alter or affect the outcome of this situation. What you've done in the past is all that matters. Everything else is out of your control. Put down your tools and admire your own work. Take the time to dream a bit. Watch for the signs that a thing's time has come. At that moment only, spring into action, and rake in the proceeds. *Reversed.* You may have to make a last-ditch effort to save a pet project.

8 OF COINS

This is a card about wages. *Look at your card.* A man works at his bench hammering out gold medallions, which is the way he earns his living. You probably have to work for your bread and butter too. Whether you stamp out goods or deliver services, you must develop your skills in order to increase your wages. A carpenter, plumber, or electrician may be coming into your life. Someone is doing some tinkering around the house. *Reversed.* There is still work to be done before you complete an apprenticeship. You may feel pressured about having to fill a lot of back orders or at having to catch up with your paperwork; but what the heck, you get paid, don't you?

For WORK questions. Salary and compensation! A skill or a trade still comes in handy even in this day and age. Quality may not be job one, but if achieved, it will result in better wages or an overall increase in your benefits. Electronic equipment—perhaps computer chips—may be involved. Someone is called in to repair the photocopier or the fax machine. *Reversed.* A few bugs need to be worked out in a computer program. Or something needs to be adjusted down the assembly line. Shoddy performance carries a penalty in your paycheck.

For LOVE questions. Fringe benefits! This relationship has enough perks that it's worth investing some time and effort in it. There may be a few rough edges to sand down and some things that need to be worked out along the way. But if you keep tinkering with it, this arrangement will pay you back handsomely. Someone is making a gift for you. *Reversed.* Your relationship settles into a routine. Be careful that you don't start taking each other for granted.

For MONEY questions. An honest day's wages! The money or time that you have invested in a business puts a little money in your pocket at the end of the day. Now that you are actively working on it, you start to chip away at your debts. A little money is put aside. A little money is earned. Or a little money is coming along to you. *Reversed.* A little money is spent. Savings are being chipped away.

For STRATEGY questions. Negotiate for more money! The situation requires you to demonstrate your skills or show what you can do. Put your personal hallmark on the things you turn out or the presentations you make. Take personal pride in your work. Always put forward your best effort, even if the task seems small or insignificant. Then go in and ask for a raise! *Reversed.* Practice and perfect your skills. Do things again and again, if you must, until they are next to perfect. You'll see the difference on your pay stub.

9 OF COINS

This is a card about the value of money. *Look at your card.* A stately woman dressed in flowing clothes stands in her garden, a pet falcon perched on her gloved hand. We each choose how we will spend our money. You have chosen how to spend yours. Clothes, flowers, or things of lasting beauty may be involved. Purchases have improved your environment or enriched your surroundings. A pet remains loyal to you. *Reversed.* Money is spent on frivolous pursuits or things that do not last.

For WORK questions. T.G.I.F.! You are looking forward to something you have planned for the weekend, even if it just involves hanging around the house. A little rest and relaxation are in order. You have worked hard for your life-style. On your day off, do something nice for yourself. Take it easy. *Reversed.* Someone wants to be pampered. Your pet may need to be boarded or taken to the vet.

For LOVE questions. Dress sharp! Clothes make this relationship. It's the little finishing touches that keep the spark alive here. Lipstick is touched up. A stray hair is brushed back into place. A bit of lint is picked off the lapel. Meaningful glances are exchanged. Someone admires you in a mirror or from behind sunglasses. *Reversed.* The clothes rustle as they tumble to the floor. Someone gives you a little peck on the nape of the neck.

For MONEY questions. External appearances! Money goes into the things that show. Landscaping, exterior paint, designer clothes, imported cars, and exotic pets may be involved. Perhaps someone is sent to charm school or modeling class. Money is spent on photographs to capture the moment. *Reversed.* Money is frittered away. You get an extravagant gift.

For STRATEGY questions. Material objects! Your money is yours to spend as you choose. Collect around you the things you are attracted to or the things that are attracted to you. Gather strength from these material objects. Bring stones and flowers in from the outdoors. *Reversed.* Plant something that attracts birds and snails. Protect the environment. Provide a refuge for wildlife in your backyard.

10 OF COINS

This is a card about material wealth. *Look at your card.* A family of means strolls through the grounds of its castle, accompanied by a matched pair of Great Danes. An old man looks on in the shadows. Perhaps you, too, have enough money to satisfy both your needs and caprices. At any rate, you live in a style to which you have grown accustomed. Someone you have not seen in a while, or a relative you have never met, comes to visit. *Reversed.* Others envy you. Others expect something from you. Others want something of yours.

For WORK questions. Profits! Great success is implied by this card.
Business, the entertainment industry, professional sports, or politics may be involved. Perhaps you reap the profits from a family-owned enterprise. You will return safely from a business trip. *Reversed.* Your efforts are going to put money in somebody else's pocket. Or others want to increase their own wealth at your expense. Things are not as pretty as the picture they paint.

For LOVE questions. House beautiful! On a scale of 1 to 10, this
relationship is at the top when it comes to household budgets and living expenses, but what the heck, you can afford it. Money may not be all that matters, but it's hard to tell for sure. You can expect a little bauble to be brought home from a business trip. *Reversed.* This lap of luxury carries a hefty price tag. Be careful—a gift you receive could be given out of guilt.

For MONEY questions. Interior decoration! Home expansion or
beautification projects are financed in cash. Drywalling, carpeting, or wall-papering may be involved. Fabrics are matched to paint chips. Quarry tiles are laid in the entrance hall. Central heating is updated or replaced. Walls are knocked out to make a master suite. You name it, you've got it. *Reversed.* If you've got it, flaunt it. The rich get richer.

For STRATEGY questions. Real estate! Whenever possible, ac-
quire land. Pay cash for everything. Live on the interest from liquid assets and put the rest into securities or objets d'art. Insure everything you've got against theft, loss, and bank failure. You will live happily ever after. *Reversed.* In the unlikely event that your fortunes should reverse, sell off tangible assets and make do on your good looks.

PAGE OF COINS
This is a card about visions. *Look at your card.* A young, dark-haired man peers into the reflection of a gold coin. He is about to get a glimpse of the future. There could be a message about money soon or some news about an artistic pursuit. Omens and premonitions might also be involved. Perhaps something is revealed to you in a dream. This messenger has something very specific to tell you. To hear your fortune, draw another card. *Reversed.* The future is cloudy and uncertain. No news comes today.

For WORK questions. Scenarios! The future is mapped out at work, and you are in it. You may be sent on an important mission or entrusted with something that needs to be handled delicately. A visionary comes into the workplace, someone with grand ideas and big plans. Vision statements are crafted at upper management meetings before being hung on the wall. There might be a little money in it for you. *Reversed.* The company lacks vision. It might be time to seek your destiny someplace that doesn't.

For LOVE questions. Beautiful dreamers! This is a relationship based on a shared vision of the future. Someone young and idealistic may be involved, or someone who has just gotten a second wind and taken a new lease on life. The future looks bright. Believe in it. Someone gives you a ring. *Reversed.* A bubble is burst. A dream runs its course. Beware the man with piercing eyes. A brunette is coming into your life.

For MONEY questions. Ante up! A couple of one-eyed Jacks may be in your future, or a winning combination of numbers. Someone has a hunch about how the game will come out, which horse will win a race, or how a particular stock will rise or fall in the next few days. It's a long shot, but what the heck, it's only a couple of bucks. *Reversed.* Easy come, easy go; win a few, lose a few; etc., etc.

For STRATEGY questions. Play the hunches! If this feels like your lucky day, it probably is. But don't be confused by the butterflies that tend to get loose in an empty stomach. A real vision comes out of nowhere. A real vision sticks in your head, like a dream that wants to be figured out. If something is supposed to be, it feels right. Draw another card and meditate on it. *Reversed.* Close, but no cigar. This ball slips through your fingers. Better luck next time.

KNIGHT OF COINS

This is a card about defensive behavior. *Look at your card.* A warrior dressed for battle sits on his dark steed, waiting perhaps for the signal to attack. The coin in his hand means that he is ready and willing to fight to protect what is his. Perhaps you've been feeling a little defensive yourself lately . . . or at least you've been ready for action. Someone in your life is dressed up fit to kill. A stocky man may be involved. *Reversed.* Somebody is calling your bluff. Somebody backs off. Somebody folds a hand without revealing the cards.

For WORK questions. Saddle up! Something threatens the peace of the workplace, the competitive position, or the entire future of the business. Management gets bent out of shape. A call to arms goes out. Staff is mobilized. Orders come down. You might want to consider wearing your good suit to an upcoming business meeting. *Reversed*. Someone invades your space or steps on your turf. Your good looks don't buy you much this time.

For LOVE questions. Dark strangers! He or she may not be tall, but there's a good chance a mysterious stranger is about to cross over your threshold. A strong, silent type may be involved. The situation may be a little risky, reckless, or accompanied by a sense of danger. Keep your guard up. Be on the defensive. *Reversed*. All talk and no action. Once you get to know him, he's not so bad.

For MONEY questions. Insurance! Take time now to review and update your coverage. There isn't necessarily anything ominous in the future, but it never hurts to be prepared. Protect the sheen on that new turbo-charged car of yours with a thick coat of wax, or put the hood cover on the grille. Get your dry-clean-only clothes pressed so they will be ready to wear when you need them next. *Reversed*. You are invited to a formal dress occasion, but you have nothing to wear.

For STRATEGY questions. Don't let 'em see you sweat! Play this situation with a cool, calm expression on your face. Use a firm but non-threatening tone of voice. State your position clearly. Look in their eyes and let them know you are dead serious in your convictions. Someone could be bluffing, but you have to pretend that the person means business. *Reversed*. Know when to back off. Somebody reveals something they weren't supposed to tell you.

QUEEN OF COINS

This is a card about the environment. *Look at your card.* A raven-haired woman sits in the arbor holding a gold coin in her lap. Surrounded by natural wonders, she protects the riches of the land. Perhaps you, too, are marveling over nature's beauty. The outdoors speaks to you. Watch for the signs and omens of the new season you are entering. You hold the future in your hands. *Reversed*. The weather turns ominous. The seasons come and go without your noticing. Someone reads the future in your palm.

For WORK questions. Work climate! Office landscaping is moved into place, living plants are brought indoors, the lighting is cooled down, the height of the computer keyboard is adjusted, or the ventilation system is improved. The atmosphere grows more congenial. You are treated like a human being. *Reversed*. The workplace is a poor substitute for your natural habitat. Things have gotten a little too hot—or too cold—for you.

For LOVE questions. Atmosphere! Moonlight enchants you. Candlelight brings a twinkle to the eye. The wind chimes sing in the breeze. And you look into each other's eyes. Perhaps you should stop off at the next scenic view. Mother Nature has been good to you. *Reversed.* Someone takes you to a place where you can see for miles, but the mist obstructs an otherwise panoramic view. Oh well, a little rain can be romantic too.

For MONEY questions. Save the whales! Devote some of your money to the protection and preservation of your natural habitat. Help preserve the plants that replenish the air supply. Help to purify the waters that we all must drink. Take care of the animals who once fed and clothed you or provided the oil for your lamps and the art for your mantel. Watch for a little money to fall into your lap or your cause to get funded. *Reversed.* Funding dries up. An environmental group you just contributed to goes bankrupt.

For STRATEGY questions. Coexistence! Whatever situation you are in, you are in it together. The environment is sometimes friendly and sometimes hostile. You neither want to overrun the place nor let the place run over you. There is a balance to be struck in this. Seek an equitable solution. *Reversed.* Maintain a safe distance. Blend in with your surroundings until the coast is clear.

KING OF COINS

This is a card about life at the top. *Look at your card.* An imperial gentleman in rich, flowing robes sits on his throne, with a coin in one hand and his foot propped up on the back of an armadillo. Perhaps you know someone who lives like a king . . . or thinks he ought to be treated that way. Lineage, heritage, or bloodlines are involved. Grapes may be hand-fed to you, or a bottle of vintage wine opened at your table. *Reversed.* Graft or corruption may be involved. Someone takes the bull by the horns. The wine is sent back to the kitchen or poured on the floor.

For WORK questions. The buck stops here! Something has to go all the way up the line for approval. Or a memo gets sent all the way down. You may have to be on your best behavior at a business dinner. The cork is popped in celebration of something that made someone richer. All the boss has to do is nod his head at you. He does. *Reversed.* Proposals are rejected out of hand. Money is cut off. Your request is waved off. Thumbs are turned down.

For LOVE questions. Most eligible! Looks don't really count so much in this relationship. Clothes do make the man, and fashions, the woman—but what matters most here is the wallet. This arrangement improves your general standard of living and allows you to move in the most exclusive of circles. Nothing is over your limit. And nothing is out of the question. Enjoy it while it lasts. *Reversed.* The money runs out, and so does the relationship.

For MONEY questions. Gold cards! Your money is good wherever you go; and when that runs out, you've got plastic coming out your ears. Clerks fawn over you. Bankers call you by name. When you get on the plane, you fly first-class. Dream on! *Reversed.* You may be in hock up to your hat, but then again, you only live once.

For STRATEGY questions. Throw money at it! One way to handle the situation you are in is to buy your way out of it. Put more financial resources into an effort. Add more people to a project. Invest more time and personal effort. Or seek the support of someone who has oodles of dough and connections in high places. *Reversed.* Write it off. Minimize your losses and put your efforts into something that shows more promise.

ACE OF SWORDS

This is a card about success from out of nowhere. *Look at your card.* A hand from the clouds produces a mighty sword dripping with the symbols of sure, swift victory. You have had a moment of glory recently or are about to have success with work, love, or money. Maybe you will win a political contest or an athletic competition. At any rate, a decisive move pays off big for you. Medals are awarded. Prizes are handed out. Spoils are divided. You can't believe your luck. Someone wants to see you take the upper hand. *Reversed.* Smoke the peace pipe. Bury the hatchet. Watch out for surprise attacks.

For WORK questions. Power politics! The sword cuts both ways—and it can be razor-sharp. This time, the powers that be come down on your side. Points are scored. The playing field is leveled. You could be the hero of the hour if you play your cards right. Stars and bars are handed out. There may be a promotion in rank for you. *Reversed.* Someone is out to get your job . . . or have your head. You risk being overpowered or outranked.

For LOVE questions. War of the roses! This is a relationship that overpowers you. Someone is determined to win you and is prepared to go to any length. Long-stemmed flowers may be involved. Bold moves come into play . . . and lots of strategy. Thumbs-up on your love life. *Reversed.* Someone is trying to butter you up or get into your good graces. Careful not to be blindsided. There are ulterior motives.

For MONEY questions. Buying power! A fistful of dollars comes your way unexpectedly, or you get your fair share of the spoils when something is divided up. A thing of great value drops into your lap or falls from the sky. A material object calls out your name. Something in the window draws you like a magnet. . . . Will that be cash or credit? *Reversed.* Get a handle on your money, before it flies away. Someone wants to rain on your parade. Your request for a loan is turned down.

For STRATEGY questions. Seize control! It's time for taking matters into your own hand or for making power plays. Physical strength may be involved, or the utmost resolve and personal courage. If you don't believe in yourself right now, who will? Make your mark on the world. Go after what you want. If someone hands you the torch, pick it up. *Reversed.* It's time to put down your weapons. Make peace.

2 OF SWORDS

This is a card about balanced forces. *Look at your card.* A blindfolded woman sits on the beach under a setting Crescent Moon. She holds two swords crisscrossed over her breast. The tides are neither going out nor coming in. No progress can be made at this time—but no progress is necessary. An equilibrium between opposing forces has been reached. You feel calm. Something has been settled between two people. *Reversed.* There is a standoff. A situation ends in stalemate. Your mood swings—one way or the other.

For WORK questions. Balance of power! Labor and management have come to an agreement. The new motto in the workplace is "Live and let live." An equal employment opportunity may be extended soon, regardless of race, creed, age, or gender. Two points of view even each other out. Everyone receives the same treatment. *Reversed.* Negotiations have led to an impasse. The sides are evenly divided on an issue. Same old !@#$, different day.

For LOVE questions. Truce! The two parties in this relationship may not always see eye to eye, but at this time you are both content. Perhaps you have recently kissed and made up. I see you locked in an embrace. A spectacular sunset may be involved. Take a moonlit walk. *Reversed.* A new lover is sure to come into your life. Make a wish over your shoulder as the Crescent Moon sets.

For MONEY questions. Making ends meet! Things are neither good nor bad on the money scene right now. You appear to be breaking even, more or less. The picture may not be as great as you'd hoped, but

you can't complain really, and after all, things could be worse. Accounts balance. Assets cancel out liabilities. *Reversed*. Your checkbook is way off at the end of the month. If you expected to have less in your pocket, you have more. If you expected to end up with more, you find you have wound up with less.

For STRATEGY questions. Strike a bargain! You have negotiated a win/win situation. Keep to the common ground you agreed to establish. Hold up your end of a compromise or bargain. Someone wants to meet you halfway on something. Come halfway yourself. Lock arms. Shake hands. *Reversed*. There are competing interests. A split decision is reached. Or no common ground can be found. A partnership splits up.

3 OF SWORDS

This is a card about getting hurt. *Look at your card*. Storm clouds have gathered. Rain is beating down upon three swords that pierce a wounded heart. You are suffering from a bruised ego, an unrequited love, or a period of stormy weather in a relationship. It rains on your parade. Someone, though unintentionally, wounds you just the same. *Reversed*. Someone tugs at your heartstrings. Something moves you to tears. Or someone hurts you on purpose.

For WORK questions. Shot down! Your brilliant ideas or hard efforts are unappreciated by the powers that be. An approach is rejected. A slight is received. A comment cuts like a knife. There are emotional outbursts in the workplace. Everyone's a critic. You may shed a few tears, or help dry someone else's. *Reversed*. You have a bad day, but it's nothing that can't be fixed tomorrow. You're feeling a bit under the weather.

For LOVE questions. Brokenhearted! You're going to be needing a strong shoulder to cry on. Or perhaps you would prefer curling up into a fetal position for a while or rocking back and forth in a chair. It's likely that a relationship is dealt a fatal blow. Perhaps someone walks out on you. A third person may be involved. The truth is blurted out, without consideration of your feelings. *Reversed*. Someone is having a midlife crisis or experiencing some other kind of temporary lapse. There is a good chance you will weather this storm.

For MONEY questions. Bleeding hearts! You have a disappointment with money. Money that was supposed to come in gets stopped before it's sent. An investment that was supposed to appreciate goes belly-up instead. A relationship that was supposed to improve your net worth ends abruptly. *Reversed*. Your credit card gets cut in half at the checkout counter. See where you can cut back.

For STRATEGY questions. Bypass! Try not to wear your heart on your sleeve right now. It makes for too easy a target. Develop a thicker skin. Let the arrows glance off you. Let a cutting remark run off your back like rain. Don't let it get you down. Don't let them get to you. Protect your vitals. *Reversed.* You may be inclined to make a snide comment yourself or to twist the knife a bit. It doesn't get you anywhere but in deeper.

4 OF SWORDS

This is a card about preparations. *Look at your card.* An effigy lies at peace on the lid of a sepulcher, his hands folded in eternal prayer. The soul waits calmly, preparing itself for the moment when the body shall be summoned again. In your own life, there is something you need to rest from or something you need to get psyched up for. To prepare, take a few deep breaths. Exhale slowly. Clear the cobwebs of worry from your head. Relax. Rest. Meditate. *Reversed.* To get command over a problem, let it go for a while. Take a breather. Think about something else. Sleep on it overnight.

For WORK questions. The pause that refreshes! Everybody deserves a little time to stare out the window. Take the two 15-minute breaks you deserve. Take your full lunch hour. Get ready for an important meeting in the morning by getting a good night's sleep. Prepare for an appearance in the afternoon by remaining calm. *Reversed.* Someone is lying down on the job. A period of probation, or a time of waiting, is just about at its end. New life is breathed into a poor old soul.

For LOVE questions. Good night, sweet prince! You are tossing and turning, thinking about someone, thinking about how you want it to be. Perhaps tomorrow is the big day. To prepare, relax your neck. Relax your arms. Relax your toes. Count backward from 400,444,444. Sleep tight. *Reversed.* Someone is so anxious for tomorrow to come that he or she goes to bed dressed. Who's expecting a baby?

For MONEY questions. Give it a rest! You've worried enough about your money for one day. Don't lose any more sleep over it. Tomorrow's another day . . . easy come, easy go . . . you can't take it with you— and all that jazz. Dismiss your worries with a heartfelt prayer. Place a coin under your pillow for good luck. *Reversed.* Keep a little money in your mattress. Make a donation in memory of someone. Put an envelope in the offering plate.

For STRATEGY questions. Twiddle your thumbs! This is a time of waiting. There is nothing you can do to make the hours pass any faster.

Tomorrow will come in its own time. You might as well fold your hands in your lap and wait patiently for the dawn's early light. *Reversed.* The answer comes to you in your sleep. You have a dream in living color. Or suddenly you see the light.

5 OF SWORDS

This is a card about self-defense. *Look at your card.* A man stands victorious over two enemies who have laid their weapons down and retreated. Perhaps you, too, have overcome great odds by standing up to your opponents or taking on a challenge that was presented to you. The thrill of victory is experienced by someone—and the agony of defeat, by someone else. A conflict is resolved in your favor. *Reversed.* You win some, you lose some. A victory is only temporary. Those who are defeated return to settle the score another day.

For WORK questions. Skirmishes! Someone has challenged your authority, made a bid for your job, or attempted to overthrow you. An outright personality clash may be involved—perhaps between staff and management. Perseverance and performance pay off in the end. You prove your point, but more important, you prove yourself in the process. Live up to your name. *Reversed.* There are competing interests in the workplace. Some subtle plot is hatched to undermine management's authority.

For LOVE questions. Squabbles! Someone fights over you or fights with someone who has said something crude about you. An actual fistfight among would-be suitors is not out of the question. One person emerges as the clear-cut winner in a relationship that involves several contenders. A love triangle is broken up. Unwelcome advances are rejected. *Reversed.* Someone is unapproachable. You suffer rejection.

For MONEY questions. Spoils of war! Others may be losing their shirts or throwing in the towel right now—and for this very reason, it's a good time for you to pick up assets cheap. Their loss, your gain. Perhaps a recent windfall has put you in a better financial position, or a fight for market share has swung in your favor. You laugh all the way to the bank. *Reversed.* A sudden streak of good fortune reverses when you take on more than you can chew. Some of your assets need to be abandoned.

For STRATEGY questions. Winner take all! Your reputation is on the line here, and bluffing your way out of this situation will not work. You need to be ready to take decisive action to protect your good name or to defend your position. Gather up your full resources and call upon your complete reserve of strength in order to measure up to this ultimate test.

When the dust settles, you emerge the winner. *Reversed.* There comes a time, too, for giving up while you are still ahead. Minimize your losses.

6 OF SWORDS

This is a card about fleeing to safety. *Look at your card.* A man pilots his family from one shore to another in search of a better life. It seems as if they are escaping something in the past. You yourself have just come through quite an ordeal or are going through a dramatic and profound transition. A place of employment or residence is changed. A journey across water is taken. Someone is running away from something, or running away *to* something. Someone bails you out of a jam. *Reversed.* You can run, but you can't hide. Your cares and woes travel with you. A move is only temporary. A journey is delayed.

For WORK questions. Jump ship! A current job is abandoned due to dissatisfaction, troubled conditions, or personal difficulties. You move to a place where jobs promise to be in better supply. You trade one line of work for something that promises to be more rewarding or fulfilling. Or a job transfer comes through. It's also possible that business interests will require you to travel to a distant place, a trip that perhaps involves a personal or family hardship. *Reversed.* Old work habits and attitudes are transferred with you. The grass is no greener on the other side.

For LOVE questions. Pick up roots! Someone is leaving the scene. Perhaps there is no question but that you will pack up and go with the person, but there are mixed emotions just the same. The past is being left behind—both the good and the bad. A chapter in your life together is ending. To continue this relationship requires giving up just about everything else, except being with the one you love. You share a long journey together. *Reversed.* Someone goes ahead, leaving the others behind for at least a while. Or a planned departure is not made after all.

For MONEY questions. Bail out! Gather up your possessions, cash in your chips, claim your vested interest, sell off stocks and bonds, close your accounts, and convert your assets into a transferable form. Gather important papers up into your briefcase. Moving or relocation expenses may be involved. Traveler's checks may be needed. Don't leave home without your credit cards. *Reversed.* You may be left with only the clothes on your back and the money in your pocket.

For STRATEGY questions. Get out of town quick! The only way to deal with the situation you are in is to leave it behind you just as fast as you can. You need to establish distance. Take with you what you can, leave the rest behind . . . and good riddance. Good luck to you in your new life. *Reversed.* You can never go home again.

7 OF SWORDS

This is a card about escaping undetected. *Look at your card.* A man, possibly a spy, sneaks away from the encampment with five swords in his arms. Perhaps you, too, are trying to get away with something. A secret is kept. A shoulder is looked over. Someone is up to no good—is it you? Or is something going on while your back is turned? Stealth plays a role in your life. Something sinister happens in broad daylight. *Reversed.* Objects of real or sentimental value come up missing. There is the pitter-patter of footsteps in your life. Plots turn sour overnight.

For WORK questions. Industrial espionage! Nondisclosure agreements are violated, secrets are leaked, or someone claims an idea that is not his or her own. It's possible someone is going through your trash or has patched into your computer. Or perhaps it's just that you want to cut away a little early from the job, maybe on a Friday afternoon in order to get a head start on the weekend. *Reversed.* Inventories come up short. Perhaps someone is taking a few office supplies home.

For LOVE questions. Dangerous liaison! There's a little sneaking around going on in this relationship. Something besides fast food is happening at lunch, or something clandestine—even sinister—is involved. You sneak off together, maybe for a weekend in the mountains or at the shore (but you never leave the room). Someone is not telling you everything there is to know. *Reversed.* Check for the telltale white band or permanent indentation on the ring finger of a married man. Be wary of strangers.

For MONEY questions. Highway robbery! Money is disappearing mysteriously from the cookie jar, from your wallet, or from your desk drawer, but in amounts too discreet to notice. Perhaps a little gas is siphoned from your tank in the middle of the night. Con jobs may be involved. Something you thought was a good deal turns out to be a rip-off. *Reversed.* Something that you thought was lost or stolen turns up in a different place from where you put it. Don't give your credit card number to the person who calls on the phone. Destroy your carbons.

For STRATEGY questions. Quick on your feet! The situation you are in requires you to act swiftly and quietly. If you get caught in the act, you'd better come up with a good story fast—but you also have the right to remain silent. A speeding ticket may be involved, or a parking violation. You will need to be prepared with a good excuse. *Reversed.* An alibi—or a paper trail—comes in handy. Buy yourself a new pair of sneakers.

8 OF SWORDS

This is a card about being captured. *Look at your card.* A woman has been taken prisoner. She has been bound, blindfolded, and imprisoned on a part of the beach below the high-tide line. You, too, may soon be in over your head. You are all wrapped up in fine details, red tape, or feelings of guilt. Monumental obstacles seem to be in the way, and tremendous odds. You are at the mercy of someone—perhaps someone who is not very nice— or of things totally outside your span of control. You desperately want to escape from your current situation. *Reversed.* A timely rescue is afoot. A thorny problem is unraveled. You overcome the odds.

For WORK questions. Hands are tied! The chances for making progress right now are nil. A decision made higher up cannot be reversed down the line. You are stuck with the consequences of past loyalties. A sacrificial lamb may be needed—someone to take the blame for a widespread problem. (Don't let it be you.) A series of pointed questions is addressed to you. You have no choice but to answer truthfully. *Reversed.* You are hung out to dry. You are sent off to cool your heels. You are stuck in a job you despise.

For LOVE questions. Ball and chain! This relationship is not answering your needs—even the most basic ones. It confines, restricts, maybe even strangles you. It may set you up. Someone wants to control your every move. Someone wants to own you, body and soul. You feel as if you have no choice. There seems to you to be no way out. And yet, escape, you must. *Reversed.* You are playing the role of a martyr. Personal sacrifice is involved in any relationship, but this is going too far.

For MONEY questions. Encumbered! Money troubles weigh you down. Your debts and long-term obligations have imprisoned you in your own house. Or the bill collectors won't get off your back. Before you declare Chapter 13, make a last-ditch effort to bail yourself out. Avoid loan sharks. *Reversed.* Your money is all tied up right now in accounts that carry a substantial penalty for early withdrawal. Or you are meeting your obligations, but you have nothing left to call your own.

For STRATEGY questions. Plot your escape! Things appear desperate right now, but it is too soon to give up hope. This situation requires a miracle, so you must work one. Remain calm. Go over the alternatives in your head. . . . Run through the Tarot cards for suggestions. Consider your options. Develop your plans. Time things out carefully. When your window of opportunity opens, be ready to jump through it to safety. *Reversed*. Tie up loose ends. Cover up tracks. Keep a low profile.

9 OF SWORDS

This is a card about mental anguish. *Look at your card*. A man sits upright in bed weeping. Perhaps you, too, have been awakened by a bad dream recently. Guilt, sorrow, or despair may be involved. A memory haunts you. You cannot get something out of your head. Or you are having trouble getting over something that happened to you. A subliminal thought that gnawed at you during the day becomes painfully obvious by the end of a dream cycle. *Reversed*. A warning is delivered in a dream. You lose a little sleep over a nagging problem. You worry too much.

For WORK questions. What have you forgotten! A nagging thought troubles you. Something is left undone at work. Something was overlooked. Something was not followed up on. Maybe you forgot to go to class all semester, and tomorrow is the final exam! You awake in the middle of the night remembering suddenly what you were supposed to do. It's not too late to do it. *Reversed*. A lot of minor worries add up to one big one. Or many concerns reduce to a single problem. Were you the one who left the coffeemaker on?

For LOVE questions. What have you done! A sudden realization comes a little too late to undo the damage done to a good relationship— too late to unsay the things that were said, too late to undo the disloyalty that has been committed, too late to express the truth with any credibility . . . or so it seems at this moment. Such depth of remorse is a message in itself. Someone would like to make amends. Hear the person out. *Reversed*. A minor indiscretion is weighted too heavily. Quit punishing yourself. Forgive the offender.

For MONEY questions. Where did it all go! Your money has been flushed down the toilet, blown, or swindled out of you. The financial damage may not be all that extensive, but the loss cannot be recovered— moreover, you feel like an absolute fool. It is not as if you haven't made it through hard times before, but at this moment, it all weighs on you. All you really need to do is make it through the night. You'll be all right. *Reversed*. You awaken in a cold sweat from a dream in which all the money in the world could not help you. Sleep on a purchase decision. Invoke the 24-hour cancellation clause on a contract.

For STRATEGY questions. What you should have said! It's all water under the bridge at this point, but suddenly the words come to you. When you are tempted to reconstruct a conversation in your head—only this time saying all the right things at the right time—go ahead. It will teach you how to handle the situation better next time, and it will make you feel better tonight. Blow off some steam in the quiet of your own room. *Reversed.* Cry your eyes out. Catharsis is a good thing too.

10 OF SWORDS

This is a card about betrayal. *Look at your card.* A poor guy lies facedown on the sand with 10 swords stuck in his back. He feels betrayed by everyone and everything. Perhaps you, too, feel as if you haven't got a friend in the world. Whoever was out to get you has got to you good; you are hurting pretty bad; or to say the very least, you're certainly down in the dumps. There is someone you'd just as soon never see again. It looks like the feeling is mutual. *Reversed.* Be careful whom you trust. Don't be so hard on yourself.

For WORK questions. Backstabbing! Office politics are a bit cut-throat these days. In order to get ahead, someone decides to eliminate enemies or find scapegoats. You may be an easy target for underhanded schemes or plots to hand off the blame. Keep your own backside covered and your nose clean. *Reversed.* You run the risk of getting caught in the cross fire of a power play. Keep your belly to the ground and your head down.

For LOVE questions. Shot through the heart! Here's living proof that "you always hurt the one you love." A relationship not only comes to its conclusion, but it ends on a pretty sour note or with an incredibly low blow. The truth hurts. It cuts you to the quick. But at least now you know what it is. *Reversed.* You may think you know someone pretty well, but you don't. Be careful.

For MONEY questions. Blood money! You don't want any part of the money that comes out of a particular money-making venture. A curse of sorts may accompany a piece of property. Nothing but financial ruin results from a shady business proposition. *Reversed.* Someone is far too envious of your personal property to be trusted. Watch out for muggers.

For STRATEGY questions. Et tu, Brute! In times like these you need to screen your contacts and associates carefully. There are apparently big stakes involved. Trust absolutely no one farther than you can see them. Ruin is a distinct possibility. Keep your guard up. Turn on all of your security systems. Don't take any risks. *Reversed.* Just because you're paranoid doesn't mean people really aren't out to get you.

PAGE OF SWORDS

This is a card about early warning signals. *Look at your card.* A redheaded youth stands on a ridge brandishing his unsheathed sword. He boldly conveys the message he has been sent to deliver: The winds of war are brewing in the west. You, too, are about to receive advance notice. Keep your eyes peeled and your ears open for signs that things are about to change. There may be a sudden change in the weather that tips you off or causes a ball game to be canceled. Be ready. For more details, draw another card at random from your deck. *Reversed.* There is no advance warning that things are about to change. A rumor of change turns out to be misinformation or an intentional leak to distract attention from what's really happening.

For WORK questions. Open and shut doors! Something big is happening at work—you can feel it in the air. And besides, management is meeting behind closed doors—a dead giveaway. A heavy hitter comes onto the work scene, or someone of relatively low rank is sent to deliver an urgent message from the higher-ups. Someone wants to give you the opportunity to prove yourself. A door is opened. You strike a home run. *Reversed.* The "new guy" is all talk and no action. You need to get a little more experience under your belt before you are ready for a big move.

For LOVE questions. Come-ons! What's going on in this relationship can be predicted. The signs are clear. It would seem that someone has a few wild oats to sow, is using this relationship to prove something, or is playing with love as if it were a game of skill. All well and good, as long as you appreciate what the score is. A redhead may be involved. *Reversed.* Someone is not easily dissuaded from a mission of conquest. A can of mace might come in handy on this date.

For MONEY questions. Communiqués! Changes in the financial situation are presaged by the drafting of papers for dispatch, by news buried in the paper, or by the updating of personal records. There may be rumors of changes in economic indicators, or news from an insider who tips you off. Look for a private, confidential, and personal notice in your mailbox. *Reversed.* A change in the financial situation happens without advance warning. You receive a summons of some kind.

For STRATEGY questions. Call to arms! This is a situation in flux. Developments are occurring quickly, the atmosphere is changing rapidly, or an emergency situation is about to break loose. You have the option of running for cover or of jumping into the thick of things. Either way, keep monitoring conditions and adjusting your actions accordingly. Keep your eye on the ball. *Reversed.* A crisis passes quickly, leaving winners and losers in its wake. A victory is pulled out in the bottom of the ninth.

KNIGHT OF SWORDS

This is a card about aggressive behavior. *Look at your card.* A knight on horseback leaps into the thick of things waving a sword over his head. He is charging off into stiff head winds. Perhaps you, too, have thrown caution to the winds in your efforts to accomplish your mission, get ahead of the game, or prove yourself. Physical-contact sports may be involved, or political maneuvers and strategic power plays. The adrenaline is pumping in your veins. Someone—perhaps a green-eyed man—rushes into your life. *Reversed.* You are left behind in a cloud of dust. You run up against a heavy-duty defense or a brick wall. A physical injury is possible if you don't slow down.

For WORK questions. Pass rushers! You want to pick up as much yardage out of a single effort as possible. There is a tendency to sail over the heads of those who stand in your way or to suddenly rise above your competitors in a bold power play. A quick maneuver at this time adds to your image if it not only carries an element of surprise but accomplishes something. *Reversed.* A goal you have been working toward is now in sight, but the enemies you have made along the way attempt to undermine you. A play is ruled incomplete.

For LOVE questions. Swift moves! Someone is attempting to get through your defenses in this supercharged relationship. Things may be happening so fast that you can hardly catch your breath. Be careful or you may be headed off at the pass. Someone is aggressively pursuing you. *Reversed.* Don't rush into anything. A relationship comes to a sudden, screeching halt. As the dust settles, you will have the opportunity to think things out.

For MONEY questions. Forward motion! You are making rapid progress in achieving your financial goals. A plan has been put into effect for paying back debts, cashing in on an idea, or getting your accounts to come out even. A major purchase may be involved, perhaps something with a gearshift and leather seats. *Reversed.* Someone pressures you to make a purchase decision, but this may not be the right time.

For STRATEGY questions. Rapid progress! You are charging ahead of the pack just now—but don't stop to look back. This situation is some kind of a race to the finish, and you can't let up until you complete your mission and reach the finish line. It's possible you will get some help from those who are young and eager to please—remember to reward them when the battle is done. *Reversed.* A critical milestone is reached. Be careful not to jump into an internal fray. Someone huffs off in a rage.

QUEEN OF SWORDS

This is a card about dominance. *Look at your card.* A redheaded woman sits on a throne. She gestures in a way that lets her subjects know that it is safe for them to rise from their knees and speak. Perhaps you have a dominating personality yourself—or it could be that someone is attempting to dominate you. At any rate, you are getting your own way right now on a matter of the utmost importance. Your request is heard. Awaited permission is granted. *Reversed.* An audience is received with an important personage. An appointment is set up. Or the okay travels down the line without any meeting.

For WORK questions. Humble requests! The whim of a person in great power stands between you and the realization of your ambitions. The job you want, the requisition you make, or the plan of action you have proposed needs to be blessed by someone in a higher position. It looks as if you will get the go-ahead if you present a good case and don't step too far out of line in the process. *Reversed.* If possible, delay a request until the recipient is in a better mood. A plea will be rejected.

For LOVE questions. Permission! You need to ask first before you proceed any further. A parent is asked to bless a marriage, a woman to give her consent, or a man to receive permission. The answer to a popped question would appear to be yes, perhaps following a reasonable period of consideration. *Reversed.* The answer is decidedly no. On this count, no argument will convince another person otherwise.

For MONEY questions. Supplication! Since you are dependent on somebody else's money here, there are a few hoops you have to jump through. Forms are filled out. Applications are submitted. A request is put in. The word comes back that you are approved. A powerful woman is involved. *Reversed.* There is too much red tape to go through. The criteria for approval are too high, or this is not the right time for your request to be heard. Try again later.

For STRATEGY questions. Diplomacy! In this situation, you are expected to stay in your place. There is a certain role you are expected to

play. There are certain protocols involved. Keep your cool. Remain dip-
lomatic. Ask things in a roundabout way and couch your answers in an
appropriate level of politics. Play the part assigned you. A firm decision is
made in your favor. *Reversed.* A decision is pending or left up in the air.
Negotiations will have to continue another day.

KING OF SWORDS

This is a card about endurance. *Look at your card.* A stern red-haired
man sits rigidly on his thrown, holding up a mighty sword. He looks like
a statue. Perhaps you, too, are as firm as a rock in your resolve to see a
matter through to its bitter end. Just as likely, someone is putting up a
strong resistance to your efforts at making inroads. An established way of
doing things stands in the way of progress. Stop and reconsider your options. Patience and perseverance pay off in the end. *Reversed.* There is a
monumental barrier in your path. Things won't budge. You get the cold
shoulder.

For WORK questions. Written in concrete! The established way
of doing things at work is far from perfect. The rules are the rules, but every
rule has its exception and every regulation can be bent—or else no progress
will ever be made. The secret is to modify and modernize rather than
revolutionize. Work within the system. *Reversed.* Be satisfied right now
with making incremental progress. Chip away at the old ways.

For LOVE questions. Etched in stone! Initials are carved in the
trunk of a tree, a heart is drawn in wet cement, a message is spray-painted
on a concrete overpass, or a name is tattooed on a biceps. As flattering as
these gestures are, nothing is certain in love and war—and all's fair. This
much is sure: For all intents and purposes, this relationship promises to last
for a long time, providing you both keep working on it. *Reversed.* Someone
is acting awfully bullheaded. A line is drawn in the sand, and you are dared
to cross it.

For MONEY questions. Cold as ice! Put your money into things
of lasting value—blue-white diamonds perhaps, or precious metals—or in
things that appreciate over time, like U.S. savings bonds. Take care of
whatever you possess. Employ assets for the whole of their useful lifetime.
Remain firm in your resolve to control spending. *Reversed.* Hedges against
inflation themselves depreciate over time. Liquid assets freeze up.

For STRATEGY questions. Sharp as a knife! This situation requires physical strength, willpower, and lots of intestinal fortitude. Now

that you have built a stronghold over something or assembled the things that matter to you, the challenge is to hold on to everything. Keep your wits about you. Remain keen and alert. It's not only lonely at the top, it can be pretty scary. *Reversed.* Enjoy the things you have worked so hard for, for as long as they last.

INDEX

ALL THE QUESTIONS YOU CAN ASK

*Consult the Extra Credit section of this Reading.
**Consult Extra Extra Credit!

What kind of life-style do I need?	24 *
What message will I receive?	21
What role does money play in my life?	14
What should my strategy be with regard to _____?	19
What will this personal relationship come to?	11

WHAT CARD AM I...

Reading #

What Tarot cards am I?	1, 5, 9, 12, 14, 17, 20, 23
What is my Tarot Key Card?	1
What is my Tarot Spirit Card?	23
What Tarot Coin describes me?	14
What Tarot Cup describes me?	9
What Tarot King or Queen describes me?	12
What Tarot Page or Knight describes me?	20
What Tarot Sword describes me?	17
What Tarot Wand describes me?	5

WHAT AM I...

Reading #

What am I influenced by?	24 *
What am I most resistant to?	24 *
What am I open to?	24 *
What am I supposed to accomplish?	27 *
What am I trying to work out?	25 *

WHAT ARE MY...

Reading #

What are my career prospects?	8
What are my motivations?	24
What are the three things I need to learn?	28 *

WHAT DO I...

Reading #

What do I aspire to?	24 *
What do I dream of?	24 *

*Consult the Extra Credit section of this Reading.

Index: All The Questions You Can Ask

*Consult the Extra Credit section of this Reading.
**Consult Extra Extra Credit!

WHERE | Reading

WHERE	Reading #
Where am I?	2
Where should I go on my honeymoon?	13
Where should I go on vacation?	13
Where will I be happiest living?	13
Where will I travel on business?	13

WHO	Reading #
Who am I?	1
Who am I deep down inside?	23
What kind of fool am I?	20
What kinds of fools am I up against?	20 **
What's my future with so-and-so?	9 *

YES/NO	Reading #
Yes or no?	22
Should I invest my time in _____?	16 *

AND	Reading #
Everything else you want to ask . . .	29

*Consult the Extra Credit section of this Reading.
**Consult Extra Extra Credit!

ACKNOWLEDGMENTS

I would like to acknowledge the following recording artists and song-writers, whose music touched me during the writing of this book, adding immeasurably to the inspiration.

Madonna: *The Immaculate Collection*, Sire Records: 1990; especially the songs: "Like a Prayer," by Madonna and Patrick Leonard; "Into the Groove," by Madonna and Stephen Bray; and "Lucky Star," by Madonna.

The Neville Brothers: *Yellow Moon*, A&M Records: 1989; especially: "My Blood," "Yellow Moon," and "Voo Doo," all by The Neville Brothers; with D. Johnson, C. Moore, W. Green, and B. Stolz.

Roger McGuinn: *Back from Rio*, Arista Records: 1991; especially: "Your Love Is a Gold Mine," by McGuinn and Dave Stewart; "King of the Hill," by McGuinn and Tom Petty; and "The Time Has Come," by McGuinn and S. Cutler.

Material Issue: *International Pop Overthrow*, Polygram Records: 1991; especially: "Chance of a Lifetime," "Crazy," and "Trouble," all by Material Issue: Ted Ansani, Jim Ellison, and Mike Zelenko.

Tom Petty: *Full Moon Fever*, MCA Records: 1989; especially: "Love Is a Long Road," by Petty and Mike Campbell; "Running Down a Dream," by Petty, Jeff Lynne, and Campbell; and "Alright for Now," by Petty.

Robert Plant: *Now & Zen*, Atlantic Records: 1988; especially: "Ship of Fools," by Plant and Phil Johnstone; "The Way I Feel," by Plant, Johnstone, and Doug Boyle; and "Why," by Plant and Robert Crash.

Midnight Oil: *Diesel and Dust*, Columbia Records/CBS Records: 1988; especially: "Bullroarer," "Sell My Soul," and "Put Down That Weapon," all by Midnight Oil: Peter Gifford, Jim Moginie, Martin Rotsey, Peter Garrett, Rob Hirst, and Gary Morris.

Acknowledgments

R. E. M.: *Out of Time*, Warner Brothers Records: 1991; especially: "Losing My Religion," "Texarkana (Catch me if I fall . . .)," and "Near Wild Heaven," all by Bill Berry, Peter Buck, Mike Mills, and Michael Stipe.

Jon Bon Jovi: *Blaze of Glory*, Mercury Records: 1990; especially: "Bang a Drum," "Santa Fe," and "Justice in the Barrel," all by Jon Bon Jovi.

Wild Bill Cox: *The Songs of Wild Bill Cox*: 1991; especially: "The Quandary," "High Time," and "Good to Be Alive," all by Bill Cox.

Starship: *Love Among the Cannibals*, RCA Records: 1989; especially: "Send a Message," by Mickey Thomas, Mark Morgan, and Steve Diamond; "Wild Again," by John Bettis and Michael Clark; "We Dream in Color," by Thomas, Morgan, and Phil Galdston; and "Healing Waters," by Martin Page.

With eternal love and endless gratitude to Tory.
Special thanks to Addie from Daddy.

FASCINATING BOOKS
OF SPIRITUALITY
AND PSYCHIC DIVINATION

THE DICTIONARY OF MIND AND SPIRIT
compiled by Donald Watson
71792-1/$12.50 US

SECRETS OF SHAMANISM:
TAPPING THE SPIRIT POWER
WITHIN YOU
by Jose Stevens, Ph.D. and Lena S. Stevens
75607-2/$5.99 US/$6.99 Can

TAROT IN TEN MINUTES
by R.T. Kaser
76689-2/$10.00 US/$12.00 Can

THE LOVERS' TAROT
by Robert Mueller, Ph.D., and Signe E. Echols, M.S.,
with Sandra A. Thomson
76886-0/$11.00 US/$13.00 Can

SEXUAL ASTROLOGY
by Marlene Masini Rathgeb
76888-7/$10.00 US/$12.00 Can